Jack

The Blind Watch

Philosophy in Dialogue
Philosophie im Dialog

Edited by

Prof. Dr. Janez Juhant
(University of Ljubljana)
and
Ass. Prof. Dr. Vojko Strahovnik
(University of Ljubljana)

Volume / Band 8

LIT

Jack E. Brush

The Blind Watch

Technological Atheism and the Theology of Nature

LIT

This book is printed on acid-free paper.

Bibliographic information published by the Deutsche Nationalbibliothek
The Deutsche Nationalbibliothek lists this publication in the Deutsche Nationalbibliografie; detailed bibliographic data are available in the Internet at http://dnb.dnb.de.

ISBN 978-3-643-91395-1 (pb)
ISBN 978-3-643-96395-6 (PDF)

A catalogue record for this book is available from the British Library.

Flössergasse 10
CH-8001 Zürich
Tel. +41 (0) 76-632 84 35
E-Mail: zuerich@lit-verlag.ch https://www.lit-verlag.ch
Distribution:
In the UK: Global Book Marketing, e-mail: mo@centralbooks.com
In North America: Independent Publishers Group, e-mail: orders@ipgbook.com
In Germany: LIT Verlag Fresnostr. 2, D-48159 Münster
Tel. +49 (0) 2 51-620 32 22, Fax +49 (0) 2 51-922 60 99, e-mail: vertrieb@lit-verlag.de

Contents

1 “The Attack of the Atheist: Richard Dawkins” 11

2 “The Wisdom of the Philosophers: Heraclitus and the Stoics” 39

The Transition 87

3 “The Message of the Apostle: Paul” 97

4 “The Doctrine of the Theologian: Augustine” 123

5 “On Thinking” 167

6 “On Nature” 189

7 “Nature and Life” 219

Conclusion 245

Epilogue 255

Bibliography 265

Preface

The present work has a twofold purpose. Firstly, it aims to expose some of the salient inadequacies and fallacies of modern atheism. Secondly, and more fundamentally, it is intended to expand our thinking about nature in general and about the meaning of nature for a Christian understanding of human beings. By "modern atheism" I mean that form of atheism that employs modern scientific theories in an attempt to discredit traditional religious beliefs of Christianity. As a point of logic, I do not consider the views of the modern atheist and those of the Christian theologian to be contradictory in the sense that the refutation of the one would establish the truth of the other. Rather, I view them as contraries, allowing the possibility that both could be false, although both cannot be true.

In approaching the topic, one must take into account at the outset the often adversarial attitude of modern atheists and try to avoid as much as possible a confusion of their unbecoming hubris with defects in their thought. I am thinking in particular of the four well-known proponents of atheism: Richard Dawkins, Sam Harris, Christopher Hitchens and Daniel Dennett, who convened in 2007 at the residence of Hitchens for a discussion on religion. Of the four, the writings of Dawkins and Dennett seem to be the best known in non-academic circles. Unfortunately, their writings are imbued with an arrogance and aggressiveness that render them difficult reading for those who do not share their views. Not only religious leaders, but also philosophers such as John Searle have complained about Dennett's near abusive writing style. As we shall see, the style of Dawkins is hardly an improvement. None of this, of course, is a matter of substance. As already noted, we need to distinguish between their often unpleasant style and the actual content of their arguments.

Following their meeting in 2007, the four members of the aforementioned group became known as "The Four Horsemen" – an epithet that they themselves apparently adopted. Those readers familiar with the Book of Revelation in the New Testament will recognize the allusion to the "Four Horsemen" of the apocalypse, who were prophesied to bring catastrophic destruction upon the earth at the end of time. For these four atheists to adopt an eschatological title is particularly odd, given the fact that none of them seems to have studied Christian thought in any depth. The educational background of the group lies, generally speaking, in the area of science and behavioral psychology – in Dennett's case with a veneer of philosophy that he acquired from Gilbert Ryle. What is striking about the group is the disparity between its desire to criticize religion and its actual knowledge of religion in general and of Christianity in particular. All four of these men are intelligent and well educated in their respective fields, and one would have expected them to seek out discussion partners in the field of religion who stand on equal footing with them. A contest between a professional soccer player and the soccer star at a local high school is really not a fair contest. But instead of inquiring about Christianity from the best minds in the field, these atheists are content to attack the simplest ideas of the fundamentalists such as the verbal inspiration of the Bible and an anthropomorphic concept of God, as though these ideas were representative of the entire Christian religion. Are the "Four Horsemen" unaware that fundamentalism is primarily an Anglo-Saxon version of Christianity that developed in the post-World War II period? Take the idea of verbal inspiration, for instance. They show no recognition of the fact that the modern understanding of verbal inspiration is indeed *modern* and is in no way an essential element of Christian thought.

The modern concept of verbal inspiration, according to which every single word of the biblical text was divinely inspired, was unknown before the rise of Protestant Orthodoxy. Even Martin Luther, the German reformer of the sixteenth century, knew nothing of this modern concept. To be sure, the Reformers assumed that the Bible was the Word of God, but the hermeneutical distinction between the *letter* and the *spirit* of the text rendered the modern concept of verbal inspiration impossible. Luther himself was very critical of the biblical Book of James because he found it to be inconsistent with the letters of Paul. According to Luther, it was not the *written* scripture that was the Word of God, but rather the *spirit* manifested in the written word. The modern idea of the infallibility of the written text was a Protestant reaction to the papal infallibility of the Roman Catholic Church, and ironically it developed under the influence of modern science itself. It is interesting to note that the concept of verbal inspiration bears some traits that are similar to those of modern science; in both cases, one encounters the minute analysis of detail in the object of investigation.

In any case, it strikes me as naive for these four men to pronounce the death of a tradition about which they know so little. I would not presume to instruct an evolutionary biologist like Richard Dawkins on the fundamentals of evolutionary biology, and yet he seems confident that he is in a position to instruct Christians on the fallacies of their religious beliefs. Of course, an objection to this criticism lies close at hand. The "Four Horsemen" might well retort that they are simply pointing out the untenability of fundamentalism, which seems to be so predominant among Christians today, and that they gladly acknowledge that there are other forms of Christian thought. If this is really the case, then they should acknowledge it openly. Such openness might provide a basis for a more civil and fruitful discussion.

For systematic reasons, I have chosen to limit my comments to a discussion of Richard Dawkins' well-known book *The Blind Watchmaker,* which was originally published in 1986 and then supplied with a new Introduction in 1996. This self-imposed restriction seems justified seeing that Dawkins is without question the best known of the group in popular culture and that his book *The Blind Watchmaker* has become a classic work on modern atheism. The allusion to Dawkins' work in my title *The Blind Watch* can be understood in a twofold sense, in the sense of a portable timepiece that is often worn on the wrist and in the sense of the careful, but limited observation of the hunter looking out from behind his blind. Regarding the portable timepiece, it should be noted that Dawkins himself alluded in his title *The Blind Watchmaker* to William Paley's classic argument for the existence of God. According to Paley, there must be a Watchmaker (i.e. a divine designer) if there is a watch (i.e. a designed universe including human beings, stars etc.). As we shall see, Dawkins redefines the watchmaker in biological terms and designates it as "blind". In contradistinction, I am describing the *watch*, i.e. the atheistic scientist, as "blind" insofar as he can no longer perceive his relationship to the Watchmaker. Combining both senses of the "blind watch", the expression becomes a metaphor for the modern scientific-technological mind that calculates everything, but sees very little. The "blind watch" is no longer capable of thinking outside the parameters of scientific inquiry, and therefore its objects of investigation are restricted to those aspects of nature that fit into the scientific mode of thought. Of course, scientists consider themselves to be very open to new ideas and new thoughts. As they are fond of saying, they are always in search of truth and are constantly questioning the accepted concepts. That's true to a point. But as soon as the new ideas become transforming for science itself as an enterprise, the touted openness often turns into rigidity and narrow-mindedness.

In my opinion, the "timepiece" has become so blind that it is now blind for its own blindness. It calculates ad infinitum, but it no longer recognizes its own deficiencies and limitations. To be sure, it recognizes that there are still many unanswered questions in science, and the more flexible minds in the scientific community will acknowledge that there are anomalous experiences that do not fit well into the current scientific framework. But fundamentally new ideas that challenge the scientific mode of thinking are usually rejected without serious consideration. Returning to my metaphor, the act of observation has become so restricted that things appearing are no longer seen. As Jesus of Nazareth once said: "This is why I speak to them in parables, because seeing they do not see, and hearing they do not hear, nor do they understand" (Matthew 13:13). Or as Heraclitus of Ephesus said: "Those who hear and do not understand are like the deaf. Of them the proverb says: 'Present, they are absent'" (Frag. III). And further: "Eyes and ears are bad witnesses to men having rude souls" (Frag. IV). There is an odd sort of comfort in these sayings inasmuch as they indicate that the modern problem of blindness is not totally unique to our times. What is unique in the modern era is the *form* of the blindness, and in the following chapters, we will see that this form is inseparable from the development of technology.

It is my hope that this book will appeal to an audience outside the narrow bounds of the academic community. The topic of atheism and nature is certainly one that affects the thinking and conduct of the public in general. For this reason, I have endeavored to provide a translation wherever the English-speaking reader encounters a foreign word or phrase. In particular, all Latin titles of the works of Cicero appear in English translation with the original Latin title in parenthesis. Furthermore, the occurrence of a Greek word or phrase in the text is routinely provided with a translation so that the sense of the argument can be easily grasped. Regarding footnotes, the situation is a bit more complicated. References to classical works or to academic literature usually assume an acquaintance with standard abbreviations that are unfamiliar to the wider public. The references to the writings of Plato utilize the so-called Stephanus numbering system, whereas references to Aristotle employ the Bekker system of pagination. Once familiar with these systems, the non-specialist will find them enormously useful in locating classical passages. For instance, the reference in the writings of Aristotle to 413b24–27 designates the four lines (24–27) in Aristotle's *On the Soul* (De anima) where he hints at the separate existence of the soul. The designation is unambiguous and unique, thus allowing the reader to locate the passage very easily. The same holds true for the Stephanus pagination in the dialogues of Plato. The large corpus of writings left by Augustine is available in several different series, and at times the designations of particular passages vary from one series to another. In an attempt to facilitate the reader, I have often included in the references the location of a particular passage in the older and somewhat outdated *Patrologia Latina* by Migne because this series is easily accessible on the internet. Admittedly, the *Patrologia Latina* contains only the Latin text, but for students and others who have a basic knowledge of Latin, the Migne references should be helpful.

Finally, I would like to express my sincere gratitude and thanks to my companion and wife Susan L. Brush who has worked side by side with me in the preparation of this book. In addition to making substantive comments about the content, she has proofread the completed manuscript and provided a detailed bibliography at the end.

The Villages, Florida, in Eastertide, 2021

Jack Edmund Brush

Introduction

Since this book is concerned with the problem of modern atheism, it might be helpful to review in brief the history of atheism. It is often claimed that atheism has a very long history, reaching back to early Greek philosophy. In the pre-Socratic period, the names Diagoras of Melos, Leucippus and Democritus are usually mentioned. Diagoras (born ca. 468 B.C.) is particularly interesting because his poetic writing is found in one of the oldest surviving Greek manuscripts, the so-called Derveni Papyrus, which is really a collection of 200 fragments more or less. Some writers have claimed that he was an outspoken atheist, but the Derveni Papyrus testifies rather to his abandonment of the traditional Greek gods and to his shift toward a version of monotheism.[1] In the Hellenistic period, Epicurus is the chief witness to whom modern atheists usually appeal. To be sure, the word "atheism" (ἄθεος) occurs in the writings of Epicurus, but it does not have the modern denotation of the English word "atheism" or the German word *Atheismus*. Also in Plato we find isolated references to the related word "godlessness" (ἀθεότης), e.g. in *Statesman* 308e and in *Laws* 967c, but in none of these instances does the word have the same meaning as it does today. For Plato, it meant the neglect of the gods of the State, whereas for Epicurus it meant that the gods are irrel-

[1] See DAVID I. ORENSTEIN and LINDA FORD BLAIKIE, *Godless Grace*, 2015. Orenstein writes: Diagoras "examined the arguments for the divine and concluded there was no evidence for gods" (p. 107). Orenstein fails to recognize that in abandoning the traditional Greek gods, Diagoras did not espouse atheism in the modern sense that there is no God. Diagoras was a part of the fifth century B.C. movement that struggled to interpret the mythological elements of Homeric poetry using allegorical methods.

evant for the lives of human beings. That is, the gods exist, but they do not care about humans and do not interact with them.

In the English language, the word "atheism" appeared for the first time around the middle of the sixteenth century, and its proponents followed more or less the lead of the ancient Epicureans.[2] They did not deny the existence of God, but they refuted certain Christian doctrines such as the divine order of the universe and the providential intervention of God in human affairs. Oddly enough, the word "atheism" predated the root word "theism" in English. The latter is first documented in 1678 in the Preface of a voluminous work by the Cambridge Platonist Ralph Cudworth: *The true Intellectual System of the Universe.* Several years later in 1699, Anthony Cooper, the Third Earl of Shaftesbury, published *An Inquiry concerning Virtue or Merit*, in which he set forth the beliefs of the theists as well as those of the atheists: "To believe therefore that everything is governed, ordered, or regulated for the best, by a designing principle or mind, necessarily good and permanent, is to be a perfect Theist. To believe nothing of a designing principle or mind, nor any cause, measure, or rule of things, but chance, so that in Nature neither the interest of the whole, nor of any particulars can be said to be in the least designed, pursued or aimed at, is to be a perfect Atheist."[3] So in this passage we see the battle lines drawn between the theists and the atheists, and at this point the existence of God is not yet in question.

We need not pursue the history of atheism in great detail. Suffice it to say that the eighteenth century, the so-called Enlightenment Period, produced various currents of thought that advanced the notion of modern atheism. On the one hand, there was the rejection of tradition and the concomitant praise of human reason. On the other hand, the natural sciences were continually expanding their ability to explain natural phe-

---

[2] Cf. INGOLF U. DALFERTH, "Theismus", *Theologische Realenzyklopädie*, Studienausgabe, Vol. 33, 2006, pp. 196–205.

[3] SHAFTESBURY, ANTHONY COOPER, *An Inquiry Concerning Virtue or Merit*, (1699), 1904, p. 23.

nomena. All of this paved the way for the full-fledged version of atheism that emerged in the nineteenth century in the works of philosophers such as Feuerbach, Marx and Nietzsche as well as in biologists like Thomas Huxley. This type of atheism incorporated many of the previous criticisms of theism, but it was distinctive in that it included as fundamental a denial of the existence of God.

The modern atheistic view is not, however, without its own problems. One of the most serious problems facing contemporary proponents of atheism is an ambivalent relationship to history and more generally an inadequate understanding of history. The ambivalence of contemporary atheists to history is evidenced by their repeated appeal to ancient Greek philosophers such as Epicurus in order to legitimize their views. Just as the Roman Catholic Church places great value on its historical development out of the first century A.D., modern atheists have the apparent need to trace their views back to ancient Greece. If one considers tradition and history to be of paramount importance, then such an endeavor makes sense. However, a fundamental tenet of Enlightenment thought out of which modern atheism developed was the rejection of tradition as authoritative as well as a general disregard for history. Atheism is supposedly based on human reason and empirical evidence, in which case it would be totally irrelevant whether this or that ancient philosopher was an atheist. A second instance of the ambivalence of modern atheism to history is its appeal to historical concepts such as human rights. As soon as the atheist argues that he is defending the human rights of various individuals or groups, he is tacitly assuming that the works of men such as Thomas Hobbes and John Locke are authoritative. Again, this is a blatant contradiction to the "official" position of the atheist on history and tradition.

Modern atheism's inadequate understanding of history has resulted in an apparent reluctance to critically examine its own history and presuppositions. This situation has led to an obvious stagnation of thought. To be specific, the battle lines today between the theists and the atheists are more or less identical with those of the nineteenth century. In addition, many arguments brought forth by contemporary atheists are rooted in nineteenth century thought and have become hopelessly outdated. Like the famous debate in 1860 between Thomas Huxley and Bishop Wilberforce in Oxford, evolutionists such as Richard Dawkins and creationists such as Stephen Meyer[4] focus today on the organic world as though the entire question about the existence of God could be decided in this arena.

Although the parameters of this discussion are very narrow, the aim of the atheist seems to be much more comprehensive. Atheism is not simply a theoretical position on one particular issue nor is it an element in the lifestyle of particular individuals. That is, it is not simply a private matter of how one chooses to think and live. Instead, modern atheism has the unmistakable marks of a movement. Many atheists are not content to be atheists themselves, but rather they seem to have a mission to convert others to their way of thinking. In view of this, one is inclined to call atheism a movement, and from the standpoint of phenomenology, one might well classify it as a religion, albeit a godless religion. The atheistic substitute for God is an ideology to which the adherents cling with all the passion and intolerance of an evangelical Christian. This is quite evident in Orenstein's little book entitled *Godless Grace*. At least two-thirds of the book consists of testimonials of atheists who converted to atheism from some other form of religion. Orenstein writes: "Just as the religious hold dear their beliefs regarding faith and want to spread the 'good news' of their religion, I, too, have the same interest and the same civil rights to share my values and ideas with others."[5]

As a semi-religious movement, modern atheism strives to accomplish two goals, namely to discredit religion in any traditional form and to replace it with an atheistic anthropology and ethic. To date, neither of these goals has been reached. It would go beyond the scope of this "In-

[4] Stephen C. Meyer, *Darwin's Doubt: The Explosive Origin of Animal Life and the Case for Intelligent Design*, revised ed. 2014.
[5] David I. Orenstein and Linda Ford Blaikie, *Godless Grace*, 2015, p. 6.

troduction" to discuss in detail the philosophical attempts in the nineteenth century to discredit religion in general. One thinks immediately of Schopenhauer, Feuerbach, Marx, and Nietzsche. Of these, the weakest argument was proposed by Feuerbach who took as his starting point the idea of creation. Then in the spirit of idealism, he reversed the biblical order and argued that man had created God, instead of God creating man. Although this argument made a lasting impression on the young Karl Marx, it was based on a logical fallacy. The proposition: If man projects an image of God, then God does not exist, is a premise, not a conclusion, and it has no more truth value that the proposition: If man projects an image of God, then God must exist. Despite Feuerbach's faulty logic, Marx followed his lead and became the most influential proponent of atheism worldwide. Whether in the form of Maoism or in the form of the Critical Theory of the so-called Frankfurt School, neo-Marxism has had a dramatic impact on American and European societies since the 1960s. Unfortunately, the dogmatic character of Marxism has seriously hindered a debate on atheism. Furthermore, the cultural approach of Marxists such as Herbert Marcuse disguised to some extent the ultimate goal of overthrowing the economic systems of Western societies.

While the Marxist atheists were combining liberal ideas such as equality and human rights with Critical Philosophy in an effort to erode traditional values and institutions, the scientific community became fixated on refuting the Christian doctrine of creation as a means of discrediting religion. Among biologists, the attack on Christianity took the form of an inflexible canonization of Darwinism in a concerted effort to combat the doctrine of creation. It is puzzling why the atheistic biologists have adopted such a narrow focus. It should be obvious that a refutation of a literal reading of the creation narrative in Genesis, Chapters 1–3 does not discredit eo ipso the entire breadth of Christianity. Even within Christianity itself, there are viable traditions that do not depend on the idea of a literal divine creation. Nor would a refutation of Christianity in all of its forms – assuming that this were even possible – entail a refutation of

Islam, Judaism, Buddhism and all other forms of religion. If the goal is to discredit religion, then the victory of an evolutionary theory over the biblical account of creation does not really accomplish very much.

Finally, we come to the topic of mythology. Out of their arsenal of weapons against Christianity, the atheists often bring forward the charge that the Bible contains myths. In particular, they label the creation account in the Hebrew Bible and the resurrection account in the New Testament as mythological and therefore claim that both are untruth. Unfortunately, it never occurs to them to clarify the concept of myth. An awareness of this deficit might have prompted the atheists to consider the topic of mythology in more depth before criticizing its occurrence in the biblical tradition. Granted, there is convincing evidence that the cited accounts are indeed mythological, but the assertion that myths are untrue is a highly dubious claim that usually goes unanalyzed. The assumption seems to be that only *historical* accounts can qualify as true. If this were really the case, then purely mathematical statements such as "two plus two equals four" would not qualify as true since there is nothing historical about this claim. With all due respect, one cannot avoid the conclusion that the atheistic rejection of myth as untrue simply reflects a lack of historical knowledge and an ignorance of the available scholarship on the topic.

In the late nineteenth and early twentieth centuries, abundant literature was produced on the development of historical consciousness, and groundbreaking work on the interpretation of myths was published. To anyone acquainted with this literature, the atheists' arguments against myth seem quite beside the point. As a matter of historical fact, it was a Christian theologian (D. F. Strauss), not an atheist, who first wrote about mythology in the New Testament. Since the first half of the 20th century, many other Christian scholars have recognized the mythological elements in the Bible, and in many cases, they have interpreted the myths in existential terms. To say that an account is mythological does not mean that it is untrue. Instead, it signals that the truth of the account does not lie in its historical accuracy, but rather in its existential meaning for human beings. If an atheist wishes to discredit the creation myth, he must demonstrate in some convincing manner that the existential meaning embedded in the myth is destructive to human nature and society. So a mere labeling of an account as mythological accomplishes nothing. More effort and more thought are required in order to refute it.

As previously noted, modern atheism not only strives to discredit Christianity, it also aims to replace it in certain fundamental ways. However, its failure to provide a viable alternative to Christianity either with regard to an understanding of human nature or in the area of ethics has been very apparent in modern philosophy. Without doubt, the philosophy of Jean Paul Sartre represents one of the most serious attempts of the twentieth century to develop an understanding of human nature from an atheistic point of view. In his most famous work *Being and Nothingness* (*L'Être et le Néant*, 1943), Sartre sketches out an existential view of human nature based on the concept of freedom and the possibilities of choice. According to the slogan "existence precedes essence", we *are* what we *choose* to be. For Sartre, there is no human soul, no essential qualities of human beings, no relation to God and, of course, no God; there is only freedom and the responsibility to make authentic choices. To Sartre's credit, he recognized the necessity of the concept of transcendence for understanding human nature, but the transcendence of *Being and Nothingness* turned out to be inadequate for the purpose of developing a theory of ethics. The key word in Sartre's ethics was "authenticity", which meant living in accordance with one's true situation. That is, authenticity is a style of life and lacks any definable ethical content. In colloquial terms, authenticity means being true to oneself. In this context, any choice would seem authentic as long as it is lived with a clear awareness of one's situation. Following Sartre's line of thought, it becomes difficult, for instance, to bring ethical charges against an "authentic Stalinist".

In comparison with the serious attempt of Sartre, the attempts of current atheists such as Richard Dawkins and Daniel Dennett appear quite superficial and trivial. As soon as human nature is reduced to a collection of DNA or to neutrons analyzable by neuroscience, any talk of ethics becomes ludicrous. In a thoroughgoing materialistic world, there is no place for ethics, and it is simply disingenuous to claim otherwise. Consider Dennett's voluminous *Consciousness Explained* (1991). After 430 pages in which he argues that the Cartesian *cogito* does not exist, that there is no such thing as a mind in human beings, and that we should abandon any spiritual or otherwise non-materialistic view of humans, he acknowledges that his ideas present a challenge for the notion of responsibility and ethical conduct. Unfortunately, Dennett makes no serious attempt to meet this challenge. Instead, he distracts from the poverty of his own thought by ridiculing his opponents who still talk about human consciousness and ethics. If one looks for something positive in Dennett's views, it is his consistent adherence to Darwinian principles. Darwinism knows nothing about transcendence, and some understanding of transcendence is a *conditio sine qua non* of ethics, even if it is only a finite transcendence as in the case of Martin Heidegger. Without a sense of transcendence there is no way to distinguish between "is" and "ought". There is no contrast to the present state of affairs, and therefore there is no way to decide what is right and what is wrong. Furthermore, if there is no overarching moral order in the universe, the foundation for pursuing ethical conduct is simply lacking.

A comparison of Sartre and Dennett is very instructive inasmuch as it highlights an underlying contradiction in the thinking of many contemporary atheists. Both Sartre and Dennett are atheists, but Sartre was a humanist, whereas Dennett is a Darwinist. Humanism and Darwinism simply do not mix. Humanism in whatever form one considers, be it the Renaissance type of Pico della Mirando or the psychological version of Carl Rogers, is essentially anthropocentric. It places the human being at the center of its reflection; it praises the unique capacities of humans; and it rejects a materialistic view of human beings. Darwinism, on the other hand, emphasizes the continuity of humans with other animal forms; it adheres to a materialistic view of human beings; and it downplays human capacities such as language acquisition. For an atheist to claim that he is both a Darwinist and a humanist is a contradiction in terms that should be abandoned for the sake of intellectual integrity. Humanism elevates man to be the measure of all things; Darwinism dethrones man from any privileged position. It is difficult to see how these two views could be reconciled.

One might argue, perhaps, that "transhumanism", which is now quite in vogue, holds the key to bridging the gap between humanism and Darwinism. Given, however, that the major proponents of transhumanism are trained in the area of technology and computer science, the "trans" part of the term seems to communicate the dominant thrust. Instead of being a legitimate form of humanism, *trans*-humanism is a moving-*beyond* humanism to "something else", and this "something else" is to be determined by technology. It would be more appropriate to call this new movement "trans-Darwinism" since it is basically a continuation of evolution in the area of information technology. Clearly, trans-humanism is just as atheistic as Sartre's humanism or Dennett's Darwinism. However, it distinguishes itself from both of these in that it promises to bring immortality to humankind – once again indicating the religious undertone of the atheistic movement. Hopefully, this brief Introduction to the problem of atheism will provide a context in which to understand the more specific topic to be pursued in this book.

In Chapter 1 of the present work, we will analyse in some detail Richard Dawkins' book *The Blind Watchmaker* and explain our objections to his philosophical and theological comments and/or conclusions. Chapter 2 will broaden the perspective from a narrow biological focus to a more general consideration of nature by turning to the wisdom of the ancient philosophers. We will begin with the fragments of Heraclitus and continue with a discussion of Stoic views on nature, especially as presented in the works of Cicero. Chapter 3 will demonstrate the way in which the Stoic understanding of nature was adopted by the Apostle Paul and interpreted in the context of his Christian message. The early Christian theology of Augustine concerning nature and creation is the topic of Chapter 4. In the writings of Augustine, we observe a more conscious integration of biblical and philosophical thought than was the case with Paul. Whereas Chapters 2, 3 and 4 are primarily historical, Chapters 5, 6 and 7 are systematic in character, while drawing on the results of the previous historical chapters. In Chapter 5, we will consider the type of thinking that is dominant in modern science and suggest an alternative mode of thinking for attaining more insight into nature *as* nature. Chapter 6 will employ the natural mode of thinking acquired in Chapter 5 in order to present a coherent understanding of nature. Returning to Richard Dawkins in Chapter 7, we will investigate his understanding of life in some detail and then consider the relationship between nature and life from the perspective of natural thinking. In the Conclusion, we will reflect upon some of the interesting similarities and differences between the evolutionists and the creationists, noting how both are trapped in the dialectic of technology and religion. In the Epilogue, we turn our attention briefly to Dawkins' later work *The God Delusion* (2006).

Chapter 1

"The Attack of the Atheist: Richard Dawkins"

We have chosen Richard Dawkins' book *The Blind Watchmaker* for a more in-depth analysis because Dawkins is a highly respected evolutionary biologist, and his book has become a classic in the atheists' arsenal against Christianity. Richard Dawkins was born in British Kenya in 1941; he received an outstanding education in zoology and biology at Oxford; and today he is internationally known for his theory of gene-centered evolution. The evolutionary biologist Ernst Mayr once commented on Dawkins's reputation. "The funny thing is if in England, you ask a man in the street who the greatest living Darwinian is, he will say Richard Dawkins. And indeed, Dawkins has done a marvellous job of popularizing Darwinism. But Dawkins' basic theory of the gene being the object of evolution is totally non-Darwinian. I would not call him the greatest Darwinian."[1] Aside from Mayr's dispute with Dawkins over the role of the gene in evolution, Mayr is certainly correct about the significance of Dawkins in the English-speaking world. Without doubt, the reason for his influence in England is not just his accomplishments in the area of evolutionary biology, but also his unwavering Anglocentric focus with regard to the philosophical or theological currents of the nineteenth and twentieth centuries.

---

[1] Ernst Mayr, "What Evolution is", *Edge* (www.edge.org), 12. 31. 1999, ed. John Brockman.

In reading Dawkins' book, one is struck immediately by the extent to which his Anglocentric thinking affects his understanding of Christianity. The only theologians that he mentions are William Paley (1743–1807) and Hugh Montefiore (1920–2005), the Bishop of Birmingham. Of the two, Paley plays the lead role in Dawkins' presentation. To be sure, William Paley had a tremendous impact on the theological thinking of the English clergy for generations. He was born in 1743 in Peterborough, England as the son of an Anglican clergyman, and he later studied theology at Christ's College in Cambridge. As a clergyman and theologian, his main works were *The Principles of Moral and Political Philosophy* (1785), *Evidences of Christianity* (1794), and *Natural Theology* (1802). These were among the best apologies written against English Deism at that time, and *Evidences of Christianity* was soon incorporated into the theological curriculum of the Anglican State Church. As the young Charles Darwin completed his theological studies in Cambridge in 1831, it was precisely Paley's theology that he was required to read. Bishop Montefiore seems to have followed more or less in Paley's footsteps, although he has made modifications that were necessary in view of modern science. Although both of these men were representative of the views held by the Church of England, neither of them can be regarded as great thinkers within the Christian tradition. There were many developments in theology that took place outside of England, but none of these is acknowledged by Dawkins. It is as though the entire Continental tradition did not exist. As a result, we find Dawkins setting up for himself two opponents that are relatively easy to conquer: Paley and Montefiore. Otherwise, Dawkins directs his negative comments about Christianity toward the "creationists", whom he never really identifies and variously belittles as "backwoodsmen" or "rednecks". Such abusive language coming from an Oxford professor is really quite unbecoming. It is true that many proponents of creationism do not have the intellectual ability or the superior education of the Oxford elite. Nevertheless, they deserve in my opinion more respect than this language suggests.

Significantly, Dawkins never addresses in this book the views of any theologian on his own intellectual and educational level. Had he felt constrained to remain within the English-speaking world, he could have engaged the views of Paul Tillich, Edward Farley or John B. Cobb, Jr., and if he had braved crossing the channel, he could have entered into conversation with Gerhard Ebeling or Karl Barth. Instead, Dawkins limits his discussion to the watchmaker argument of William Paley and then attempts to draw conclusions that are much more comprehensive in scope. The argument goes something like this: If Paley's watchmaker argument is wrong, then atheism is right. In addition to the obvious provincialism of Dawkins' method, his argument fails on purely logical grounds. He attacks a particular form of Christian thought about creation and then claims that his refutation has consequences for the whole of Christian theology. In conclusion, let me say – perhaps to the surprise of the reader – that I agree with Dawkins about the weakness of Paley's argument, but I do not think that he has accomplished a great deal by refuting a rather simple nineteenth century argument.[2]

Apart from his choice of opponents, Dawkins' work suffers from generalizations that are often presented without argumentation. Take, for example, this statement: "Darwin made it possible to be an intellectually fulfilled atheist". First of all, I do not know what an "intellectually fulfilled atheist" would be, but more importantly, the scientific correctness of Darwin's theory does not disprove in any way the existence of God or more appropriately the reality of God. At most, it disproves Paley's argument from design. In *The Blind Watchmaker* Dawkins does not consider classical arguments for the existence of God such as the so-called ontological argument presented by Anselm, the eleventh century Archbishop of Canterbury,[3] nor does he show any recognition of the argument from

[2] The watchmaker argument appeared in WILLIAM PALEY's book *Natural Theology*, 1802.

[3] See my discussion in the "Epilogue" regarding DAWKINS' *The God Delusion*, in which he briefly comments on ANSELM and THOMAS AQUINAS.

contingency presented by the Scotsman Duns Scotus. Admittedly, both of these theologians belong to the Scholastic Period of the Middle Ages, but this fact in itself does not render their arguments invalid since the arguments are logical, not empirical. Still, if Dawkins were to insist on a contemporary thinker, he could have mentioned the modal proof for the existence of God formulated by Charles Hartshorne who was professor of philosophy at the University of Chicago and who developed Anselm's argument in the context of modern logic.

A third problem that one encounters in reading Dawkins' book is his failure to define critical terms, particularly those central for his conclusions. As an evolutionary biologist, he is as a rule very careful about his definition of scientific terms, but when he ventures into philosophy or theology, the terms become very blurred, if not completely incomprehensible. Already in his Introduction, Dawkins uses terms like "life", "exist", "existence", "essence" and "nature" as though their meanings were self-evident. Consider, for instance, this sentence: "Darwinism encompasses all of life – human, animal, plant, bacterial …" (p. x) One notes that the words "human", "animal", "plant" and "bacterial" are used as though they were further descriptions of life, but life itself remains undefined.[4] Later in the book, he combines "life" with "existence" and "essence" as though the meaning of these terms emerged from his discussion of evolutionary biology. If he actually intends to use these classical philosophical terms in a biological sense, he begs the question about the meaning of "life" before he enters the discussion with Christian thinkers. It seems more likely, however, that he simply does not recognize the need for definitions as a basis for discussion. For our purposes, the most grievous omission of definitional clarity involves the

[4] Jürgen Hübner discusses the problem of definition in his book *Die Welt als Gottes Schöpfung ehren*, 1982: "So werden denn auch in der biologischen Literatur keine Definitionen im strengen, eigentlichen Sinne gegeben. Angeführt werden vielmehr Merkmale, die lebende Systeme charakterisieren, die das beschreiben, was Lebewesen tun" (p. 29).

word "nature". The words "nature" and "natural" (e.g. natural selection) occur throughout the book, but we are never told how the author understands nature. Dawkins provides detailed information on DNA, genes, replicators etc., but nature *as* nature remains a mystery.

A final problem confronting the reader of Dawkins' book is his unstated, underlying assumption that science is the key to understanding all of reality. So when he, for instance, speaks about "evidence", he means "scientific evidence" – evidence that can be verified within the framework currently accepted by the scientific community. The consequences of this bias are manifold. It leads among other things to the surprising statement that Darwinism is the bedrock of all the humanities. This is consistent, of course, with the so-called Cognitive Revolution of the second half of the twentieth century – a movement that began at MIT in 1956, adopting a thoroughgoing materialistic point of view, denying the reality of the human mind and emphasizing the analogy between humans and computers.[5] Problematic is this: The claim that one can explain "everything" on the basis of one's own narrow discipline elevates that discipline to the level of a speculative philosophy or a metaphysics. The mathematician and philosopher Alfred North Whitehead, a fellow countryman of Dawkins, defined metaphysics or speculative philosophy in this way: "Speculative philosophy is the endeavour to frame a coherent, logical, necessary system of general ideas in terms of which every element of our experience can be interpreted. By this notion of 'interpretation' I mean that everything of which we are conscious, as enjoyed, perceived, willed, or thought, shall have the character of a particular instance of the general scheme."[6] If one wishes to develop a speculative philosophy and incorporate evolutionary biology into it, one utilizes at least a viable procedure, but if one tries to inflate evolutionary biology

---

[5] See Noam Chomsky, "Language and Cognition", *The Future of the Cognitive Revolution*, ed. David Johnson and Christina Erneling, 1997, pp. 1–31.

[6] Alfred North Whitehead, *Process and Reality*, (1929), Corrected Edition, ed. by David Ray Griffin and Donald W. Sherburne, 1978, p. 3.

itself into a speculative philosophy, the attempt runs amok because the concepts are too narrow to cover the breadth of topics involved. Additionally, it leads to an untenable absolutizing of evolutionary biology and to a claim of certainty that the history of science itself refutes. Then the history of science teaches us that every scientific insight and theory is relative and subject to fundamental change. The overconfidence with which Abraham Michelson presented his views on theoretical physics around the turn of the twentieth century is a classic example of absolutizing a relative point of view. As we know today, Einstein's "Special Theory of Relativity" demonstrated the fallacy of Michelson's claim and stands as a constant reminder that no scientific theory can attain absolute certainty. It would behove Dawkins to remember such classic examples before making absolute claims about evolutionary biology or unsubstantiated claims about matters outside the realm of biology. The present framework of evolutionary biology should be respected as a serious attempt to understand a segment of nature, but its claims must be regarded as relative and subject to fundamental change at some point in the future.

With these introductory remarks to Dawkins' work, we now turn to a more detailed analysis of *The Blind Watchmaker*. In his Introduction to the 1996 Edition of this work, Dawkins launches immediately into a series of sweeping generalities. He claims that "Darwinism encompasses all of life" and that it "provides the only satisfying explanation for why we exist …" According to Dawkins, Darwinism is the bedrock on which all of the humanities rest – the humanities being history, language, music, visual arts etc. The reason for this privileged position of Darwinism is that all of the humanities are products of brains, which are simply "evolved data processing devices". Dawkins apparently feels justified in making such claims because he finds support in the writings of Daniel Dennett and Steven Pinker. The reader should be aware, however, that all three of these men belong to the same club of materialistic reductionists. Dennett, a former student of Gilbert Ryle in Oxford, represents a very narrow stream of twentieth century philosophy and has not really added very much to Ryle’s critique of the Cartesian dualism. From totally different perspectives, both Whitehead and Heidegger have called Descartes’ dualism of mind and body into question, but neither has taken the narrow position that the brain is a data processing device responsible for all human endeavours. In effect, Dawkins and Dennett do not really solve the Cartesian problem; they simply eliminate the half of the duality that strikes them as problematic.

If the reader wishes to join this small club of materialistic reductionists, he will have little difficulty in accepting most of Dawkins’ claims in the subsequent chapters and will meet Dawkins’ requirements to be considered an “intellectually fulfilled atheist”. However, if the reader finds the broad claims of this Introduction unfounded, if he is convinced that these claims require thorough verification, if he thinks that the mental capacities of humans exceed qualitatively those of computers, if he is not willing to accept the assertion that *all* evidence is *scientific* evidence, then Dawkins will label him a “backwoodsman” who is too dumb to understand how things really work. This is the “either/or” logic of Dawkins, and he never wavers from it. Either the reader must accept Dawkins’ version of life or he will be disregarded as a “backwoodsman”. *Tertium non datur*! There is in Dawkins’ mind (or brain) no viable alternative. The intolerance with which Dawkins pursues his project exemplifies well the “evangelical fervour” of the new atheists.

Dawkins begins the Preface to his book with this astonishing statement: “This book is written in the conviction that our own existence once presented the greatest of all mysteries, but that it is a mystery no longer because it is solved. Darwin and Wallace solved it, though we shall continue to add footnotes to their solution for a while yet.”[7] In reading this statement, one is reminded again of the situation of classical physics around the turn of the twentieth century. In his book *Light Waves and*

[7] Richard Dawkins, *The Blind Watchmaker*, (1987), 1996, p. xv. For those readers not familiar with Alfred Wallace, he was the co-founder of the theory of evolution who worked independently of Darwin.

Their Uses, 1903, Albert Abraham Michelson wrote these words concerning the future "footnotes" to classical physics: "What would be the use of such extreme refinement in the science of measurement? Very briefly and in general terms the answer would be that in this direction the greater part of all future discovery must lie. *The more important fundamental laws and facts of physical science have all been discovered, and these are now so firmly established that the possibility of their ever being supplanted in consequence of new discoveries is exceedingly remote.*"[8]

Michelson's words reflect the optimism of the time that theoretical physics had been worked out to the point of near absolute certainty and that the future work would simply involve the refinement of measurement techniques and minor corrections to the theoretical framework. Two years later Albert Einstein published his groundbreaking article on the "Special Theory of Relativity", thus placing the foundation of classical physics in question and ushering in a revolution in scientific thinking. The history of science itself should make Dawkins somewhat more cautious about his claims. Of course, he admits that his views reflect a "conviction", but the reader is left with the question as to whether Dawkins' "conviction" is more trustworthy than the "intuition" of the backwoodsman. In "The World as I see it" Einstein later wrote: "I am satisfied with the mystery of the eternity of life and with the awareness and a glimpse of the marvelous structure of the existing world, together with the devoted striving to comprehend a portion, be it ever so tiny, of the Reason that manifests itself in nature."[9] This is not to say that Albert Einstein was religious in any usual sense of the word nor that he would question the correctness of today's evolutionary biology. Nevertheless, I think that he would find Dawkins' overconfidence about the validity of evolutionary biology extremely nearsighted.

---

[8] Albert Abraham Michelson, *Light Waves and Their Uses*, 1903, pp. 23–24 (italics added).

[9] Albert Einstein, *Ideas and Opinions*, 1954, p. 11.

In describing his approach in *The Blind Watchmaker* Dawkins tells us that he is assuming the role of an advocate in order to convince us of his views on Darwinism. He writes: "it sometimes isn't enough to lay the evidence before the reader in a dispassionate way. You have to become an advocate and use the tricks of the advocate's trade. This book is not a dispassionate treatise."[10] One must admire Dawkins' honesty about his method and style in this book, and presumably this statement about his adversarial tone is intended to excuse his rude and belittling comments toward his opponents. Still, those who do not appreciate his approach will be inclined to criticize it as an example of poorly conceived sophistry. Be that as it may, it is undeniable that Dawkins' style and tone have much more in common with Thomas Huxley than with the fair-minded Charles Darwin. Finally, it should be noted that Dawkins' style sometimes creates uncertainty about the strength of his argument in a particular case. Is he intentionally distorting the views of his opponents as a "trick of the advocate's trade"? Is he strategically suppressing information that does not support his claims? Or is he simply ignorant of important facts and significant evidence that contradict his views? Often the reader finds it very difficult to judge him fairly.

Chapter 1 is entitled "Explaining the very improbable" and is in my opinion the intellectually weakest chapter of the entire book. Before beginning his detailed account of the Darwinian theory of evolution in the subsequent chapters, Dawkins wishes to devote this chapter to "philosophical" problems, setting the limits of the investigation and defining terms. One must give Dawkins credit for perceiving the need for such a chapter, but the results are disappointing because the crucial philosophical terms are never really clarified. For instance, his discussion about "complexity" in nature is interesting, but terms such as "nature" and "existence" are employed as though they were self-evident. He sets the limits of the investigation by defining "hierarchical reductionism", noting that the analysis of the whole into its parts must halt at some level.

[10] Richard Dawkins, *The Blind Watchmaker*, (1987), 1996, p. xvi.

That is, the evolutionary biologist cannot continue down the scale of hierarchical reductionism until he reaches the level of particle physics. On this point, Dawkins is certainly correct; limits to the investigation must be set. But his reductionism involves another presupposition that must be accepted "on faith" – a presupposition that he never seriously questions. As a reductionist, Dawkins is convinced that the behavior of a body as a *whole* will emerge from the interaction of its *parts*. I know of no logical proof for this presupposition, and any appeal to empirical evidence must assume a utilitarian concept of truth. That is, truth must be considered as a predication of something that produces certain results, whether these results are known in advance or not. In more colloquial terms: If it works, it's true. Furthermore, there is scientific evidence from other fields of investigation that contradicts Dawkins' presupposition. Internationally known is the work of Ilya Prigogine on the thermodynamics of nonequilibrium systems. Prigogine's research on thermodynamic systems far from their equilibrium point has demonstrated that such systems do not obey the whole/part model. Lest I be misunderstood: I do not object to Dawkins' utilizing the part/whole method of analysis. It is after all a standard procedure in scientific work. I do object, however, to his tendency to absolutize the claims that follow from this procedure.

The reductionistic approach of Dawkins finds expression repeatedly in his claim that humans have brains, but no minds, that their bodies are like machines and that there is a close analogy between evolution and computer technology. Needless to say, he rejects the concept of a "life force" (*élan vital*), but he neither acknowledges the philosophy of Henri Bergson nor provides any argumentation against the concept of vital force. He simply asserts that there is no life force in living matter and that there is nothing supernatural about it. Although the word "supernatural" appears throughout Dawkins' book, he never seems to realize that its meaning depends upon one's definition of "natural". In the Scholastic theology of Thomas Aquinas, the "natural" was understood in the sense of Aristotle's philosophy, and the "supernatural" was thought to *complete* the natural, not to *contradict* it. However, one suspects that Dawkins' understanding of "supernatural" was taken not from Thomas Aquinas, but from William Paley who was a part of the Supernaturalist movement against the Deists of the eighteenth century. In this context, the words "natural" and "supernatural" acquired new meanings which were conditioned by the development of classical physics. Is Dawkins' failure to define these terms simply an advocate's trick? Or is he unaware of the importance of the terms for the claims that he wishes to make. One is inclined to think the latter when one reads some of his statements about history that are blatantly false.

Regarding historical inaccuracy, consider the following statement: "Almost everybody throughout history, up to the second half of the nineteenth century, has firmly believed in the opposite [of Darwinism] – the Conscious Designer theory."[11] I defy Dawkins to present historical evidence for this claim. He will not find the Conscious Designer theory in the fragments of Heraclitus, nor in the *Physics* or *Metaphysics* of Aristotle, nor in the *Summa Theologiae* of Thomas Aquinas[12]. Neither Luther nor Zwingli knew anything about this theory, and the German theologian Schleiermacher who was roughly a contemporary of Paley would have found it impossible to incorporate the design argument into his own theological thinking. In its original form, the theory of conscious design was developed by the Stoics, and it found its clearest expression in the writings of Cicero. The Christian theologian Augustine of the early church adopted the Stoic idea, but modified it in accordance with his Neoplatonic philosophical views and his Christian orientation. In subsequent chapters, we will investigate these matters in detail. Suffice it for the moment to say that the Conscious Designer theory was a product of the eighteenth century, and as we know, it was employed by William Paley as an argument for the existence of God. Dawkins' claim about the Con-

---

[11] DAWKINS, p. 7.

[12] THOMAS AQUINAS' fifth argument for the reality of God is an argument from final causation, not from design. See *Summa Theologiae*, Pars Prima, Question 2, Article 3.

scious Designer theory reflects not only his Anglocentric mindset, but also his historical myopia. He seems to be oblivious to the entire theological tradition prior to William Paley. Were he simply addressing the views of the Anglican Church, one might overlook his narrowmindedness, but since he is making broad philosophical and theological claims that are intended to have validity beyond the shores of England, it is incumbent upon him to broaden his perspective.

In Chapter 2 ("Good Design") Dawkins takes up the matter of design and presents his arguments against the views of William Paley and Bishop Hugh Montefiore. Although Dawkins quotes Paley's Watchmaker argument in Chapter 1, it would have been more appropriate in Chapter 2 where he addresses explicitly the matter of design. For clarity, let us take a look at Dawkins' quotation in Chapter 1 from Paley's argument:

"In crossing a heath, suppose I pitched my foot against a *stone*, and were asked how the stone came to be there; I might possibly answer, that, for any thing I knew to the contrary, it had lain there forever: nor would it perhaps be very easy to show the absurdity of this answer. But suppose I had found a *watch* upon the ground, and it should be inquired how the watch happened to be in that place; I should hardly think of the answer which I had before given, that for any thing I knew, the watch might have always been there. ..." Dawkins breaks off Paley's argument at this point and summarily comments on the intricacy of the watch as the basis upon which Paley concludes "that the watch must have had a maker: that there must have existed, at some time, and at some place or other, an artificer or artificers, who formed it for the purpose which we find it actually to answer; who comprehended its construction, and designed its use."[13]

Significantly, Dawkins quotes a truncated version of Paley's argument and omits the detailed description of motion in the parts of the watch. As we shall see in Chapter 7 of the present work, the concept of motion in the

---

[13] Richard Dawkins, *The Blind Watchmaker*, (1987), 1996, p. 8.

watch foreshadows the celestial motion in the inorganic world and was not considered by Paley to be a trivial detail. Moreover, Dawkins never really attempts to refute Paley's argument, but rather he begins Chapter 2 with his own conclusion: "Natural selection is the blind watchmaker, blind because it does not see ahead, does not plan consequences, has no purpose in view. Yet the living results of natural selection overwhelmingly impress us with the appearance of design as if by a master watchmaker, impress us with the illusion of design and planning."[14] So the purpose of Chapter 2 is twofold: to strengthen our impression of design in nature and then to expose this impression as an illusion by demonstrating that the apparent design is really the result of the evolutionary process. To this point, Dawkins' argument is clear and cogent. Unfortunately, he confuses the matter by insisting on a technological analogy and pursuing the investigation in the following three steps: 1) he describes the problem that a "living machine" would face, 2) he considers solutions that an engineer might suggest, and finally 3) he explains the solution that nature has actually adopted. As an example, Dawkins offers a long section on bats in which he concludes that the brains of bats are "delicately tuned packages of miniaturized electronic wizardry, programmed with the elaborate software necessary to decode a world of echoes in real time".[15]

Near the end of the chapter, we discover why Dawkins introduced the analogy of electronic technology in the case of the bat. He wants to convince the reader that the impression of design in nature is largely, if not exclusively, the result of the technological mode of thinking. He writes: "Our experience of electronic technology prepares us to accept the idea that unconscious machinery can behave as if it understands complex mathematical ideas. This idea is directly transferable to the workings of living machinery. A bat is a machine. ... So far our intuition, derived from technology is correct. But our experience of technology

---

[14] DAWKINS, p. 29.
[15] DAWKINS, p. 34.

also prepares us to see the mind of a conscious and purposeful designer in the genesis of sophisticated machinery. It is this second intuition that is wrong in the case of living machinery. In the case of living machinery, the 'designer' is unconscious natural selection, the blind watchmaker."[16] Clearly Dawkins is departing here from the area of biology and proposing a psychological explanation of our impression of design in nature. Since engineers design machinery, we easily transfer, according to Dawkins, this thought to nature and assume that some designer must have designed it. It may well be that the technological mindset has produced its own characteristic way of thinking about design, but the fundamental intuition that there is design in nature predates modern science and can be traced back to the ancient Stoics who knew nothing about technology in the modern sense.

In Chapter 3, which is entitled "Accumulating small change", Dawkins presents an interesting and clear argument for the non-random cumulative process of evolution over time. Employing again his analogy between evolution and computer technology, he leads us step by step through a computer simulation in an effort to demonstrate that Darwinism is not simply a random process. Admittedly, the argument becomes a bit confused at points because he finds it necessary to correct the hypothetical computer program several times in order to make it fit the actual process of evolution. Nonetheless, the point of the chapter is clear. Those opponents of Darwinism who criticize evolution as a process based on random chance simply do not understand the important distinction between the *mutation* of genes and the *selection* of genes. It is true that the mutations themselves are random, but the selection of genes over time demonstrates a trajectory through genetic space because "there is a statistically limited number of mutations at any point in time which can survive".[17] Dawkins continues: "This belief, that Darwinian evolution is 'random', is not merely false. It is the exact opposite of the

[16] DAWKINS, p. 52 f.
[17] DAWKINS, p. 61.

truth. Chance is a minor ingredient in the Darwinian recipe, but the most important ingredient is cumulative selection which is quintessentially *non*random."[18]

When we remember that natural selection itself is the *blind* watchmaker, it seems strange at first that the selection of genes turns out to be *non-random*, but this is precisely Dawkins' claim. The "blind forces of nature" have led to a non-random process. We will comment on this claim later. Although it does not alter the validity of his argument, many readers will find Dawkins' comments about religion demeaning. It is regrettable that Dawkins lacked the decorum to address his opponents respectfully. The result has been that his work has wrought divisiveness instead of promoting fruitful dialogue.

Midway through Chapter 4 ("Making tracks through animal space") Dawkins quotes the following passage from Charles Darwin's *The Origin of Species*: "If it could be demonstrated that any complex organ existed which could not possibly have been formed by numerous, successive, slight modifications, my theory would absolutely break down".[19] Since opponents of Darwinism do indeed claim that organs such as the human eye could not have developed through slight modifications, Dawkins presents the evidence of evolutionary biology for the development of the eye and other complex structures. He also deals with the phenomenon of convergent evolution, "in which independent lines of evolution appear to have converged, from very different starting points, on what looks very like the same endpoint."[20] In actual fact, however, the convergence is not total, and numerous details betray the independent origins of the evolutionary lines. From a philosophical point of view, Dawkins notes that evolution is not in principle irreversible and that it has nothing to do with the idealistic concept of progress toward some goal – a philosophical point with which I totally agree.

[18] DAWKINS, p. 71.

[19] DAWKINS, p. 128.

[20] DAWKINS, p. 133.

Chapter 5, entitled "The Power and the Archives", deals with DNA and replication, and Dawkins' aim in this chapter is to discredit any notion of a "life force" and to dispel any lingering thoughts about the mystery of life. "What lies at the heart of every living thing is not a fire, not warm breath, not a 'spark of life'. It is information, words, instructions. ... If you want to understand life ... think about information technology."[21] Although Dawkins does not mention the Stoics, the idea of the fire or the warm breath in nature originated within Stoic thought. As the chapter proceeds, Dawkins continues to stress that there is nothing special about living things. They are simply collections of molecules. "What is special is that these molecules are put together in much more complicated patterns than the molecules of nonliving things, and this putting together is done by following programs, sets of instructions for how to develop. ..."[22] Pursuing his analogy between life and information technology, he insists that living cells are no more mysterious than the computer. The storage of information in the computer is electronic, whereas it is chemical in living cells. Having asserted that there is very little difference between information technology and the process of evolution, Dawkins notes that only about one percent of the genetic information in human cells seems to be used. "Nobody knows why the other 99 per cent is there."[23] One wonders if this fact alone does not indicate a flaw in Dawkins' theoretical model just as the absence of the interference lines in the famous Michelson-Morley experiment indicated a fundamental flaw in classical physics. Dawkins gives no indication, however, that he entertains such a possibility. Nor does his lack of knowledge about the 99 percent seem to shake his confidence that the mystery of life has been completely resolved.

As the chapter progresses, Dawkins' enthusiasm about DNA overflows into philosophical speculation when he shares with us "a central

[21] DAWKINS, p. 159.
[22] DAWKINS, p. 158.
[23] DAWKINS, p. 164.

truth about life on Earth". "This is that living organisms exist for the benefit of DNA rather than the other way around. … The messages that DNA molecules contain are all but eternal when seen against the time scale of individual lifetimes."[24] The shift in terminology is noticeable. When Dawkins is explaining evolutionary biology, the words are: cells, DNA, replication, molecules etc. But when he wishes to share his philosophical views, he shifts to traditional philosophical terms like "existence", "eternal" and "life". His claim that the messages contained in DNA molecules are "all but eternal" is truly remarkable. It borders philosophically on the notion of eternal truths and imbues Dawkins' views with a quasi-religious tone characteristic of modern atheism. Finally, let it be noted that the word "life" remains undefined throughout the entire book.

In spite of the fact that living things, according to Dawkins, are not fundamentally different from nonliving things, he asserts that there must be some ingredient or ingredients that account for life. Furthermore, "these very same ingredients, at least in some rudimentary form, must have arisen spontaneously on the early Earth, otherwise cumulative selection, and therefore life, would never have got started in the first place".[25] The occurrence of the word "spontaneously" in this passage is significant. If there was no first cause of life, if life was not created by a Creator, then life must be traced back to a spontaneous event. But what is a *spontaneous* event? It is a self-acting event, i.e. an event which is its own cause. Dawkins himself arrives implicitly at the same concept of *causa sui* (i.e. cause of itself) when he explains the first ingredient of life. "It is not breath, not wind, not any kind of elixir or potion. It is not a substance at all, it is a *property,* the property of self-replication. This is the basic ingredient of cumulative selection. There must somehow, as a consequence of the ordinary laws of physics, come into being *self-copying* entities or, as I shall call them, *replicators.*"[26]

---

[24] Dawkins, p. 180.
[25] Dawkins, p. 182.
[26] Dawkins, p. 183.

So the fundamental ingredient of life is a *property*, namely the property of making copies of itself. Dawkins' meaning here is far from clear. In normal usage, properties are understood to be qualities or traits of things or individuals. If I say: "The roses in my garden are red", it is understood that "red" is a quality or trait of the roses. Or if I say: "The man is very polite", again it is understood that "polite" is a trait of this man. Of course, the man will have many other traits, but none of these traits alone describes him completely. Nor would a combination of traits exhaust the meaning of being this particular man. So when Dawkins says that the fundamental ingredient of life is a property, the question immediately arises: a property of what? If he means that the fundamental ingredient of life is a property of life, then the statement is hopelessly circular and therefore meaningless. In this case, he would have simply exchanged the word "ingredient" for "property" without clarifying in any way the meaning of "life". Or does he vaguely sense that events are ontologically more fundamental than things? In this case, his use of the word "property" is misplaced; he should have said that life itself is the event of self-copying. But then his insistence on self-replication, i.e. on an event causing itself, would seem to imply a relativizing of the cause/effect relationship in biology. Were this the case, it would seem to undermine all of his arguments based on cause and effect. Unfortunately, his use of language here is confused. Expressions like "somehow", "we may suspect" and "it seems likely" betray his inability to clearly dispense with the notion of a vital force in life.

"Origins and Miracles" is the title of Chapter 6, and this is certainly not Dawkins' finest chapter. It requires a great deal of patience on the part of the reader to wade through 40 pages of text in order to learn that the author does not know how life originated. Possible scientific explanations include "the primeval soup" and "the inorganic mineral" theories, but the only point of certainty in Dawkins' mind (or brain) is that the origination of life was not a miracle. "My thesis will be that events that we commonly call miracles are not supernatural, but are part of a spectrum of more-or-less improbable natural events.”[27] Once again we are confronted with Dawkins’ Anglocentric thinking. The contrast of natural/supernatural, characteristic of English supernaturalism of the nineteenth century, is the only possibility that he considers, but as in previous sections he makes no attempt to define either term. In contrast to Paley and Dawkins, Augustine did not consider miracles to be contrary to the natural order at all. This is a topic that we will consider later. Dawkins, for his part, recognizing that his inability to explain the origin of cumulative selection appears to be a flaw in his theory, assures us that a *theological* explanation would be even worse. Lest we turn to the Christian Church for an answer, Dawkins dismisses it a priori as backward: “I am heartily thankful that we have escaped from the small-mindedness of the medieval church”.[28] In his typically unscientific way, Dawkins resorts to ridiculing his opponents when a scientific explanation eludes him. There is no middle ground for him; either you agree with his views or you are hopelessly dumb. One is reminded of Hans Christian Andersen’s short tale “The Emperor’s New Clothes”, in which the two weavers claim that the new suit of clothes for the emperor is invisible only to those who are unfit for their positions or are stupid and incompetent.

Chapter 7 (“Constructive Evolution”) is very informative because it provides more detail about Dawkins’ gene-centered approach to evolution. “In natural selection, genes are always selected for their capacity to flourish in the environment in which they find themselves. We often think of this environment as the outside world, the world of predators and climate. But from each gene’s point of view, perhaps the most important part of its environment *is all the other genes that it encounters*.”[29] It is well known that Dawkins deviates significantly from Charles Darwin on this point and that he was opposed for this reason by the evolutionary biologist Ernst Mayr. This is an interesting dispute between two competent

---

[27] DAWKINS, p. 197.
[28] DAWKINS, p. 203.
[29] DAWKINS, p. 240 f.

biologists, but it is not relevant to our topic. In addition to the discussion of genes, Dawkins reiterates an important point that he made earlier. Although he maintains that complexity is attained in the process of evolution, he rightly rejects the enlightenment concept of steady progress.[30] That is, the process of evolution does not necessarily lead to progress in the political or social sense.

In Chapter 8, entitled "Explosions and spirals", Dawkins takes up two phenomena that do not seem at first glance to fit into the usual framework of evolution: the peacock's fan and cultural development. The peacock's fan appears to be a case of unstable, uncontrolled explosive development, and Dawkins explains it in terms of positive feedback, utilizing once again an analogy from technology. His argument about the peacock is interesting, but it is not as philosophically relevant as his excursion into matters of culture and history. In this regard, Dawkins goes well beyond Charles Darwin, and one cannot avoid reminding him that Darwin himself found the application of evolutionary theory to history and culture in the work of Ernst Haeckel very disturbing.[31] As he proceeds in this chapter, Dawkins tries to disassociate himself from Social Darwinism with its racist overtones, but it is difficult to see how he can reject the whole of Social Darwinism and still apply evolutionary concepts to history and culture. Of course, Dawkins admits that cultural evolution is not really evolution "if we are being fussy and purist about our use of words"[32], but he insists that there is a valid analogy. "It has frequently been pointed out – indeed any fool can see – that there is something quasi-evolutionary about many aspects of human history."[33] As we have now learned, Dawkins typically turns to belittling remarks such as "any fool can see" when he is on shaky ground, and indeed he is on very shaky

[30] DAWKINS, p. 257.

[31] The nineteenth century writings of ERNST HAECKEL were utilized later by the Nazis as a justification for persecuting the Jews.

[32] DAWKINS, p. 308.

[33] DAWKINS, p. 309.

ground with his claim about history. I know personally a number of professional historians, but I do not know a single one who would agree with Dawkins on this point. To find any support for Dawkins' claim, the reader must adopt the views of nineteenth century historicism or those of some other ahistorical ideology. One can only speculate as to why Dawkins even wants to make this claim since he is clearly out of his area of expertise. A possible explanation would be this: Unless he can transform evolutionary biology into a form of metaphysics that can explain in principle the whole of the humanities, there remains the possibility that religion could have a certain validity, and he is dedicated to an atheist view of the world that does not allow for religious phenomena.

Apropos religion, Dawkins begins Chapter 9 "Puncturing Punctuationism" with a fictitious story about the children of Israel migrating across the Sinai desert. Ostensibly the story is intended to introduce a controversy among the students of evolutionary biology, but the subliminal message is intended to mock both the biblical story and the historians who interpret it. At the end of the chapter, Dawkins returns to the topic of religion, branding those who do not share his views as "rednecks". Sandwiched in between these two attacks on religion are some rather interesting observations by Dawkins on the problem of gaps in the fossil evidence for evolution. As he notes, there are various ways of explaining these gaps, but none of them deviate significantly from Darwinism.

There is one further point at the end of the chapter that requires comment. In rejecting the views of his opponents, Dawkins claims that some of them refuse to accept Darwinism because the theory offends their sense of dignity. He writes: "some find the idea of natural selection unacceptably harsh and ruthless; others confuse natural selection with randomness, and hence 'meaninglessness', which offends their dignity. ..."[34] Although Dawkins glosses over this objection as though it were self-evident nonsense, the problem of the meaninglessness of human existence from the perspective of evolutionary biology is very real, and his-

[34] DAWKINS, p. 358.

torically it was one of the reasons that the original opponents of Darwin reacted so strongly to his views. Dawkins recognizes correctly that Darwin's theory was problematic for the Anglican Church because it provided a plausible alternative to Paley's interpretation of living things. But he fails to recognize that there was a second issue at stake that was rooted not only in Christian thought, but also in Aristotelian philosophy.

The scientific work of Galileo and Newton in the seventeenth century had already called into question the Aristotelian view of the physical world including the movement of the heavenly bodies, but until Darwin's work in the 19th century, the organic world as Aristotle had conceived it was not really in doubt. In his well-known treatise *On the Soul*, Aristotle had proposed an hierarchical structure of living beings, beginning with plants, extending through animals and concluding with human beings as the pinnacle of the organic world. The primary trait of plants was self-preservation; animals added to self-preservation the ability of sense perception; and humans were thought to possess not only self-preservation and sense perception, but also the unique capacity of reason. Thus we have the Aristotelian definition of man as the rational animal (*animal rationale*).

This hierarchical structure was adopted by the Christian Church and combined with biblical passages such as Psalm 8:4–5: "What is man that thou art mindful of him, and the son of man that thou dost care for him? Yet thou hast made him little less than God and dost crown him with glory and honour. Thou hast given him dominion over the works of thy hands; thou hast put all things under his feet. ..." The dignity of man and his superiority over all other animals was so well established in European culture that Pico della Mirandola of the Italian Renaissance could write an entire treatise entitled *Oration on the Dignity of Man* (*Oratio de hominis Dignitate*, 1486). The unity of Christian thought and humanistic philosophy concerning the dignity of man and his position in the universe was from the standpoint of public opinion a tremendous problem for Darwin when he first published his *On the Origin of Species*. To be sure, the full implication of the theory of evolution for the dignity of man was not apparent until Darwin's publication of *The Descent of Man*, but for astute readers of *On the Origin of Species* the handwriting was on the wall.

Charles Darwin published his groundbreaking work entitled *The Descent of Man* in 1871. In its first edition, the word "evolution" occurred for the very first time in any of Darwin's writings; in the following year, it appeared in the sixth edition of *On the Origin of Species*. The word "descent" in the title of Darwin's treatment of humankind is interesting. One can employ the term in the sense of "derivation from an ancestor", but the word also has the more general meaning of "descending from a higher to a lower level, rank or state". Darwin used the word, of course, in the former sense, and in the two volumes of *The Descent of Man* he applies the principles of evolution to human beings in order to demonstrate their derivation from a more primitive ancestor. It is fair to say that the results of Darwin's work in its broad features have become an indisputable theory in the scientific community. At the same time, *The Descent of Man* has had unexpected consequences due to the elimination of the traditional, fundamental differences between human beings and animals. At the outset of Chapter III of Vol. 1, Darwin presents a comparison of the mental powers of man and those of lower animals. Initially he confirms his agreement with those authors who view the conscience or the moral sense as precisely *that* trait which distinguishes humans from other animals.[35] But then, Darwin relativizes this statement through the formulation of his own thesis: "The following proposition seems to me in a high degree probable – namely, that any animal whatever, endowed with well-marked social instincts, would inevitably acquire a moral sense or conscience, as soon as its intellectual powers had become as well developed, or nearly as well developed, as in man."[36]

[35] CHARLES DARWIN, *The Descent of Man*, Vol. 1, 1871, p. 70.

[36] DARWIN, p. 71 f.

The very fact that Darwin entertained the possibility that other animals could develop the intellectual capacity of humans and that these animals would inevitably develop a conscience like humans amounts to an elimination of the traditional boundary between humans and animals. This was not simply a religious issue for Europeans of the nineteenth century nor is it simply a religious issue for us today. If there is no qualitative difference between humans and other animals, what does it mean to talk about the dignity of man? This is a deeply rooted cultural issue extending as far back as classical Athens, and Dawkins seems to be unaware of its significance when he pushes aside possible objections about the meaninglessness of human existence. Of course, the concept of meaning requires clarification, but historically, it has been associated with patterns of events and human relationships that were perceived to be purposeful. Admittedly, these reflections lead us into an area where simple answers are not to be found. Nevertheless, Dawkins does his reader a disservice by pretending that there is no issue to discuss. He continually emphasizes that natural selection is non-random, while admitting that mutations occur randomly. That may be the case. Still, there is no way to remove the random element from the evolutionary process. The process begins with the role of the dice, and from chance beginnings it is impossible to postulate a purposeful outcome – unless, of course, one adopts the concept of a guiding force which is precisely what Dawkins rejects. In the end Dawkins' entire thesis speaks against the concept of meaning; natural selection really is the *blind* watchmaker.

By the time the reader reaches Chapter 10, "The one true tree of life", he has become accustomed to Dawkins' undefined terms and inaccurate characterizations of Christianity. This chapter is mainly about taxonomy, the science of classification, which is supposed to assist us in understanding "nature" – a term that is used throughout the book, but whose meaning is never clarified. Furthermore, Dawkins inaccurately blames Christianity for the idea that humans are to be valued more than other animals. It is difficult to believe that Dawkins does not know that his statement is inaccurate; as a member of the Oxford elite, he has certainly read Cicero[37], if not Aristotle. In any case, he presents here a bogus argument that can be easily refuted by citing pre-Christian classical authors.

Having pointed out these weaknesses in Dawkins' presentation, one must admit that the content of his scientific understanding is quite interesting. Dawkins discusses various approaches to classification and explains how DNA has been used in the process of classification of living things. Problematic for him is, however, the following: Some of the scientists working in the area of classification have concluded that their results call Darwinism itself into question, and this opens the door to the creationists who – in Dawkins' opinion – exploit these views for their own purposes. In addressing this problem, Dawkins takes a two-pronged approach. On the one hand, he interprets the scientists in question as near-Darwinists, if not purists; on the other hand, he characterizes the creationists' ideas as absurd. To Dawkins' credit, he concedes toward the end of the chapter that there are certain difficulties with the Darwinian theory. Since "most of the evolutionary change that goes on at the molecular level is *neutral*", it follows "that it is not due to natural selection but is effectively random. ..."[38] Such problems should not, however, shake our confidence in Darwinism, if we remember that the actual evolutionary adaptations are non-random. Yet as we have already noted, it is questionable whether a non-random selection from random possibilities can really free itself from the charge of randomness. My

---

[37] DAWKINS is certainly familiar with CICERO's *On the Ends of Good and Evil* (De finibus bonorum et malorum), Bk. III, Sec. 67: "Praeclare enim Chrysippus, cetera nata esse hominum causa et deorum, eos autem communitatis et societatis suae, *ut bestiis homines uti ad utilitatem suam possint sine iniuria*" (*so that men can make use of beasts for their own purposes without injustice).* I am not espousing such a relationship between humans and animals; I am simply pointing out that Dawkins unjustly charges Christianity with an attitude that was very common in the ancient world and certainly predated Christianity. If Dawkins knows better – and I assume that he does –, then his comments are very disingenuous.

[38] RICHARD DAWKINS, *The Blind Watchmaker*, (1987), 1996, p. 385.

judgment is that Dawkins overstates his case in an effort to refute his opponents.

Chapter 11, entitled "Doomed Rivals", is the most disappointing chapter of the entire book. The reader expects Dawkins, the advocate of Charles Darwin and the worthy successor of Thomas Huxley, to offer a convincing summary account of his case. At the beginning of the book, Dawkins declared that he was an advocate for evolutionary biology and that his opponents were supporters of Paley's design argument. Given this initial framing of the topic, one is surprised to find that he devotes almost the entire last chapter to a discussion of Lamarckism, followed by a critique of neutralism and mutationism. Equally surprising is that he abandons his previous insistence on scientific evidence and takes, in his words, a "more armchair" approach. To be specific, Dawkins selects one property of living things for consideration and attempts to show that Darwinism is the only theory capable of explaining it adequately. This property turns out to be "adaptive complexity". Dawkins' "logic" is this: If Darwinism is the only known theory capable of explaining *adaptive complexity*, then Darwinism is the only plausible theory for explaining *life*. Evidence for or against the rival theories is no longer decisive; crucial is simply that Darwinism can account for adaptive complexity.

Dawkins' argument suffers both from a confusion of terms and from circularity. Clearly, *evolution* is not synonymous with *adaptive complexity*, although it includes the latter. So drawing any conclusions about the entire process of evolution from this one property seems highly dubious. Specifically, Dawkins sets out to demonstrate that only Darwinism is capable of explaining *adaptive complexity*; then he incorrectly assumes that only Darwinism can explain *life*. The phrase "to explain life" prompts him to explain what he means by "explain", but it never occurs to him that the word "life" is left unexplained. Regarding circularity, it is obvious that Dawkins chose the property of adaptive complexity, knowing that it is a primary element in the Darwinian theory. Thus he has assumed fortuitously the conclusion at the outset.

When Dawkins turns to the rival theories of neutralism and mutationism, he admits that "large quantities of evolutionary change may be non-adaptive ... but only in the boring parts of evolution, not the parts concerned with what is special about life as opposed to non-life."[39] Since neutralism and mutationism cannot account for adaptive complexity, they are not capable of explaining evolution or life. In the last three pages of the book, Dawkins finally comes to deal with the views of his declared opponents who follow the design argument of William Paley. "We have dealt with all the alleged alternatives to the theory of natural selection except the oldest one. This is the theory that life was created, or its evolution master-minded, by a conscious designer."[40] Overlooking the fact that creation is not a *theory*, but a *belief*, the reader now anticipates a discussion of Paley's theology and the way in which it has been appropriated by contemporary conservatives. Additionally, one expects a serious confrontation in summary form between creationism and evolutionism. Instead, Dawkins offers some rather elementary and to some extent inaccurate information about the creation myth of the Hebrew Bible. Oddly enough, he then acknowledges that creation is indeed a belief, as he writes: "All that we can say about such beliefs is, firstly, that they are superfluous and, secondly, that they *assume* the existence of the main thing we want to *explain*, namely organized complexity."[41] One hardly knows where to start in order to unravel the confusion in this passage. Of course, the Christian doctrine of creation is superfluous to an evolutionary biologist who is not interested in anything that does not fit within the narrow limits of scientific thinking. This seems to be a very obvious point. And Dawkins' second point also states nothing more than the obvious. Of course, the traditional doctrine of creation does not explain organized complexity in Dawkins' sense because it was never intended to explain organized complexity. Furthermore, the idea

---

[39] DAWKINS, p. 429.
[40] DAWKINS, p. 448.
[41] DAWKINS, p. 449.

of creation involves the entire *universe*, not simply *living beings*. What all of this has to do with William Paley is left to the reader's imagination. For Dawkins closes the book with a few philosophical phrases such as "essence of life" and "existence of life", which are, of course, meaningless in the context of his scientific thought.

In conclusion, I would like to acknowledge once again the expertise of Richard Dawkins in the area of evolutionary biology. That notwithstanding, his criticisms of Christianity are often ill-informed and his logic faulty. His entire argument against Christian views on creation can be simplified and summarized by saying that these views do not fit within the framework of modern biology. But then, neither does Sartre's concept of existence nor Heidegger's description of "Dasein" nor Whitehead's concept of creativity, and the list goes on. If Dawkins simply wanted to say that he does not acknowledge any truths beyond the narrow limits of evolutionary biology, he could have said that in less than 451 pages.

In the following chapter, we will broaden our perspective by stepping back from the narrow restraints of modern scientific thinking in order to consider the tradition of thought originating among the ancient Greeks. For this purpose the fragments of Heraclitus are well suited, as are the extant writings of the Stoics. Both sources will provide us with insights that are neither scientific nor Christian and will aide us in establishing a foundation for further discussion. Unfortunately, the current debate between evolutionists and creationists lacks any such foundation. On the one side of the debate, creationists either adopt a quasi-scientific mode of thinking and argue about the details of biology or they retreat into a rigid belief-system that renders dialogue impossible. On the other side, the evolutionary biologists demonstrate the same rigidity by clinching to their assumptions about the world and refusing to seriously consider any point of view that deviates from the accepted scientific position. Given this constellation, meaningful dialogue becomes impossible and the end result is a poverty of thought on both sides.

Chapter 2

"The Wisdom of the Philosophers: Heraclitus and the Stoics"

Heraclitus, the Obscure

At the beginning of Greek philosophy stood one of the most enigmatic figures of Western thought: Heraclitus. Profound, aggressive, lonely, and – by all accounts – obscure, this thinker from Ephesus has troubled philosophers for millennia. Nietzsche wrote once of Heraclitus that such men live in their own solar system.[1] Diogenes reports: "He [Heraclitus] was lofty-minded beyond all other men, and over-weening, as is clear from his book in which he says: 'Much learning does not teach understanding; else would it have taught Hesiod and Pythagoras, or again, Xenophanes and Hecataeus.' For 'this one thing is wisdom, to understand thought, as that which guides all the world everywhere.' And he used to say that 'Homer deserved to be chased out of the lists [the place of contest at the games] and beaten with rods. …" Heraclitus' contempt for other writers was equaled by his eccentric behavior. "He would retire to the temple of Artemis and play at knuckle-bones with the boys; and when the Ephesians stood round him and looked on, 'Why, you rascals,'

[1] Nietzsche, *Die Philosophie im tragischen Zeitalter der Griechen*, Späteres Vorwort, Abschnitt 8.

he said, 'are you astonished? Is it not better to do this than to take part in your civil life?'"[2]

Certainly one of the difficulties facing the modern interpreter of Heraclitus is the paucity of material available about his life and work. There is very little known about his life; our primary source is Diogenes Laertius who devoted several sections to Heraclitus in Book IX of his *Lives of Eminent Philosophers*[3]. From him we learn that Heraclitus lived in the Greek-inhabited city of Ephesus in Asia Minor (modern Turkey) sometime around 500 B.C. According to Diogenes, Heraclitus wrote an extended treatise entitled *On Nature*, but unfortunately the entire work has been lost except for 126 fragments which appear in the writings of other philosophers who refer to Heraclitus.[4] Some of these fragments appear in the writings of Stoics who adopted certain ideas of Heraclitus. Other fragments are found in opponents of the Stoics where the views of the Ephesian are criticized. Needless to say, both types of fragments undergo interpretation in the context in which we now have them. A further difficulty lies in the fact that there is no apparent structure reflected in these fragments. We simply have an arbitrary list of fragments excerpted from various sources, and any attempt to organize them involves at the outset an interpretation of their meaning.

However, the obscurity of the fragments cannot be explained solely on the basis of their poor transmission. Already at the time when the book of Heraclitus was still intact and being read by other thinkers, he was called "Heraclitus, the Obscure" (ὁ Σκοτεινός), and stories circulated about his

[2] DIOGENES LAERTIUS, *Lives of Eminent Philosophers*, Bks. VI–X, trans. by R. D. HICKS in Harvard's Loeb Classical Library, Bk. IX, Ch. 1, Sec. 4.

[3] Written in the early third century A.D.

[4] Both HERMANN DIELS and G. T. W. PATRICK have published lists of HERACLITUS' fragments: HERMANN DIELS, *Die Fragmente der Vorsokratiker*, Vol. 1, 1903, pp. 58–88 and G. T. W. PATRICK, *The Fragments of Heraclitus*, 2013. DIELS considers 126 known fragments to be authentic, whereas PATRICK has included 130 in his list. Also the order of the fragments in the list of DIELS and of PATRICK differs considerably. The following discussion will refer to the fragment numbers of DIELS.

odd behavior. Aristotle relates a story about how Heraclitus would sit in an oven to warm himself and would tell onlookers that the gods were also present in there.[5] Still, not even such eccentric behavior accounts for the epithet "the Obscure". Instead, it was the originality and depth of his thought that made Heraclitus so enigmatic and obscure. He looked at the world around him and saw things that others did not perceive. Unlike his predecessors such as Anaximander, he saw nature not just as a substance, whether it be air, water, fire or earth, but as an unfathomable mystery, whether one describes it as an event or as a process or as Being itself. In any case, the question around which an understanding of Heraclitus revolves is this: How did he understand nature?

To begin, it seems that Heraclitus discovered in nature the philosophical problem of the one and the many – a problem that has persisted in the history of philosophy until the present day. But what exactly is the problem of the one and the many? An answer to this question can be approached in different ways, but the most helpful in understanding Heraclitus is in the context of permanence and change. Take, for example, an oak tree. The changes that take place in an oak tree are observable. It grows, it produces acorns annually, it sheds its leaves, and so forth. Amid all such changes, we still think that it is the same oak tree as before. It is *one* oak tree, not *many*. It is the same oak tree in summer as it is in winter. In an attempt to explain the permanence of the oak tree amid change, Aristotle postulated the idea of a form or substance inherent in the tree. The appearance of the oak tree undergoes changes, but these changes have no impact on the basic substance of the tree. That is, there are many different appearances of the tree, but the substance or form remains one and the same. This solution to the problem was embraced in the Middle Ages by theologians such as Thomas Aquinas, and it provided the basis for the doctrine of transubstantiation (i.e. change of substance) of the eucharistic elements. Only in this case, it was the outward appearance of the elements that remained the same, whereas the

[5] ARISTOTLE, *Parts of Animals* (De partibus animalium), Bk. I, Ch. 5 (645a17 ff.).

substantial form was thought to change. However, this was not the solution of Heraclitus. Although he discovered the problem of the one and the many, he never envisioned a permanence of the Aristotelian sort. In the following, we seek to elucidate Heraclitus' thought on this problem. We will consider selected fragments that relate to the topic of nature, and we will arrange them under italicized rubrics that are intended to assist our interpretation.[6]

> *All things are in constant change.*
>
> Frag. 6: "The sun is new everyday."
>
> Frag. 91: "It is not possible to step in the same river twice nor twice to touch a perishable substance in a fixed condition (κατὰ ἕξιν), but by the sharpness and quickness of change, it disperses and gathers again; it both approaches and retreats."
>
> Frag. 12: "To those stepping into the same river, other and other waters flow."

Fragment 6 testifies to the uniqueness of the world in the midst of its rhythmic motion. Every morning the sun rises, and every evening the sun sets. But these events are never the same; the sun is new everyday. That the world is in constant flux comes to expression again in Fragment 91, where not the rhythm of physical processes, but rather a human act comes into view. If you wish, you can step into a river, but you cannot step into the same river twice. The river is not only flowing; it is itself *as* river in constant flux. There is a variant to Fragment 91 that reads: "To those stepping into the same river, other and other waters flow" (Frag. 12), and some commentators have suggested that Heraclitus is making a distinction between the permanence of the river and change of the waters. However, such an interpretation finds little support in the other frag-

[6] Regarding the English translation of the fragments, I have followed in some cases the translation of G. T. W. Patrick in *The Fragments of Heraclitus*, 2013, but in other cases, I have provided my own translation of Heraclitus' Greek.

ments that we possess. Even the second half of Fragment 91 would seem to exclude the idea of permanence. For Heraclitus says further: "It is not possible to step in the same river twice nor twice to touch a perishable substance in a fixed condition (κατὰ ἕξιν), but by the sharpness and quickness of change, it disperses and gathers again; it both approaches and retreats." The continual *approaching* and *retreating* accounts for the flux of all things.

> *Nevertheless all things are one.*
>
> Frag. 50: "It is wise for those who hear, not me, but the logos, to confess that all things are one."

In this succinct, but deeply meaningful sentence, Heraclitus places himself in the background and admonishes the reader to heed the *logos*. But what is the *logos*? Unfortunately, the Greek word λόγος cannot be translated simply into English. Indeed it can mean "word" in the sense of a saying, but not in the sense of individual words listed in a dictionary. The verb from which *logos* is derived has the basic meaning of "gathering" or "gleaning", and *logos* itself as a noun can mean "counting" ("reckoning") or "recounting" ("explaining"). In the sense of "counting", *logos* has a strong rational connotation so that it could mean "reason" (i.e. man's ability to think). Additionally, it was used in mathematics to mean "proportion" or "relation". In the sense of "recounting", it could mean "speech", "language" or "narrative". In sum, *logos* could be translated in Fragment 50 either as "word" or as "reason". In either case, however, we must guard against a subjectivistic interpretation. For Heraclitus *logos* constitutes not only humans in their true being, but also the entire cosmos. Apparently, it was Heraclitus who first maintained that *logos* – let's call it "Word" with a capital letter – is the fundamental relationship between human beings and the world, between human beings and the gods, and finally among human beings themselves. As Heraclitus says in Fragment 1, the Word is eternal, and although it is not understood by men, all things happen through this Word. Human beings are bound by the Word, but they do not see it or understand it.

In Fragment 50, Heraclitus tells us that it is wise for those who do hear the Word to confess that all things are one. It is indeed surprising, after we have been told that all things are in *flux*, to hear that all things are *one*. The idea that the sun is new everyday and that it is impossible to step into the same river twice points not only to the uniqueness of things and events, but also to the sheer multiplicity of the world. As an apparent contradiction to the "many" in the world, Fragment 50 asserts that all things are ultimately "one". How this "one" is to be understood is crucial. The modern research into the fragments of Heraclitus was initiated by Hegel and Schleiermacher.[7] Particularly, Hegel saw in these fragments a confirmation of his own concept of the dialectic: the positing of opposites (the many) that are then unified into a new whole (the one). This is not the place to embark upon a criticism of Hegel's dialectic. Suffice it to say that his interpretation of Heraclitus is very questionable. For the moment we leave the question about the meaning of the "one" unanswered; we will return to it later.

> *The harmony of opposites.*
>
> Frag. 8: "The opposition is bringing together; and out of the differences the most beautiful harmony; and all things take place through strife."
>
> Frag. 10: "Connections are: whole and not whole, agreement and disagreement, accordant and discordant; and out of all things one and out of one all things."
>
> Frag. 60: "The way upward and downward are one and the same."

---

[7] See FRIEDRICH SCHLEIERMACHER, *Herakleitos, der dunkle, von Ephesos*, 1808, *Kritische Gesamtausgabe*, 1. Abteilung, Bd. 6, S. 101–241.

Frag. 51: "They do not understand how that which is drawn apart agrees with itself. It is a turning-back harmony just as in the case of the bow and the lyre."

Frag. 54: "The hidden harmony is better than the visible."

In reading Fragment 8, we can understand why Hegel considered Heraclitus' harmony of opposites to be a dialectical process. When the thesis and the antithesis are united, they form a beautiful harmony. Yet in Hegel's thought, this harmony soon breaks up again into a new thesis and antithesis, and the whole process advances to higher and higher stages of reality, being driven by the concept of the Absolute. Heraclitus' thought is otherwise. There is no Absolute bringing the opposites together into a new unity; rather it is the opposition itself that draws the opposites together. Furthermore, there is no indication that strife ceases even for a moment when the harmony of opposites is established. The Greek word for "strife" is interesting because it was personified as the goddess Eris who incites war. Eris was the goddess of discord, and it is precisely the discord that establishes harmony.

Fragment 10 states: "Connections are: whole and not whole, agreement and disagreement, accordant and discordant; and out of all things one and out of one all things." Again Heraclitus refers to the process of the one and the many. Out of the many oppositions comes the one, and out of the one come the many. Out of agreement, disagreement and out of accordant, discordant. The Greek word for "accordant" (συνᾴδω) is a musical term meaning "to sing with or together" or "to be in unison", whereas the meaning of the Greek word for "dissonant" is less certain. To be sure, it can mean "to be dissonant", but it can also mean "to contend in song", for instance, in order to win a prize. The idea of contending or striving certainly fits Heraclitus' understanding of the harmony produced out of opposites. If this is correct, Fragment 10 bespeaks a striving that produces a harmony.

We have referred to the process of the one and the many as if Heraclitus were thinking along the lines of Whitehead in his well-known

Process and Reality. This is certainly not true. The one out of the many and the many out of the one should not be understood in any way as a temporal succession. Consider Fragment 60: "The way upward and downward are one and the same." The way up and the way down are not sequential, but rather they are one and the same. Paradoxical as that may sound, it is exactly what Heraclitus meant, and the task of interpretation is one of bringing this paradox to light so that it is understandable.

Fragment 51 reads: "They do not understand how that which is drawn apart agrees with itself. It is a turning-back harmony just as in the case of the bow and the lyre." The word "harmony" (ἁρμονία), which appears in Fragments 8, 51, and 54, was used in Greek culture in connection with music and meant "harmony" or "concord". Its root meaning, however, indicated a means of joining or fastening things together. It could refer in anatomy to a suture or in cosmology to the framework of the universe. The harmony of the opposites is one of connectivity, but we must guard against the static image of a suture or framework. Heraclitus' connectivity of the opposites involves a *dynamic tension* as is clear from his reference to the bow and the lyre. Both of these are illustrations of a harmony of opposite straining tension.[8] The old Greek bow was constructed with its arms bent back at the ends, and this construction produced a tension much like that of the lyre.

Finally, we learn in Fragment 54 that the dynamic connectivity of oppositions is in no way visible: "The hidden harmony is better than the visible." What we see in our daily lives are the oppositions: day and night, hot and cold, up and down, accordant and discordant. Nevertheless the straining tension that holds them together and gathers them into the one is always present. The hiddenness of this harmony was possibly the most profound insight of Heraclitus.

The appearing and hiding of nature.
Frag. 123: "Nature loves to hide herself."

[8] See G. T. W. Patrick, *The Fragments of Heraclitus*, 2013, p. 50, footnote 19.

In his interpretation of Heraclitus, Martin Heidegger considered this fragment to be the second most important for an understanding of the obscure Ephesian.[9] Problematic, however, is that Heidegger's translation of the Greek deviates considerably from that of reputed philologists. As much as I am indebted to Heidegger for my understanding of Heraclitus, I prefer in this case to retain the standard translation: "Nature loves to hide herself".

Although Fragment 123 is the only one in which the word "nature" (φύσις) occurs, nature was presumably the central topic of Heraclitus' thought. As we have noted, Diogenes reports that the entire work of Heraclitus was entitled *On Nature*. For this reason, the task of understanding Heraclitus' philosophical thought revolves around the difficulty of fathoming his unique view of nature. Certainly he did not understand nature as we do. We think of nature as the sum total of living and non-living, organic and inorganic beings, and we organize beings and things into categories so that we can investigate them. Since the advent of modern science in the seventeenth century, the categorization and analysis of nature have advanced to a point of specialization where not even the most gifted scientist can claim to understand nature as a whole. Perhaps a common dictionary definition of "natural science" would be instructive. According to Merriam Webster, "natural science" is defined as "any of the sciences (as physics, chemistry, or biology) that deal with matter, energy, and their interrelations and transformations or with objectively measurable phenomena". None of this would have made any sense to Heraclitus. It would never have occurred to him to measure nature or to dissect it into parts such as biology, chemistry etc. He was not even interested in the less abstract divisions later proposed by Aristotle such as living and non-living. To be sure, nature included for him such things as trees, mountains, rivers, animals and human beings, but it included them as "the one and the many", as the "harmony of oppositions".

[9] MARTIN HEIDEGGER, *Der Anfang des abendländischen Denkens: Heraklit*, Gesamtausgabe, II. Abteilung, Vorlesungen, 1923–1944, Bd. 55, 1979.

The Greek word for "nature" is *physis* (φύσις) from which English derived the word "physics", but the meaning of *physis* is quite different from the English "physics". The root verb of *physis* is *phuo* and means "to grow" or "to spring up". "Nature", then, meant for Heraclitus not the sum total of things living and non-living, but rather nature was "a springing up" or "a growing" of these things. It is not the trees, the mountains and the rivers that he had in mind, but rather "the springing up" of the trees, the mountains and the rivers. This does not mean that he was thinking of springing up or growing in the sense of a biologist or a horticulturist. It was the sheer *appearing* of things that amazed him. And the wonderment of the appearing finds expression in Fragment 123 precisely in the tension between "nature" and "hiding". When nature appears, it hides itself. When the trees, the mountains, the rivers and human beings spring forth, there is both an *appearing* and a *concealing*.

Just as the idea of appearing is inherent in the Greek word for "nature" (φύσις), the idea of withdrawing is connotated in the word for "hiding" (λανθάνω). In its active sense, the word means "to escape notice", and in the middle-passive, it means "to forget", "to let something escape one". When we are unable to recall something, we can say in English: "It escapes me." Thereby we do not mean that the matter is not present at all. On the contrary, we are aware that the matter is escaping us. It is withdrawing and for the moment it is beyond our control. For Heraclitus the withdrawing, escaping, hiding cannot be separated from the appearing, which is itself nature. In the context of the present study, we cannot pursue further the originality of Heraclitus' thought on this topic. Let us simply content ourselves with the assertion: Something shines forth and is hidden at the same time. And let us name the hiddenness "mystery". So nature is the sheer springing forth of things that always involves a mystery – not a mystery that at some point in the future could be explained or clarified, but rather a mystery that is profoundly hidden in the very appearing of nature.

The governing power of the universe.

Frag. 64: "The thunderbolt steers all things."

Frag. 30: "This world, the same for all, neither any of the gods nor any man has made, but it always was, and is, and will be an ever-living fire, kindled in due measure and in due measure extinguished."

In Greek thought, the thunderbolt was a symbol of Zeus. So the meaning of this fragment may simply be that Zeus guides the universe with his providential care. However, there is the further possibility that Heraclitus considered Zeus to be a symbol for the light that suddenly appears. When the thunderbolt strikes in the night, all things suddenly shine forth out of the darkness. The emphasis on light finds support in Fragment 30 which reads: "This world, the same for all, neither any of the gods nor any man has made, but it always was, and is, and will be an ever-living fire, kindled in due measure and in due measure extinguished." Just as we found in Fragment 123, something shines forth and something is hidden. The simultaneous appearing and concealing is expressed in the image of the eternal, living fire that is kindled in due measure and in due measure extinguished.

One world, one Word, one law.

Frag. 89: "To those who are awake there is one world in common, but of those who are asleep, each is withdrawn to a private world of his own."

Frag. 2: "Although the Word is common to all, most people live as though they had thoughts of their own."

Frag. 114: "Those who speak with understanding must hold fast to that which is common to all, even more strongly than a city holds fast to its law. For all human laws are nourished by the law of God, for this rules as far as it wills, and suffices for all, and prevails over all."

It is perhaps tempting for the modern reader to interpret Fragment 89 as support for a globalized world. "To those who are awake there is one world in common, but of those who are asleep, each is withdrawn to a private world of his own." That is, those who are really alert and well informed realize that it is a mistake to retreat into the narrow bounds of nationalism. Such a reading of Heraclitus, however, would amount to a crass interjection of the present into an ancient world that was very different from ours and that is very difficult for us to understand. This was the mistake of Karl Popper in his book *The Open Society and its Enemies* (1945) in which he argued that Pericles stood for an open society in Athens. Popper's shock over the events of the Second World War blinded him to the extent that he could only conceive of two possibilities: a totalitarian society like the National Socialism that he had experienced and an open society characterized by egalitarianism and individualism. Whatever merits one might find in Popper's thought, the violence that he did to historical documents is totally unacceptable. So if Heraclitus does not address a modern problem of societies, what did he mean to say in Fragment 89?

We notice first of all that this fragment is not in any way a call to action. Heraclitus is not admonishing us to take certain actions in order to produce a world that is common to all. If there is in this fragment a call to anything, it is a call to watchfulness. The Greek word in this fragment does not mean simply to be awake, but rather to watch or to keep watch. It is the watchfulness of the night guard. One is reminded of the saying of Jesus in which the same Greek word appears. "But know this, that if the householder had known in what part of the night the thief was coming, he would have watched and would not have let his house be broken into."[10] But what is it that we are supposed to see if we keep watch over the world? It is the oneness of all things. It is the harmony

[10] Matthew 24:43. All biblical quotations in English translation have been taken from *The Oxford Annotated Bible: Revised Standard Version*, ed. by Herbert G. May and Bruce M. Metzger, 1962.

of opposites, the appearing and hiding of nature, the guidance of Zeus. And as we learn in Fragment 2, this oneness comes to light in the Word that is common to all.

The Greek expression for “Word” in Fragment 2 is *logos*, and as we have seen, the word does not admit of any single translation into English. Some translators prefer to translate *logos* in Fragment 2 as “reason”, and certainly this is linguistically possible. It does not, however, accord well with the thinking of Heraclitus. Other possible meanings of *logos* are “account”, “reckoning”, “proportion”, “speech” or “saying”, but in its root verbal form, it conveys the notion of “gathering”. The *logos* gathers together and sets in order. In the context of the fragments that we have already discussed, the idea of “gathering and setting in order” is more consonant with Heraclitus’ thought than the concept of reason. If this is correct, the Word does not refer directly to a common language that all human beings share. Furthermore, it refers neither to a unique linguistic capacity of humans nor to something akin to Chomsky’s universal grammar. Instead the Word points again to the harmony of opposites, to the appearing and hiding of nature. The Word as a gathering and setting in order brings together the oppositions into a harmony. In light of the Word, nature reveals itself and hides itself at the same time. In this fragment, Heraclitus is calling our attention to the most fundamental basis of language. Beneath the differences manifested among the various languages and language families and beneath any common structures that we might be able to identify, there is a fundamental process at work that makes language what it is. Regardless of which historical language one considers, it is the gathering of the Word that makes that language what it is.

In Fragment 114 we learn that the Word has the character of law – not just any law, but rather the law common to all. “Those who speak with understanding must hold fast to that which is common to all, even more strongly than a city holds fast to its law. For all human laws are nourished by the law of God, for this rules as far as it wills, and suffices for all, and prevails over all.” The second part of this fragment makes it clear that

Heraclitus is thinking neither of a law of nature in the sense of a modern scientific law nor of natural law in a moral sense, but rather of the law of God. At first blush, this assertion may seem to clarify the meaning of law, but in fact the first impression is deceptive because it is far from clear what Heraclitus means when he speaks of the "law of God". Certainly, he is not thinking about anything analogous to the Ten Commandments of the Hebrew Bible. His emphasis on oneness would preclude a multiplicity of rules and ordinances. If we bring Fragment 94 to bear on the matter, we only complicate the situation. Whereas Fragment 114 clearly speaks about the law of God, Fragment 94 seems to point in the direction of a universal law of nature: "The sun will not overstep his measure, for if he does, the Erinyes, the helpers of Justice, will find him out." From a modern perspective, the rising and setting of the sun is a phenomenon of nature and can be understood in accordance with the laws of physics. But Heraclitus tells us that the Erinyes will *punish* the sun if it oversteps its bounds, and this reference to the Erinyes does not fit any interpretation in terms of modern scientific laws. "Justice" in this fragment is capitalized because in early Greek mythology the word referred to the goddess of all that was right and just. Justice was the daughter of Zeus and was assisted in the meting out of justice by the Erinyes, the subterranean goddesses of vengeance who punished unmercifully those who violated the law.[11] So the occurrence of "Justice" and the "Erinyes" in this fragment only confuses further the meaning of the law that is common to all. On the one hand, we have a phenomenon of nature – the rising and setting of the sun –, and on the other hand, we have as it were the moral indignation of the Erinyes who assist Justice and punish all trespassers.

Returning to Fragment 114, we find that the second half of it does indeed address the matter of civil and moral law: "For all *human laws* are nourished by the law of God, for this rules as far as it wills, and suffices for all, and prevails over all". So what conclusions can be drawn from

[11] In Latin, they were called the *Furiae*, and CICERO mentions them in *On the Laws* (De legibus), Bk. 1, Ch. XIV. Sec. 40.

these fragments? First of all, it is clear that Heraclitus had no concept of nature in the modern scientific sense and therefore no concept of a law of nature. Furthermore, the notion of positive civil and moral law separated from universal, divine law was foreign to his thinking. As we have already hinted, the key to understanding law in these fragments is the idea of oneness. The oneness of all things precludes the many distinctions that we hold important because oneness is always a gathering of oppositions. The thinking of Heraclitus, the Obscure, lacked the definitions and categorization that even Aristotle found essential. For Heraclitus *law* and *Word* cannot be separated. Just as the Word is a gathering of oppositions into a harmony, so also the law is a gathering together with the additional connotation of regularity and necessity. The necessity associated with law seems to be indicated in Fragment 16 which reads: "How can one escape that which never sets?" Admittedly, this is a particularly obscure fragment, and commentators from the time of Schleiermacher have struggled to offer a satisfactory explanation of its meaning.[12] In my opinion, "that which never sets" is best understood as eternal order or law. One cannot escape the law. It sets the bounds of human freedom. The regularity of the law was already indicated in Fragment 94 where Justice guaranteed the daily movement of the sun.

Let us summarize what we have gleaned from Heraclitus's fragments. According to Heraclitus, nature is not simply a collection of things. It is not the sum total of human beings, animals, trees, rivers, mountains etc. Instead nature is the springing up of these things; it is the appearing of things. The appearing of things is, however, always at the same time a concealing of them. Things appear and withdraw at the same time. The mystery of nature is never exposed in the appearing. Furthermore, the appearing and concealing of things involves a dynamic tension – a pulling in opposite directions as in the case of the bow and the lyre. The springing forth of things in this dynamic tension can be described as light or fire. Finally, nature as the springing forth of things in a dynamic

[12] G. T. W. Patrick, *The Fragments of Heraclitus*, 2013, p. 48, footnote 14.

tension of appearing and concealing has the character of Word and law. It is the gathering together into the light (Word), and it ultimately directs all things (law).

The implications of Heraclitus' understanding of nature bear directly on the situation of the modern individual in an organized society. Against the background of Heraclitus' fragments, the much-celebrated freedom of modern man is unmasked as an illusion. We have the freedom to think and to act only within the bounds of nature, i.e. within the bounds of that which comes to light. When the thunderbolt strikes in the night, there is an immediate illumination, and within the boundaries of this illumination, we are free to think and to act. Authentic thought must heed the light, and true morality must adhere to the Word. We may make *judgments* about right and wrong, but we do not have the capacity to *establish* right and wrong. Nature itself in its dynamic appearing and concealing provides the structure. That is, the Word gathers that which is needful into an ordered pattern and allows it to be spoken. Above all else, the philosophy of Heraclitus stands as an indictment against the hubris of the modern mind.

The Stoics: From Zeno to Cicero

Between the pre-Socratic philosophy of Heraclitus (ca. 500 B.C.) and the rise of Stoicism (ca. 300 B.C.) lay the Golden Age of Athenian philosophy as it was formulated in the works of Plato and Aristotle. Of the two philosophers, Aristotle stands closer in many ways to the scientific thought of the modern era. His interests in empirical data, his analytical mode of thought, his tendency to categorization, his focus on individual substances and his delineation of causes can be viewed as forerunners of the scientific revolution of the seventeenth century. Of course, a closer examination will also bring fundamental differences to light. The so-called four "causes" of Aristotle are not really *causes* in the modern sense; the Greek word αἰτία (cause) has a much broader meaning than the English word "cause" and has connotations of "responsibility". To ask about the Aristotelian "causes" of an event or object is to search for that which is responsible for the event or the object being thus and so. Furthermore, Aristotle's doctrine of the internal finality of each thing[13] as well as his suggestion that there is an overarching pattern of purpose in the universe[14] clearly set him apart from Galileo and Newton. As a matter of fact, the idea of internal finality or teleology was one of the points most heavily debated between the Aristotelians of the seventeenth century and the proponents of the emerging empirical science. Nevertheless, it is possible to make certain comparisons between Aristotle's physics and modern science that reveal in broad terms a continuity of thought. When we approach Stoicism, however, we find comparisons of a different sort with modern thought, and these are to be found not so much in the area of classical physics as in the area of thermodynamics and quantum physics. For instance, the Stoic emphasis on heat in the universe is an interesting parallel to the role of heat in thermodynamics, and the field concept of modern physics may well have grown out of the Stoic idea of spirit (*pneuma*).

The emergence of Stoicism in Athens is inseparably connected with the fate of Aristotle after the death of Alexander the Great. Unlike Plato, Aristotle was not an Athenian. He was born in 384 B.C. in the small town of Stagira in Macedonia, which was at that time the northwestern region of Greece. At the age of seventeen he was sent to Athens in order to learn philosophy under the tutorage of Plato who had established the Academy on the outskirts of Athens. The details of his life in Athens, his sojourn in Assos etc. need not concern us here. Suffice it to say that Aristotle, being a Macedonian, was never fully accepted in Athens, and after the death of Alexander the Great – also a Macedonian – in 323 B.C., Aristotle was forced into exile where he died a year later. With the exile and death of Aristotle a new chapter in Greek philosophy began. With astonishing

[13] ARISTOTLE, *Physics*, Bk. B.

[14] ARISTOTLE, *On the Heavens*, 271a23–33.

rapidity new schools of philosophy emerged in Athens, and one of these schools was Stoicism, whose founder was Zeno of Citium.

Born in the Phoenician-Greek city of Citium on Cyprus in 336 B.C., Zeno came to Athens sometime around 300 B.C. to study philosophy, and he eventually founded his own school, which became known as Stoicism because its adherents met daily for philosophical discussion in the Stoa Poikile, i.e. the Painted Colonnade. It has been noted that the Phoenician, i.e. Semitic, background of Zeno may have had some influence on his thought inasmuch as he brought a holistic approach to his philosophy that was quite different from the analytical method of Aristotle. Furthermore, he stressed much more than Aristotle the necessity of God in the constitution and functioning of the universe. Even more striking, however, than the possible Semitic influence was the importance of Heraclitus for Zeno's thinking. The relationship between the philosophy of Heraclitus and the development of Stoicism has been debated for centuries, and even today there is no consensus concerning the degree to which the Stoics adopted the ideas of Heraclitus or simply misinterpreted them. Certainly in the case of Zeno's successor Cleanthes, the influence of Heraclitus is very apparent. For example, Heraclitus' idea of Zeus as the ordering fire-god appears in Cleanthes' famous *Hymn to Zeus*, albeit with a different emphasis.

Stoicism as a philosophical movement is generally divided into three stages: Early, Middle and Late Stoa. The Early Stoa began with the work of Zeno (336–264 B.C.), continued under his immediate successor Cleanthes of Assos (331–232 B.C.) and was concluded under Chrysippus of Soli (280–206 B.C.). The Middle Stoa of the second and first centuries B.C. is represented by Panaetius (185–110 B.C.) and Posidonius (135–51 B.C.). Finally, the representatives of the Late Stoa of the first and second centuries A.D. were Seneca (4 B.C.–A.D. 65), Epictetus (A.D. 50–138) and Marcus Aurelius (A.D. 121–180). Ideally a study of these three periods of Stoicism would proceed by analyzing the extant texts of the respective philosophers. Unfortunately, most of the material that we possess is fragmentary and is found only in the works of other writers who simply report the words of the Stoics, sometimes approvingly, sometimes critically. Although not a Stoic himself, Cicero (106–43 B.C.) is one of our best sources for information about the Early and Middle Stoa, and for this reason we will often refer to his writings in our treatment of Stoicism. A notable exception to the fragmentary character of our sources is the celebrated *Hymn to Zeus* of Cleanthes that has been preserved intact. Cleanthes was the most religious of the Stoics, and we will begin with a consideration of his famous hymn.

Cleanthes' *Hymn to Zeus*, with some omissions, reads as follows:

> Most majestic of immortals, many-titled, ever omnipotent Zeus, originating power of nature, who with your law steer all things, hail to you. For it is proper for any mortal to address you: we are your offspring, and alone of all mortal creatures which are alive and tread the earth we bear a likeness to God. Therefore I shall hymn you and sing forever of your might. All this cosmos, as it spins around the earth, obeys you, whichever way you lead, and willingly submits to your sway. Such is the double-edged fiery everliving thunderbolt which you hold at the ready in your unvanquished hands. For under its strokes all the works of nature are accomplished. With it you direct the universal Reason/Word (κοινὸς λόγος) which runs through all things and intermingles with the lights of heaven both great and small. … No deed is done on earth, God, without your offices, nor in the divine ethereal vault of heaven, nor at sea, save what bad men do in their folly. But you know how to make things crooked straight and to order things disorderly. You love things unloved. For you have fitted together into one all things noble and worthless so that there is a single everlasting Reason/Word of all things. It is shunned and ne-

> glected by the bad among mortal men, the wretched, who ever yearn for the possession of goods yet neither see nor hear God's universal law, by obeying which they could lead a good life in partnership with intelligence. Instead, devoid of intelligence, they rush into this evil or that, some in their belligerent quest for fame, others with an unbridled bent for acquisition, others for leisure and the pleasurable acts of the body. … Let us achieve the power of judgement by trusting in which direction you steer all things with justice, so that by winning honor we may repay you with honor, forever singing of your works, as it befits mortals to do. For neither men nor gods have any greater privilege than this: to sing forever in righteousness of the universal law.[15]

In this remarkable hymn of Cleanthes, we see major aspects of early Stoicism presented in poetic form. The very first sentence introduces the idea of Zeus' omnipotence: "Most majestic of immortals, many-titled, ever omnipotent Zeus, originating power of nature, who with your law steer all things, hail to you." And the omnipotence of Zeus is manifested in a twofold manner: Zeus is the originator of nature and the director of all things through his law. That is, he is both *originator* and *sustainer* of nature, and his activity in nature is described as law. One would expect to find in this context the phrase "natural law", but it does not occur.[16] Instead Cleanthes speaks of "universal law" or "common law" (κοινὸς

[15] This is the translation found in: A. A. LONG and D. N. SEDLEY, *The Hellenistic Philosophers*, Vol. 1, with slight modification based on my own reading of the Greek text.

[16] The older Stoics did not use the phrase "law of nature" (νόμος φύσεως) or "natural law". The closest parallel to these phrases is found in CHRYSIPPUS (280–206 B.C.) who, like CLEANTHES, belonged to the Early Stoa: φύσει νόμος (i.e. law by nature) is found in Frag. 528, IOANNES ARNIM, *Stoicorum Veterum Fragmenta*, Vol. II, (1903), 1964. Instead, the early Stoics spoke of right reason or Word (λόγος ὀρθός) or common law (κοινὸς νόμος). See CHRYSIPPUS in Frag.4, ARNIM, Vol. II: ὁ νόμος ὁ κοινός, and it is precisely this phrase that appears in CLEANTHES' *Hymn to Zeus*.

νόμος). Moreover, he maintains that this universal law is identical with universal *logos* that permeates all things. Once again the Greek λόγος (transliterated: *logos*) presents a problem for the translator. In the fragments of Heraclitus, we translated it as Word, but due to the strong rationalistic bent of Stoicism – one thinks of the innovations of Stoic logic – the combination "Reason/Word" seems more accurate. In any case, the universal law with which Zeus directs all things is both rational and righteous. As rational creatures, human beings are said to be the offspring of Zeus and to bear his likeness. Of all the Stoics, Cleanthes was perhaps the most influenced by Heraclitus, and this influence is clearly seen in Cleanthes' description of the thunderbolt that Zeus holds in his hand. In traditional Greek piety, the thunderbolt was a symbol of wrath, but in the fragments of Heraclitus it emerges as an ordering power, creative and sustaining. Adopting this understanding, Cleanthes portrays Zeus as an immanent, creative, rational, and providential presence in all things.

For the modern reader, the strongly deterministic thrust of Stoic thought raises serious questions about the possibility of ethics. It should be noted, however, that Cleanthes insists that the cosmos "willingly submits" to the law of Zeus, and his criticism of bad men who do not obey the universal law would seem to preclude a strict ethical determinism. The "deterministic" aspect of his thought is better described as an overarching determinism that transforms the bad into the good: "But you [Zeus] know how to make things crooked straight and to order (κοσμεῖν) things disorderly." The ordering power of Zeus is also implied in the Greek word for "Reason/Word" (λόγος), which occurs in the following sentence: "For you have fitted together into one all things noble and worthless so that there is a single everlasting Reason/Word (λόγος)." As we have seen, the Greek *logos* conveys the notion of "gathering". The *logos* gathers together and sets in order. In connection with a particular, spoken language, this basic meaning of gathering is discernible in actual practice. We gather words together into a sentence in order to convey a meaning, and we order sentences to communicate our thoughts. Similarly, Zeus gathers together all things into a structured whole and sustains the universe.

In Cleanthes' *Hymn to Zeus* we observe the imminent activity of Zeus in the universe, which in other Stoic writings appears to border on a crass pantheism. Diogenes Laertius, the Greek philosopher of the early third century A.D., who has provided us with invaluable information about Stoicism, reports in Book VII the following concerning the philosophy of Zeno: "Zeno says that the whole world and the heaven is the substance of God. ... By 'nature' (φύσις) they [i.e. the Stoics] sometimes mean that which holds together (συνέχω) the world, sometimes that which causes terrestrial things to grow (φύω). Nature is a self-moving condition (ἕξις), which completes and sustains (συνέχω) its offspring in accordance with seminal reasons (λόγοι)."[17]

Since the question of pantheism cannot be resolved apart from a discussion of nature, we consider first of all the concept of nature portrayed in the above quoted passage. From the standpoint of interpretation, the most troubling word is ἕξις (translated: "self-moving condition") – a noun that was derived from the verb form ἔχω meaning "to have" or "to hold". In most instances, the Greek word ἕξις has the meaning "state", "condition" or "habit", which would lead to a translation of the text as "nature is a condition moving of itself" or simply "nature is a self-moving condition". To be sure, "self-moving condition" is an awkward translation of Diogenes' text, but the Loeb Classical translation: "Nature is defined as a *force* moving of itself" seems very misleading.[18] Still the question remains: What is a self-moving condition? The very fact that this condition is self-moving indicates that it is dynamic, not static, and the linguistic connection between "condition" (ἕξις) and "holding together" (συνέχω) suggests that this condition is a "holding together" that is sustaining. That is, nature is both *creating* and *sustaining*. Nota

[17] Diogenes Laertius, *Lives of Eminent Philosophers,* Bk. VII, Ch. 1, Sec. 148.
[18] Diogenes, Bk. VII, Ch. 1, Sec. 148. Long and Sedley suggest „self-moving tenor". See Long and Sedley, *The Hellenistic Philosophers,* Vol. 1, p. 266.

bene: Not just living forms, but rather all of nature is generative in Stoic thought. There is no fundamental distinction here between living and non-living. One could say that nature itself is the intelligent designer, designing its products according to a rational plan, i.e. the seminal reasons. The biologist Steven Rose comes close to this Stoic view when he discusses the self-organization of living cells: "The organism is both the weaver and the pattern it weaves. ..."[19] But then, we must transfer Rose's metaphor from the living cell to nature itself, and we must add that nature as "self-weaving" is from the Stoic point of view ultimately synonymous with Zeus as "the designing fire" or as "the breath permeating all things". Of course, the Stoics did not identify Zeus with ordinary, visible fire, but their insistence on the role of heat in the universe is intended to emphasize the fiery, creative activity of Zeus. The identity of Zeus and fire is certainly reminiscent of Heraclitus, but the Stoics developed the idea of fire and heat in the universe in a manner oddly suggestive of modern thermodynamics.

From the Stoic texts examined thus far, it appears that Zeus is considered to be coextensive with the universe. Whether one labels this point of view pantheism or not depends to some extent on the definition of pantheism. In any case, even though Zeus is coextensive with the universe, he is not the only fundamental constitutive principle of the universe. The other principle is matter. According to Diogenes, Zeno maintained that the universe is constituted through two principles, an *active* one termed Reason, Word or God, and a *passive* one termed unqualified substance or matter. "They [i.e. the Stoics] hold that there are two principles in the universe, the active principle and the passive. The passive principle, then, is a substance without quality, i.e. matter, whereas the active is the reason inherent in this substance, that is God. For he is everlasting and is the artificer of each several thing throughout the whole extent of matter".[20] So God and matter are the foundations of the world. Any

[19] STEVEN ROSE, *Lifelines: Biology Beyond Determinism*, 1998, p. 171.
[20] DIOGENES LAERTIUS, *Lives of Eminent Philosophers,* Bk. VII, Ch. 1, Sec. 134.

particular object as well as the world as a whole is a composite of matter and God. God needs matter in order to create and sustain; matter needs God in order to be a particular thing with qualities. Since God is never separated from this mixture with matter, we can say in a sense that God *is* the universe.

The creating, sustaining activity of God in matter according to a rational pattern means that the Stoic universe was thoroughly teleological. Everything is directed by Zeus. Every single thing in the universe and the universe itself as a whole move toward the end that was predetermined in the rational pattern. Since God and matter are everlasting and always mixed together, the universe always possesses vital heat. This does not mean, however, that the present universe is everlasting. On the contrary, Zeus as the designing fire leads the present world-order toward a total conflagration, out of which a new world-order will emerge under his direction. The alternation between world-order and conflagration is a basic concept in the Stoic understanding of the universe and stands in stark contrast to the Judeo-Christian idea of a universe that has a definite beginning and an end. The Stoic universe has no real beginning and no real end. Indeed the present order of the universe will end in a conflagration, but a new world-order, which duplicates the old world-order, will emerge out of the conflagration. There is in this view an infinite sequence of finite world-orders, and the transition from one to the next takes place through the fiery consumption of the entire world.

Of the four traditional elements in Greek thought, namely air, water, earth, and fire, the latter occupies the central position for the Stoics. Zeus is both the designing fire that orders and sustains the universe and the consuming fire that destroys the world-order of the universe. Contrary to what one might think, the conflagration of a world-order was not thought to be punishment for the accumulated evil in the universe. The conflagration is not the result of Zeus' wrath, but rather his providential care. He ends the present world-order when its optimal state of goodness and wisdom has been attained so that the reconstitution of the world-order will be the best possible. Seneca, who was a representative of the Late Stoa, compares the conflagration with the meditation of a wise man. "What kind of life will a man have if he is abandoned by his friends and hurled into prison or isolated in some foreign country or detained on a long voyage or cast out onto a desert shore? It will be like the life of Zeus, at the time when the world is dissolved and the gods have been blended together into one, when nature comes to a stop for a while; he reposes in himself given over to his thoughts. The wise man's behavior is just like this: he retires into himself, and is with himself."[21] The continual cycle of creating, sustaining and dissolving is actually the self-transformation of Zeus and constitutes his providence in the universe.

Regarding the notion of divine providence, it is important to distinguish the Stoic understanding from later Christian ideas. Both Chrysippus and Seneca acknowledge that necessity limits the action of divine providence. And in his *On the Nature of the Gods*, Cicero writes: "Now of all the things which are administered by nature the universe is, so to speak, the originator, begetter, parent, and supporter, and it cherishes and contains them as members and parts of itself. But if the parts of the universe are administered by nature, the same must be the case with the universe itself; at any rate there is nothing in the administration of it which can be faulted, *for the best that could have been produced from the elements which there were has been produced*."[22] That is, the current universe is the best possible universe under the given circumstances at the time of its creation. Necessity always limits divine activity. Thus the Stoic idea of divine providence stands in vivid contrast to the Christian understanding of God's omnipotence as it is reflected in the creation narrative of Genesis.

Returning to the description of Zeus as "designing fire", it is interesting to note that the early Stoics employed biological arguments for the

---

[21] SENECA, *The Moral Letters to Lucilium* (Ad Lucilium Epistulae Morales), Letter 9, Sec.16 f.

[22] CICERO, *On the Nature of the Gods* (De natura deorum), Bk. II, Ch. 34 (italics added).

role of vital heat in the world and concluded from this that the entire universe is ordered and sustained by the designing fire. In Cicero's *On the Nature of the Gods*, Balbus, the spokesman for the Stoics, presents an argument that probably has its origin in the thought of Cleanthes. "It is a fact that all things which undergo nurture and growth contain within themselves a power of heat without which they could not be nurtured and grow. For everything which is hot and fiery is roused and activated by its own movement; but a thing which is nourished and grows has a definite and regular movement; as long as this remains in us, so long sensation and life remain, but when the heat has been chilled and extinguished, we ourselves die and are extinguished. ... Therefore every living thing, whether animal or vegetable, is alive on account of the heat enclosed within it. From this it must be understood that the element heat has within itself a vital power which pervades the whole world. We shall recognize this more readily from a more detailed account of this all-penetrating fieriness in its entirety. All parts of the world (I shall speak only of the greatest) are supported and maintained by heat. It follows from this that, since all parts of the world are maintained by heat, the world itself too has been preserved over so long a time by a comparable and like nature – and all the more so because it must be understood that this hot and fiery entity is extended in every nature in such a way that it contains the power of reproduction and the cause of generation. ... It is therefore nature that sustains the whole world and protects it, and this certainly does not lack sensation and reason. ... So the world must be wise, and that nature which holds all things together in its embrace must be perfectly and outstandingly rational. Therefore the world must be God, and all the power of the world must be sustained by the divine nature."[23]

This argument for the sustaining power of the divine nature involves five major steps. First of all, the argument begins with the biological realm and maintains that heat is necessary for life. Secondly, the argu-

[23] CICERO, Bk. II, Ch. 9–11.

ment extends the range of application from the organic to the inorganic realm and claims that heat is necessary for the entire world. Thirdly, heat is identified with nature, which holds all things together. Fourthly, it is stated that this "holding together" would not be possible unless nature is perfectly rational. Finally, it is concluded that this perfectly rational nature is the divine nature or God. The second claim, which extends the argument from the organic to the inorganic world, may seem odd at first, but on reflection it does have mutatis mutandis some support from the modern understanding of thermodynamics. Until we reach zero Kelvin, it makes sense to talk about heat in the universe. On the other hand, the claim that nature, i.e. the power of heat, is rational would be more difficult to reconcile with modern science.[24]

Cleanthes did not recognize any vitalizing or sustaining power in the universe except fire. In contrast, his successor Chrysippus modified this view and maintained that the primary sustaining force of the universe is *breath* (i.e. hot air), not *heat*.[25] As Diogenes reports: "Chrysippus, however, in the course of the same work gives a somewhat different account, namely, that it is the purer part of the aether; the same which they declare to be pre-eminently God and always to have, as it were in a sensible fashion, pervaded all that is in the air, all animals and plants, and also the earth itself, as a principle of cohesion".[26] The reasoning for the shift from heat to breath was probably based on the observation that the breath of animals including humans is hot air. So the vital principle of animals was termed *pneuma* or "breath", and the further association of breath with the aether of Aristotle made it possible to extend this line of thought to the entire world. Hence the sustaining principle of the entire universe was considered to be breath or aether. Since this breath or

---

[24] There have been some physicists who have ventured into this area. See for instance: MENAS KAFATOS and ROBERT NADEAU, *The Conscious Universe*, 1990 and HANS PRIMAS, "Umdenken in der Naturwissenschaft", *GAIA*, No. 1, 1992.

[25] LONG and SEDLEY, *The Hellenistic Philosophers,* Vol. 1, p. 287.

[26] DIOGENES LAERTIUS, *Lives of Eminent Philosophers,* Bk. VII, Ch. 139.

pneuma permeates the entire universe, it builds a dynamic continuum that sustains all things.

There is, however, a further development in the thought of Chrysippus. Adopting Aristotle's idea of the activity of hot *and* cold, Chrysippus maintained that the two elements work together in breath. So in the end, breath is a blending of the two constitutive elements hot and cold, and it is precisely this blending that forms the dynamic continuum of the universe that expands from its heat and contracts from its cold. This complex motion was described as "tension" or "tensile movement". Long and Sedley describe the elasticity of this movement as follows: "The special character of this motion is its *simultaneous* activity in opposite directions, outwards and inwards, whereby we should understand fire and air to be pulling, as it were, against each other in the blend which they constitute."[27] The similarity between the Stoic concept of dynamic tension between opposites and Heraclitus' idea of the harmony of opposites is unmistakable. Equally unmistakable, however, is the fundamental difference between the two concepts. For Heraclitus, the harmony of opposites describes the *event* in which something appears and withdraws, whereas the Stoics are concerned with quasi-*substances* that form a dynamic tension.

The physicist Max Jammer who has written several books on the history of scientific concepts has traced the modern field concept back to the Stoic notion of *pneuma* or breath. Jammer writes: "The *pneuma* of Stoicism (Zeno, Chrysippus, Posidonius) can be considered the direct predecessor of the concept of field; then in contrast to the Aristotelian geometrical kinetics (circular movement) and the atomistic combinatoric (construction of atoms), the Stoics thought that the order, the unity and the connection of the cosmos was determined dynamically through the *pneuma* that permeated all material and produced a tension (τόνος). This *pneuma* was considered to be the cause of all movement and of all spe-

[27] Long and Sedley, *The Hellenistic Philosophers*, Vol. 1, p. 288.

cific qualities of matter."[28] The Stoic thought differed not only from the atomism of the Epicureans, but also from the modern atomic theory that predated the development of quantum field concepts. For the Stoics, it was the pneuma that held the world together; for the quantum physicists, there are measurable force fields that hold things together.

Since the existence of God or the gods was never seriously questioned in antiquity – the Epicureans merely argued that the gods were not concerned about human beings –, the Stoics had much more to say about the *activities* of God in the universe than about his *existence*. Nevertheless, Cicero does set forth arguments for the existence of God that foreshadow later arguments of the Deists and Supernaturalists of the eighteenth and nineteenth centuries. In *On the Nature of the Gods*, he writes: "But if all the parts of the universe have been so ordered that they could not have been better adapted for use, or more beautiful as regards appearance, let us see whether they are the work of chance, or whether their arrangement is one in which they could not have possibly been combined except by the guidance of understanding and divine providence. If, then, the things achieved by nature are more excellent than those achieved by art, and if art produces nothing without making use of intelligence, nature also ought not to be considered destitute of intelligence. If at the sight of a statue or painted picture you know that art has been employed, and from the distant view of the course of a ship feel sure that it is made to move by art and intelligence, and if you understand on looking at a horologe, whether one marked out with lines, or working by means of

---

[28] MAX JAMMER, "Feld, Feldtheorie", *Historisches Wörterbuch der Philosophie*, Bd. 2, S. 923: "Als direkter Vorläufer des Feld-Begriffs kann das *Pneuma* der Stoa gelten (ZENO, CHRYSIPP, POSEDONIUS); denn im Gegensatz zur Aristotelischen geometrischen Kinematik (Kreisbewegung) und der atomistischen Kombinatorik (Komplexionen von Atomen) ist nach den *Stoikern*, die Ordnung, die Einheit und der Zusammenhang des Kosmos dynamisch dadurch bestimmt, dass ein alle Stoffe durchdringendes Pneuma eine Spannung (τόνος) erzeugt, die die Ursache aller Bewegungen und aller spezifischen Qualitäten der Stoffe ist." (The English text is my translation.) JAMMER's observation is very interesting, but he was wrong to include ZENO in this context.

water, that the hours are indicated by art and not by chance, with what possible consistency can you suppose that the universe which contains these same products of art, and their constructors, and all things, is destitute of forethought and intelligence?"[29]

It should be noted that the Latin word *ars*, which is translated here as "art", has a much broader meaning than its English equivalent. Basically *ars* refers to the necessary "skill" to make something; from here, its meaning extends to "work of art" as well as to "knowledge". In the quoted passage from Cicero, the word means "the knowledge and skill to make something", whether in reference to a clock or to the entire universe. Cicero's argument that the design of the universe is evidence of intelligent design is without doubt a forerunner of William Paley's argument many centuries later.

Having established that the wonderful design of the universe is the work of divine providence, Cicero raises the question concerning the purpose of this design. "But it will be asked for whose sake so vast a work was carried out. Was it for the sake of trees and herbs, which though without sensation are nevertheless sustained by Nature? No, that at any rate is absurd. Was it for the sake of animals? It is equally improbable that the gods went to such pains for beings that are dumb and without understanding. For whose sake, then, would one say that the universe was formed? For the sake, undoubtedly, of those animate beings that exercise reason (*ratio*). These are gods and men. ... It is thus credibly established that the universe and everything that is in it were made for the sake of gods and men."[30] The preeminence of human beings in the universe leads Cicero to a detailed description of the superior structure

[29] CICERO, *On the Nature of the Gods* (De natura deorum), Bk. II, Ch. 34. Cf. Ch. 37. A similar thought is expressed by PHILO in *On Providence*, Fragment I; see Loeb Classical Library, number 363, p. 455.

[30] CICERO, Bk. II, Ch. 53. Whereas we have translated the Greek *logos* as Word in the fragments of HERACLITUS and as "Reason/Word" in Greek Stoic texts, we render the Latin equivalent, namely *ratio*, as "reason".

of the human body. Again his glowing comments about the human eye anticipate William Paley's *Natural Theology*.[31]

Yet as praiseworthy as the structure of the human body is, it is not the primary distinguishing characteristic of human beings. What sets human beings apart from the animals is the faculty of reason, i.e. the human mind. In Book V of his *Tusculan Disputations*, Cicero develops this basic conviction about human beings in the direction of ethics by posing the question whether virtue is adequate for the excellent life (*vita beata*).[32] Perhaps a word on the translation of Cicero's *vita beata* is necessary before we continue. In the Vulgate (Latin version) of the New Testament *beatus* is often translated as "blessed", but this imbues the word with a religious tone that is unsuitable to Cicero's thought. On the other hand, the translation of *beatus* as "happy" strikes me in our contemporary world as trivial. In my opinion, the translation "excellent" captures much better than "blessed" or "happy" the sense of the text.

In approaching the excellent life (*vita beata*), Cicero takes nature as his starting point and discusses the way in which the force of nature (*vis naturae*) has given rise to various plants and animals and how the law of nature (*lex naturae*) maintains the boundaries of the species. "What surer starting point can we have than nature our common parent? All that she has given birth to, not merely living creatures but also what springs from the earth and has to support itself on its roots, she has willed to be perfect each after its kind. ... But it is in animals that the force of nature pure and simple can be still more easily discerned, because nature has granted them sensation. ... Moreover each kind holding fast to its own instinct, seeing that it cannot pass into the manner of living of a creature unlike itself, abides by the law of nature."[33] By mentioning

---

[31] CICERO, Bk. II, Ch. 57. WILLIAM PALEY, *Natural Theology*, 1802, Ch. 3.

[32] The historical question regarding CICERO's sources cannot be treated in this context. Although ideas of the New Academy may appear in the *Tusculan Disputations*, we take the predominant thrust to be Stoic.

[33] CICERO, *Tusculan Disputations* (Disputationes Tusculanae), Bk. V, 13.

the "will" of nature, Cicero makes it clear that nature is not simply a blind force in the universe. On the contrary, the force of nature has a strong voluntaristic character that abides by the law inherent in nature itself. As we will see below, the phrase "law of nature" in the writings of Cicero usually appears as a moral or legal concept, but in the present context it refers to biological restrictions. Thus, there does not seem to be a strict distinction between the biological and the moral/legal senses of the phrase in Cicero's thought.

Cicero continues: "And as with all creatures nature has given to one, one distinguishing feature, to another another which each of them preserves as its own and does not depart from, so to man she has given something far more pre-eminent – although the term 'pre-eminent' ought to be applied to things which admit of some comparison; but the mind of man, derived as it is from the divine mind, can be compared with nothing else, if it is right to say so, save God alone. Therefore if this mind has been so trained, if its power of vision has been so cared for that it is not blinded by error, the result is mind made perfect, that is, complete reason, and this means also virtue."[34] The deep affinity of human beings to God lies in the perfection of reason in both. To be sure, Cicero acknowledges the possibility of corruption in humans, i.e. the possibility that reason in certain individuals is distorted[35], but since the unique relationship between God and man is rooted in reason, the perfection of reason in humans assumes a teleological element. Human beings were designed by nature to attain perfect reason. The identification of virtue with reason may seem odd to the modern reader who associates the word "virtue" with the conservative adherence to particular moral rules. For Cicero, however, as well as for the Greek philosophers before him, the word "virtue" (Latin: *virtus*, Greek ἀρετή) had a much broader meaning. Perhaps we should translate Cicero's *virtus* as "excellence of life". When reason is perfected in an individual, that individual attains the wisdom

[34] Cicero, Bk. V, 13.
[35] Cicero, Bk. V, 32.

to act in accordance with the will of nature, and this state of wisdom constitutes an excellence of life that is unattainable in any other way.

Let us summarize briefly our progress in understanding Stoicism. According to the Stoics, Zeus is the omnipotent, ordering fire that permeates the universe. He creates, sustains and dissolves the universe in order to produce an infinite series of finite world-orders. Zeus is coextensive with the universe and almost identical with nature. That is, "Zeus" and "nature" are in most contexts synonymous terms. Far from being blind, nature is an active force governed by an inherent law within it. As we saw, the "law of nature" can refer to strictly biological aspects of the world, but more importantly for Cicero it applies to the ethical realm. Already Zeno tells us that the end of ethics is to live in accordance with nature. For the modern reader this beginning point requires some explanation. At the time of Zeno, it was generally thought by philosophers that the life of an individual should have some goal or *telos*. As Sandbach explains: "The 'end'[of life] is at once that towards which all one's efforts should be directed and also the supreme good. It was assumed that a man's activities should be so integrated and subordinated to a single end. ..."[36] This view stands in stark contrast to the modern world in which individuals rarely give serious thought to any overarching goal in life – at least none beyond earning as much money as possible and indulging in entertainment as often as possible.

Continuing with Zeno's view on the goal of life, Diogenes reports: "This is why Zeno was the first (in his treatise *On the Nature of Man*) to designate as the end 'life in agreement with nature' (or living agreeably to nature), which is the same as a virtuous life, virtue being the goal towards which nature guides us. ... And this is why the end may be defined as life in accordance with nature, or, in other words, in accordance with our own human nature as well as that of the universe, a life in which we refrain from every action forbidden by the law common to all things, that is to say, the right reason which pervades all things, and is identical with

[36] F. H. SANDBACH, *The Stoics,* (1975), 1994, p. 52 f.

this Zeus, lord and ruler of all that is." The casual reader of this passage might interpret Zeno as a proponent of libertarianism; living according to one's own nature would seem to provide license for any and all forms of conduct. Such a reading of the Stoics would be, however, a gross misinterpretation. Then "living in accordance with nature" is not defined solely with regard to the individual person, but rather in reference to human nature in general as well as to the entire universe, both of which are permeated by law.

During the first two centuries of the Stoic school, the followers of Zeno strived in various ways to clarify the meaning of the phrase "living in accordance with nature". According to Diogenes, Cleanthes understood "living in accordance with nature" to mean "living in accordance with the nature of the universe", whereas Chrysippus interpreted Zeno to mean "living in accordance with human nature and the nature of the universe".[37] Contrary to what one might think, no Stoic ever advocated living in accordance with human nature in a narrow sense, i.e. following every impulse of one's own nature. In addition, it is clear that Cicero in his work *On Duties* stresses adherence to *universal* nature much more than to human nature of the *individual*.[38] What we can assert with confidence is this: The ethics of the Stoics were grounded in their understanding of nature, whereby preference was given to universal nature.[39]

The idea that living according to nature is virtuous, i.e. that it leads to the life of excellence, is a uniquely Stoic conception and was developed at length by Cicero in Book III of *On the Ends of Good and Evil,* which is one of the best extant summaries of Stoic ethics. In approaching Cicero's text, we encounter the initial difficulty that his understanding of nature

---

[37] DIOGENES LAERTIUS, *Lives of Eminent Philosophers,* Bk. VII, Ch. 1, Sec. 89 (italics added).

[38] CICERO, *On Duties* (De officiis), Bk. I, Sec. 110.

[39] The various formulations of Stoic ethics that we find in the writings of its proponents make it impossible to render a definitive account. In the following, we adhere to the understanding of Stoic ethics found in CICERO's *On the Ends of Good and Evil.*

differs considerably from ours. Whereas we draw sharp distinctions between biology, physics and psychology, Cicero uses the word "nature" in reference to the entire universe, to the biological life of human beings as well as to their mental/ethical development. This means that acting in accordance with nature, which constitutes the ultimate good, must be demonstrable at every level, beginning with the biological needs of the newborn baby for self-preservation. The desire of the newborn to preserve itself is in Stoic thought a form of self-love that is quite natural. However, in order to establish self-love as the basis of ethics, Cicero must insist that this natural impulse does not include pleasure (*voluptas*). "In proof of this opinion they [the Stoics] urge that infants desire things conducive to their health and reject things that are the opposite before they have ever felt pleasure or pain: this would not be the case, unless they felt an affection for their own constitution and were afraid of destruction"[40]

Just as the infant experiences affection for his own body, children and adults experience affection for the truth and repugnance for the false. According to the Stoics, nothing is more repugnant to the human mind than the assent to false propositions because this act is contrary to nature. On the biological level, nature urges us to bodily wholeness; on the cognitive level, nature urges us to discover and to give our assent to the truth. Already at this point, it is apparent that Cicero is striving for a holistic conception of the various levels of nature, and so it is crucial that the latter stages be in harmony with the primary impulses of nature just described. To this end, Cicero introduces the following distinctions:

"The next step is the following fundamental classification: That which is in itself in accordance with nature, or which produces something else that is so, and which therefore is deserving of choice as possessing a certain amount of positive value – ἀξίαν as the Stoics call it – this they pronounce to be 'valuable' (for so I suppose we may translate it); and on

[40] CICERO, *On the Ends of Good and Evil* (De finibus bonorum et malorum), Bk. III, Ch. 5.

the other hand that which is the contrary to the former they term 'valueless'. The initial principle being thus established that things in accordance with nature are 'things to be taken' for their own sake, and their opposites similarly 'things to be rejected', the first duty[41] (for so I render the Greek καθῆκον) is to preserve oneself in one's natural constitution; the next is to retain those things which are in accordance with nature and to repel those that are the contrary; then when this principle of choice and also of rejection has been discovered, there follows next in order choice conditioned by duty; then, such choice becomes a fixed habit; and finally, choice fully rationalized and in harmony with nature. It is at this final stage that the Good properly so called first emerges and comes to be understood in its true nature."[42]

We notice in this section that Cicero begins with the distinction between two types of acts: those that possess *value* and those that are *valueless*. Concerning value, he introduces a further distinction between those acts that are *in themselves* according to nature and those that *produce something* that is in accordance with nature. The former possess full moral value; the latter have only limited value. Those acts that are not in themselves according to nature, but have limited value because they produce something in accordance with nature are considered to be intermediate between absolute good and absolute bad. Since these acts are neither morally good nor bad, they are said to be morally indifferent (ἀδιάφορα) and Cicero calls them "duties" (*officia*). Both duties and morally good acts are performed in accordance with nature as well as in agreement with reason. Yet there is a fundamental difference. As the rational capacity of the individual develops, performing an act according to reason acquires two meanings; it can mean either that it is possible to render a reasonable account of the action or that reason demands the

---

[41] Contrary to RACKHAM's translation in the Loeb Classical series, I see no reason not to translate καθῆκον as „duty". This certainly accords better with CICERO's "officium".

[42] CICERO, *On the Ends of Good and Evil* (De finibus bonorum et malorum), Bk. III, Ch. 6, Sec. 20 f.

action.[43] Duties fall into the former category; morally good acts belong to the latter. Under duties, the Stoics understood such things as honoring one's parents, associating with friends, getting married and having children etc. In contrast, morally good acts are those performed by the wise individual who understands completely what reason demands. This division between duties and morally good acts is one of the odd consequences of the Stoic absoluteness in the ethical realm. Good and bad were for the Stoics absolute. Either an individual has attained wisdom and therefore absolute moral goodness or an individual lacks true wisdom and is considered morally bad, even if he performs all of his duties faithfully. Although they have no moral value, duties do possess a limited value since they are in accordance with nature and reason in a weaker sense. Therefore the individual who is striving to attain wisdom should prefer duties to those acts that have no value at all.[44]

Still the question remains why one should prefer duties to other indifferent acts since neither of these have moral value. The answer lies in the concept of nature and its role in Stoic ethics. As we have noted, Cicero is presenting a *holistic view of nature* that includes the biological needs of the newborn as well as the cognitive abilities of the mature adult. In both cases, the performance of duties ensures the attainment of the "primary needs of nature"; in the case of the newborn, this primary need is self-preservation, in the case of adults, it is among other things life in an organized civil society. To act in accordance with nature, the newborn strives to preserve himself, whereas the adult supports the society in which he lives. These are primary natural needs that form the basis for attaining moral goodness. Cicero explains: "But since those actions that I have termed 'duties' commence with the first things of nature, it is necessary that the former [all duties] be traced back to the latter [the first things of nature]. So it can rightly be said that all duties can be ascribed to the fact that we attained the primary things of nature. Yet it must not be

[43] CICERO, Bk. III, Ch. 6, Sec. 58.
[44] CICERO, Bk. III, Ch. 6, Sec. 52 f.

inferred that their attainment is the ultimate good, inasmuch as moral action is not inherent in the first agreement with nature, but is an outgrowth of this." The first duty of the newborn is self-preservation, and all subsequent duties are only possible because this first duty was performed. All such duties are performed in accordance with nature in a restricted sense, but none of them is considered to be a moral act because the reasoning capacity of the individual has not yet brought forth the act in full accordance with nature. To act in full accordance with nature requires a rational consideration of universal nature as well as human nature and may result in the denial of certain individual needs in the interest of universal nature. But ultimately there is no real conflict between human nature and universal nature since human nature at its highest is reason.

Given that nature is synonymous with Zeus, it should come as no surprise that acting according to nature is the same as acting according to the *law* of nature. It belongs to the rational character of nature that law is inherent in it. The laws of nature govern the behavior of animals, but more importantly they govern the conduct of human beings.[45] Nature is not simply a blind force[46], but rather it is the force of reason and order in the universe. Although the rational orderliness of the universe was a fundamental tenet of Stoicism from the beginning, the phrase "law of nature" (*lex naturae*) or "natural law" (*lex naturalis*) was not in common usage before the time of Cicero.[47] The Greek equivalent for the phrase "law of nature" (νόμος φύσεως) occurred for the first time in Philo of Alexandria[48], and it has been suggested that Philo and Cicero adopted

---

[45] CICERO, *Tusculan Disputations* (Disputationes Tusculanae), Bk. V, Ch. 13, Sec. 38.

[46] CICERO, *On the Nature of the Gods* (De natura deorum), Bk. II, Ch. 32, Sec. 81.

[47] See *On the Nature of the Gods,* Bk. I, Ch. 14, Sec. 36 and *On Duties*, Bk. III, Ch. 6, Sec. 27 and 30 f.

[48] Regarding PHILO, it is interesting to note that he was the first to combine the Hebrew concept of law with the Greek concept of nature; in Hebrew, there is no equivalent for φύσις. The Hebrew ארץ simply means "earth" or "land", not "nature". (See article "φύσις" in: *The Theological Dictionary of the New Testament*, Vol. 9, ed. HELMUT KÖSTER, pp. 251–277). The search results from *Thesaurus Graecae Linguae* show only

the phrase from a common source.[49] However, it seems more likely that Cicero himself coined the Latin phrase and introduced it into Roman Stoicism. In any case, the phrase has played a significant role in Western thought down to the modern era.

In *On the Laws* Cicero raises the question of universal justice and maintains that an investigation of justice must begin with a careful consideration of natural law. "The most learned men have taken their starting point from law; and they are probably right to do so if, as these same people define it, law is the highest reason, innate in nature, which commands things that must be done and prohibits the opposite. When this same reason is secured and established in the human mind, it is law."[50] And again: "I think that these ideas are generally right; and if so, then the beginning of justice is to be sought in law: law is a power of nature, it is the mind and reason of the prudent man, it distinguishes justice and injustice."[51] So "in establishing the nature of justice, let us begin from that highest law, which was born aeons before any law was written or indeed before any state was established."[52]

---

four occurrences of νόμος φύσεως in the writings of PHILO OF ALEXANDRIA (*De plantatione*, Sec. 132, line 5, *De vita Mosis*, Bk. II, Sec. 7, line 4, Bk. II, Sec. 245, line 1 and *De providentia* Fragment 2, Sec. 23, line 9). Additionally there are eight occurrences of the plural φύσεως νόμοις, but most occurrences of "law" or "laws" are not associated with "nature".

[49] The common source suggested by HORSLEY was ANTIOCHUS OF ASCALON, the head of the Academy in the first century B.C. See RICHARD HORSLEY, "The Law of Nature in Philo and Cicero", *Harvard Theological Review*, Vol. 71, Issue 1–2, 1978, pp. 35–59. Since our primary source of information about the philosophy of ANTIOCHUS is CICERO's *Academica* and Book V of his *On the Ends of Good and Evil*, we would expect to find the phrase *lex naturalis* or *lex naturae* in these sections. However, in *Academica* the phrase does not occur at all and in *On the Ends of Good and Evil* only once. Thus, I am inclined to think that the phrase either was a part of the eclectic philosophy of CICERO's time or was coined by CICERO himself.

[50] CICERO, *On the Laws* (De legibus), Bk. I, Sec. 18.

[51] CICERO, Bk. I, Sec. 19.

[52] CICERO, Bk. I, Sec. 19.

The law that is innate in nature is the highest reason and is to be distinguished from Roman law (*ius civile*) which is written and specific. Although the highest law is present everywhere in nature, human nature has a privileged position in the search for it, and therefore an understanding of natural law is inseparable from an understanding of human nature. At this point, a careful distinction must be made. Although Cicero takes human nature as the *starting point* for arriving at an understanding of natural law, he does not consider human nature to be the *foundation* of natural law. The foundation is the activity of the gods ruling in nature, whether we call this activity a force, a will or whatever.[53] Ultimately, Zeus is the foundation of law, but human nature is the most appropriate starting point for understanding law.

Having firmly established that law or reason is a force permeating all things, Cicero explains the way in which law forms the basis of society. "And therefore, since there is nothing better than reason, and it is found both in humans and in God, reason forms the first association between humans and God. And those who share reason also share right reason; and since this is law, we humans must be considered to be closely associated with the gods by law."[54] So the first "society", so to speak, is formed between Zeus and human beings, and the phrase "right reason" indicates the level of perfection attained in this society by the person who has gained wisdom. Of course, all humans possess reason and therefore a knowledge of universal law, but only the wise individual, i.e. the Stoic sage, attains *right* reason and is able to bring law (*lex*) into harmony with justice (*ius*). From the community between God and humans, Cicero infers that there is a common state of all humans and God. "Furthermore, those who share law also share justice; and those who have these things in common must be considered members of the same state (*eadem civitas*), all the more so if they obey the same commands and authorities. Moreover, they do obey this celestial order, the divine mind and the all-

---

[53] CICERO, Bk. I, Sec. 21.
[54] CICERO, Bk. I, Sec. 23.

powerful God, so that this whole cosmos must be considered to be the common state of gods and humans."[55]

The connection between right reason, law, and the cosmic city was a typically Stoic concept, which Cicero also expressed in other works.[56] The modern reader should note carefully that there is no place in this context for the concept of religious faith. The bond between humans and the gods is based on their common nature, not on the belief of humans. It is not as though human beings were being admonished to search for a relationship to God through obedience and faith. The relationship is already there. In technical terms, it is ontological. By nature, the individual has a certain knowledge of God, even if it is inadequate, and the acknowledgment of the existence of God is at the same time an acknowledgment of one's own nature.[57] No other creature on earth enjoys this special relationship to God. From this, Cicero can conclude that there is "therefore a natural similitude between God and man" (*naturalis est igitur homini cum deo similitudo*).[58] Furthermore, Cicero claims that there is a similitude among all men in virtue of their capacity for reason[59], the implication being that such similarity overrides individual differences and promotes the formation of societies. Of course, false opinions and perverse habits can obscure the similarity among human beings, but the commonality remains, as evidenced by the fact that one definition of "man" is valid for all.[60] All human beings are capable of attaining virtue because nature has endowed them with an inborn orientation toward jus-

---

[55] CICERO, Bk. I, Sec. 23.

[56] CICERO, *On the Commonwealth* (De re publica), Bk. I, Sec. 19 and *On the Nature of the Gods* (De natura deorum), Bk. II, Sec. 154.

[57] Cf. PAUL in Romans 2 as well as LUTHER's understanding of the knowledge of God and of man (*cognitio dei et hominis*) in *Enarratio Psalmi 51*, Weimarer Ausgabe, Vol. 40, Part 2.

[58] CICERO, *On the Laws* (De legibus), Bk. I, Sec. 25. Cf. *similitudo* and *imago* in Genesis 1:26 of the Vulgate text.

[59] CICERO, Bk. I, Sec. 29 f.

[60] CICERO, Bk. I, Sec. 30 f.

tice. This teleological element in human nature means that justice is not established by opinion, but rather by nature itself.[61] Cicero stresses this point with all earnestness:

"If the opinions and the decrees of stupid people are powerful enough to overturn nature by their votes, why don't they ordain that what is evil and destructive should be considered good and helpful? If law can make justice out of injustice, why can't it make good from evil? But in fact we can divide good laws from bad by no other standard than that of nature. And it is not only justice and injustice that can be distinguished naturally, but in general all honorable and disgraceful acts. For nature has given us shared conceptions and has so established them in our minds that honorable things are classed with virtue, disgraceful ones with vice. To think that these things are a matter of opinion, not fixed in nature, is the mark of a madman."[62]

Not only does law and justice depend on nature, but also logic and ethics. Without the presence of Zeus in the world, i.e. without the force of nature directing the conduct of human beings, there would be no ethics, no reliable standard by which to measure conduct. In this context, Cicero maintains that the wise man (*vir sapiens*) loves (*diligere*) his neighbor as much as himself[63], and he gives an example of such love that is in some ways similar to the Parable of the Good Samaritan in the New Testament Gospel of Luke. Cicero writes: "What will a person do in the dark if he is afraid only of witnesses and judges? What will he do in some deserted place if he encounters someone from whom he can steal a lot of gold, someone weak and alone? Our naturally just and good man will talk to him, help him, and lead him on his way; the man who does nothing for someone else's sake and measures everything by his own interest – I think you know what he will do!"[64] Cicero was very much aware of the

[61] CICERO, Bk. I, Sec. 28.
[62] CICERO, Bk. I, Sec. 44 f.
[63] CICERO, Bk. I, Sec. 34.
[64] CICERO, Bk. I, Sec. 41.

fact that nature has been corrupted in many individuals due to bad habits, but when a person really acts according to nature, that person will act in the interest of others as the above example indicates. In addition to the similarities between Cicero's example and Jesus' parable, a fundamental difference should be noted. The action of the Good Samaritan is an outgrowth of his faith in the presence of God proclaimed by Jesus; the action of Cicero's wise man is a result of his true nature and is not bound to a religious faith.

There is an interesting passage in Cicero's *On the Commonwealth* in which he addresses the matter of punishment for non-compliance with natural law. In reference to natural law he writes: "It is wrong to pass laws obviating this law; it is not permitted to abrogate any of it; it cannot be totally repealed. We cannot be released from this law by the senate or the people. ... but all nations at all times will be bound by this one eternal and unchangeable law, and God will be the one common master and general (so to speak) of all people. He is the author, expounder, and mover of this law; and the person who does not obey it will be in exile from himself (*se fugere*). Insofar as he scorns his own nature as a human being, by this very fact he will pay the greatest penalty, even if he escapes all the other things that are generally recognized as punishments."[65] There is no way to escape punishment for not obeying natural law. Even if the guilty person incurs no external punishment, he will suffer the self-estrangement of being at odds with his true nature. Cicero makes a similar point in *On the Laws*, where he argues that nature is the most effective deterrent to crime.[66] He writes: "But there is no purification for crimes against humans and for impiety against the gods, and so they pay the penalty, not so much in courts – which used not to exist anywhere and now do not exist in many places, and where they do, they are often corrupt – as through being chased and hounded by the Furies, not with burning torches as in the myths, but with the pains of conscience

[65] Cicero, *On the Commonwealth* (De re publica), Bk. III, Sec. 33.
[66] Andrew Dyck, *Commentary on Cicero's De Legibus,* 2004, p. 174.

and the tortures of delusion [possibly 'self-deception']."[67] I have rendered the Latin *fraus* as "delusion" or "self-deception", which accords quite well with the passage from *On the Commonwealth*. In both cases, it is nature, not the courts, that metes out the punishment for crime and impiety. This is, of course, consistent with the Stoic concept of natural law, which in contrast to modern science not only applies to the physical realm, but also to the moral. Particularly interesting in the passage from *On the Laws* is the way in which Cicero demythologizes the myth of the Furies and introduces the concept of conscience.

Although the concept of the conscience is often associated with the Stoics, it does not seem to have played a role in the period of Early Stoicism. There is no record that Zeno ever used the Greek equivalent (συνείδησις), and the single occurrence in Chrysippus means "awareness" and lacks any moral connotations.[68] The oldest known occurrence of the word "conscience" (συνείδησις) is found in Democritus[69], and once again it simply means "awareness". Apparently the word did not acquire a specifically philosophical meaning until late in the Hellenistic Period. The Latin equivalent *conscientia* occurs for the first time in an anonymous work on rhetoric by a Roman author sometime in the late 80s B.C.[70], and subsequently it was used frequently by Cicero and became a part of Roman Stoicism as evidenced later by Seneca.

How then did Cicero understand the concept of conscience? It would certainly be a mistake to assume that he understood the term as we do. First of all, it should be noted that the English words "conscience" and "consciousness" both derive from the Latin *conscientia*, and as one might suppose, Cicero used *conscientia* in both senses. For instance, in

---

[67] CICERO, *On the Laws* (De legibus), Bk. I, Sec. 40.

[68] See DIOGENES LAERTIUS, *Lives of Eminent Philosophers*, Bk. VII, Ch. 1, Sec. 85. In this passage, DIOGENES is quoting CHRYSIPPUS.

[69] DEMOCRITUS, Fragment 297, line 2, in: HERMANN DIELS, *Die Fragmente der Vorsokratiker*, Vol. II, 1922.

[70] *Rhetorica ad Herennium*, Bk. II, Ch. 5, Sec. 8 and Bk. II, Ch. 31, Sec. 50.

a letter to his younger brother Quintus, Cicero writes: "Nor am I making the mistake I made once before in my consciousness [or "awareness"] of the forces behind me"[71]. In this context, *conscientia* has absolutely no moral connotations; it simply refers to an awareness of something such as when we say: "I am conscious of the fact that. ..." In still another passage, the word refers to an awareness of noble deeds[72], or again, to an elevated sense of self-confidence[73]. However, when the object of consciousness or awareness is a crime as in Cicero's legal defense of Milo, the word definitely begins to assume a moral tone[74], and when Cicero introduces in the *Tusculan Disputations* the notion of the *pangs* of conscience, the word is clearly approaching our understanding of conscience. The critical passage reads: "For escape from the penalty of trespasses seems granted to those who endure disgrace and shame without pain; it is better to suffer the stings of conscience".[75] This does not mean, of course, that the conscience makes itself known only in cases of misdeeds. Cicero also refers to the "good conscience": "there is no audience for virtue of higher authority than the approval of conscience".[76] Finally, the conscience becomes a norm for guiding human conduct and behavior: "No one in any part of his life should stray a hair-breadth from the path of conscience."[77]

What appears to be emerging in these passages is the autonomy of conscience that accords with modern secular understandings of the individual. But the initial appearance is deceiving. Cicero knew nothing of

[71] CICERO, *Letters to Quintus*, Bk. II, Letter 15, Sec. 2.
[72] CICERO, *On the Commonwealth* (De re publica), Bk. VI, Sec. 12 (VIII). This is one of the extant fragments of the work.
[73] CICERO, *First Philippic* (Oratio Philippica prima), Sec. 9. This was an oration held by Cicero in September, 44 B.C. against Mark Anthony.
[74] CICERO, *Milo* (Oratio pro Milone), Sec. XXIII. 61: "Milo was returning to Rome ... without any consciousness of crime to disquiet him".
[75] CICERO, *Tusculan Disputations* (Disputationes Tusculanae), Bk. IV, Ch. XX, Sec. 45.
[76] CICERO, Bk. II, Ch. XXVI, Sec. 64.
[77] CICERO, *Letters to Atticus*, Bk. XIII, Letter 20, Sec. 4.

the modern individualism that dominates our world, and he certainly did not think of conscience as the internalized values and norms of society. Instead, he was convinced that the conscience is implanted in the human mind by the gods, as we can see in his defense of Cluentius. Speaking of the wise judge, Cicero writes: "it is not lawful for him to do whatever he wishes; but that he must employ in his deliberations law, equity, religion, and good faith; that he must discard lust, hatred, envy, fear, and all evil passions, and must value as the greatest the conscience of his mind that we receive from the immortal gods and that cannot be taken away from us."[78] When we consider Cicero's comments in *On the Commonwealth* concerning the punishment for non-compliance with natural law, it becomes clear that the human conscience is informed by precisely this law. Acting according to nature is synonymous with acting according to one's own conscience since the conscience is informed by universal, natural law.

The relationship between natural law and positive or written law was not addressed by Cicero in Book I of *On the Laws* because it was to be the subject of the remaining books. Apparently, *On the Laws* originally contained four additional books, in which Cicero dealt with the implications of natural law for written law in Roman society, but only three of these are extant and Book III is itself very incomplete. As we have seen in Book I, natural law is an unwritten law that permeates the entire world. It is identical with right reason and is shared by humans and gods alike. Out of this commonality of all human beings and the similitude between humans and the gods, the Stoics developed the idea of a world city. Given the universal character of natural law, the question arises as to how such universal law can be adapted to a particular society such as that of the Romans in the first century B.C. Unfortunately, Cicero was never able to clarify sufficiently the application of the universal to the particular. Having expounded the community of humans and gods in Book I, he undertook in Book II a discussion of written law in the

[78] CICERO, *Oration for Cluentius* (Oratio pro Cluentio), Ch. LVIII, Sec. 159.

area of religion in order to demonstrate an important application of the universal natural law, and in the extant sections of Book III, he dealt with the matter of magistracies. At times Cicero seems to be saying that the recommended positive law is the ideal law derived from natural law; at other times, however, he indicates that written law is simply the best possible formulation of natural law under the given circumstances.

In spite of the difficulties in defining and applying natural law, this Stoic concept has played a significant role in Western societies. In the thirteenth century Thomas Aquinas developed the idea theologically in his *Summa Theologiae*[79], and in the seventeenth century the Dutch jurist Hugo Grotius employed the concept of natural law as the foundation for developing positive international law. From the seventeenth century onward, theologians, philosophers and jurists have appealed to the idea of natural law in their efforts to ensure that the laws of the state are just. Anyone familiar with the problem of natural law knows the inherent difficulties in applying it to specific circumstances. On the other hand, a total disregard for natural law can lead to a situation where the most perfidious written statutes are considered to be just because there are no grounds for criticizing them. The Enlightenment concept of human rights has been employed in many Western societies in an attempt to fill the gap left by the disregard for natural law, but the highly individualistic character of the rights concept renders it a questionable substitute for natural law. Whereas the idea of human rights underscores the *claims* that the individual (or group of individuals) can place on others, natural law focuses not only on claims, but also on the *duties* of every citizen within society.

In summary: There is much in Early Stoicism that is reminiscent of Heraclitus. In Cleanthes' *Hymn of Zeus,* Zeus is portrayed as the originating power of nature who steers all things through the wielding of his thunderbolt. As originator and sustainer of nature, Zeus is described as the universal law that fits all things together into one. But the "fitting

---

[79] THOMAS AQUINAS, *Summa Theologiae*, Prima Secundae, Questions 90–97.

together" of Cleanthes is significantly different from that of Heraclitus. The fundamental insight of Heraclitus concerning the "appearing and concealing of nature" that is reflected in Fragment 123 ("Nature loves to hide herself") no longer finds expression in Stoicism. Thus, the "fitting together into one" becomes the fitting together into a rational pattern, whereby the *logos* of Heraclitus, which we translated as Word, assumes a much more rational tone and is probably best translated in Greek Stoic texts as "Reason/Word". The expression "Reason" is intended to designate the structured whole, whereas "Word" points to the gathering process through which the structured whole is established.

In the philosophy of Chrysippus, the unity of opposites and the dynamic tension of Heraclitus emerge again, but with noticeable differences. In the thought of Chrysippus, the dynamic tension is caused by the simultaneous movement of hot and cold in opposite directions, and the result of this tension is a dynamic continuum of the entire universe that is called *pneuma* or breath. In contrast, the dynamic tension of Heraclitus was the simultaneous appearing and withdrawing of nature, in which the uniqueness of each and every event was revealed.

The historical transition from Greek to Roman Stoicism involved a linguistic as well as a cultural turn. This is noticeable first and foremost in the translation of λόγος as *ratio*. Whereas the Greek λόγος had a wide range of meanings, the Latin *ratio* was much more restricted to the idea of reason. The root verb of *ratio*, namely *reor*, means to reckon or to calculate, and the noun *ratio* was used in reference to calculations, transactions of business, causes, reasons or to the faculty of the mind as the basis of performing calculations. Accordingly, Roman Stoicism focused on rational patterns and extended into the more practical regions of law and ethics. Thus it was the Latin Stoics who developed the concept of natural law and moral conscience.

The Transition

The transition from the philosophical thought of Chapter 2 to the theological reflection of Chapter 3 involves much more than a change of content. Heraclitus and the Stoics were philosophers, whereas the Apostle Paul was an early Christian theologian. One might be tempted to summarily explain this difference as a transition from rational thought to faith, and although there is some justification for this view, it does not really penetrate to the heart of the matter. Philosophy and theology have been interrelated from pre-Christian times onward. In fact, the word "theology" (θεολογία) first appeared in the writings of Plato (Rep. II 379a), where he employed the term in criticizing the traditional Greek myths and thereby establishing the legitimate talk about the gods. From the standpoint of etymology, "theology" refers in some way to the relationship between God and language (*theo-logos*), and particularly in the Reformation thought of the sixteenth century, this meaning became dominant: Theology is the word of God. In contrast, the etymology of the word "philosophy" (φιλοσοφία) points to the "love of knowledge" or the "love of wisdom". Motivated by the love of knowledge, Greek philosophers of antiquity sought to determine the possibility of talking about the gods – an endeavor that led them into the realm of theology. On the other hand, theologians have utilized from early times philosophical concepts in an attempt to clarify the relationship between God and language. As we shall see in Chapter 3, the Apostle Paul employed certain Stoic ideas in developing his theology.

This overlapping of philosophy and theology in both disciples can assume various forms. Extreme cases, whereby theologians strive to eliminate philosophical concepts altogether from their theological reflections, on the one hand, or whereby theologians develop a system of thought almost indistinguishable from philosophy, on the other hand, are easily recognized. In most cases, however, the combination of philosophy and theology is more subtle and less apparent. Rudolf Bultmann, for instance, was quite dependent upon the philosophical views of Martin Heidegger; Paul Tillich incorporated insights of Schelling; and John Cobb, Jr. was greatly indebted to Alfred North Whitehead for the basic concepts of his theology. Philosophers for their part tend to be less open about their theological views, although a careful study of their works will reveal in most cases fairly clear theological presuppositions. Certainly, this was the case with Hegel, Kierkegaard and Whitehead, but also with atheists such as Feuerbach. Precisely in his rejection of God, Feuerbach assumed a certain concept of God which he adopted from theology.

We are not suggesting, of course, that there is no difference of content between philosophy and theology. Certainly there is. The problems investigated and the methods employed differ in the two disciplines just as they differ in other disciplines that we might compare such as chemistry and geography. Nevertheless there is a more fundamental difference between philosophy and theology that is reflected *in* their respective content. The basic shift from Greek philosophy to Christian theology, i.e. from Chapter 2 to Chapter 3, involves the *experience* at the foundation of thought. Before any philosopher or theologian begins his work, there is a basic experience that motivates him. As Aristotle notes in his *Metaphysics*, it was the experience of wonderment that gave rise to philosophy. In describing the supreme knowledge of the *Metaphysics*, he writes: "That it is not a productive science is also clear from those who began to philosophize, for it is because of wondering that men began to philosophize and do so now".[80] The Greek infinitive θαυμάζειν that occurs in this sentence means "to wonder" or "to marvel", and according to Aristotle, the experience of wonderment and astonishment was the be-

[80] ARISTOTLE, *Metaphysics*, 982b11–13.

ginning of philosophical thinking. Aristotle's view was echoed two millennia later when Immanuel Kant wrote these words in the Conclusion to his *Critique of Practical Reason*: "Two things fill the mind with ever new and increasing admiration and awe (*Bewunderung und Ehrfurcht*), the more often and the more steadily we reflect upon them: the starry heavens above and the moral law within." Admittedly, there are subtle differences between Aristotle's wonderment and Kant's admiration and awe, but both expressions attest to the fundamental experience of the philosopher who is astonished and puzzled by the world around him.

In the age of modern science, it is precisely this experience of wonderment and awe that has motivated the most gifted scientists. In 1930 Albert Einstein wrote an article entitled "Religion and Science" in which he attempted to delineate three stages of religious experience. His views on religion were quite elementary, but his description of the experience that motivated him in his research was very interesting. He wrote: "The individual feels that futility of human desires and aims and the sublimity and marvellous order which reveal themselves both in nature and in the world of thought."[81] Einstein called this experience "the cosmic religious feeling" and attributed it to other great scientists such as Kepler and Newton. "I maintain that the cosmic religious feeling is the strongest and noblest motive for scientific research. ... What a deep conviction of the rationality of the universe and what a yearning to understand ... Kepler and Newton must have had to enable them to spend years of solitary labor in disentangling the principles of celestial mechanics!"[82] Although Einstein refers to this cosmic feeling as "religious", it really stands more properly in the tradition of wonderment, admiration and awe that is characteristic of the philosophical mind.

Of course, it can be objected that many contemporary philosophers no longer speak of experiences such as those of Aristotle and Kant. In particular, academicians of the analytic persuasion, those associated with

---

[81] Albert Einstein, "Religion and Science", *Ideas and Opinions*, 1954, p. 38.
[82] Einstein, p. 39.

the so-called Cognitive Revolution and the postmodern thinkers under the influence of French nihilism find no cause to inquire about the experience of wonderment. However, this experiential deficiency results in a noticeable superficiality of thought and imbues contemporary "philosophy" with a technological character that sets it apart from the entire tradition since Heraclitus. If Aristotle was right about the origin of philosophy, it is difficult to avoid the conclusion that philosophizing has ceased to be practiced in the Western world.

Be that as it may, the fundamental experience out of which theology arises is distinct from the wonderment of Aristotle or the admiration and awe of Kant. To be sure, wonderment and awe may be dimensions of the religious experience, but they are not its *conditio sine qua non*. At the very heart of the religious experience is the sense of "being addressed by an unknown presence". Although this experience is attested in many different religions, the Christian scriptures comprised of the Hebrew Bible and the Greek New Testament provide ample description of the experience, albeit in legendary form.

Consider, for example, the call of Moses as it is recorded in the Book of Exodus, Chapter 3, verses 1–6.

> Now Moses was keeping the flock of his father-in-law, Jethro, the priest of Mid'ian; and he led his flock to the west side of the wilderness, and came to Horeb, the mountain of God. And the angel of the LORD appeared to him in a flame of fire out of the midst of a bush; and he looked, and lo, the bush was burning, yet it was not consumed. And Moses said, "I will turn aside and see this great sight, why the bush is not burnt." When the LORD saw that he turned aside to see, God called to him out of the bush, "Moses, Moses!" And he said, "Here am I." Then he said, "Do not come near; put off your shoes from your feet, for the place on which you are standing is holy ground." And he said, "I am the God of

> your father, the God of Abraham, the God of Isaac, and the God of Jacob." And Moses hid his face, for he was afraid to look at God.

Leaving aside a discussion of the mythological elements in this account, we notice first of all the personal address of the experience. What Moses experienced was not an objective admiration for the universe in Kant's sense, nor was the primary element in the experience of the burning bush a sense of wonderment about the world in the sense of Aristotle. To be sure, Moses was struck initially with curiosity about the burning bush, but the experience quickly turned into a linguistic event in which he was personally addressed by name. When this happened, he experienced a fundamental distinction between the *sacred* and the *profane* – a distinction that frequently accompanies deep religious experiences. This distinction came to expression in the command of God: "put off your shoes from your feet, for the place on which you are standing is holy ground". In the religious experience, the everydayness of the world is interrupted, and the homogeneity of space is broken as the dimension of the holy emerges. All ground is not the same. There is ordinary ground and there is holy ground. And the difference between the two provides stability and orientation to the individuals who experience it.

In Book IV of his *Physics,* Aristotle analyzes and discusses in great detail the concept of space or place (ὁ τόπος). The classical Hebrew language of the Old Testament had no equivalent term for Aristotle's concept. The Hebrew word for "place" in the call of Moses means literally a "standing-place" (מָקוֹם) and is derived from a verb meaning "to arise" or "to stand up". Whereas Aristotle was interested in understanding place *as* place, the Hebrew mind was concerned to distinguish one place from another based on events associated with this or that place. In the call of Moses, it was the linguistic event that made the place "holy ground". Moses was addressed personally, and he was summoned to give a response: "'Moses, Moses!' And he said, 'Here am I.'" The experience of being addressed by the sacred and of responding to it is fundamental to the religious experience. Undoubtedly, there is an element of awe in the experience, but more fundamentally there is the awareness of a power over existential life and death. Withdrawing from the sacred would mean a loss of orientation and stability; approaching the sacred could mean destruction. "Do not come near!" So Moses hid his face in fear.

In the call of Moses, the ancient writers of the Hebrew scriptures left on record a mythological account of a fundamental religious experience. It would be possible to analyze this account and present the essential elements of the experience in philosophical terms such as the transcendence of the infinite over the finite, but in many ways the mythological mode of expression conveys much more vividly the character of the experience.

Although there is a further element in the religious experience that comes to expression in the call of Moses, this element is presented much more vividly in the call of Isaiah. The profound distinction between the sacred and the profane, between the holy and the ordinary conveys a new *awareness of one's self.* In the Book of Isaiah (6:1–9) we read:

> In the year that King Uzzi'ah died I saw the Lord sitting upon a throne, high and lifted up; and his train filled the temple. Above him stood the seraphim; each had six wings: with two he covered his face, and with two he covered his feet, and with two he flew. And one called to another and said: "Holy, holy, holy is the LORD of hosts; the whole earth is full of his glory." And the foundations of the thresholds shook at the voice of him who called, and the house was filled with smoke. And I said: "Woe is me! For I am lost; for I am a man of unclean lips, and I dwell in the midst of a people of unclean lips; for my eyes have seen the King, the LORD of hosts!" Then flew one of the seraphim to me, having in his hand a burning coal which he had taken with tongs from the altar. And he touched my mouth, and said:

> "Behold, this has touched your lips; your guilt is taken away, and your sin forgiven." And I heard the voice of the Lord saying, "Whom shall I send, and who will go for us?" Then I said, "Here am I! Send me." And he said, "Go, and say to this people: 'Hear and hear, but do not understand; see and see, but do not perceive.'"

Again we have a mythological account in which fundamental aspects of religious experience are expressed. In the distinction between the holy and the ordinary, the individual senses his profound belongingness to the ordinary and profane. The phrase "unclean lips" may refer to the need for ritual purification before entering the temple, but more generally it is an image for the imperfection of human nature – an imperfection that comes clearly to light only in the contrast between the sacred and the profane. That the experience provided Isaiah with a new orientation in his life is evident from the commission that he received. "Go, and say to this people."

It might be objected that these two accounts are relating the call of an individual to a divine mission and that they are not typical of religious experience in general. That is certainly true. The accounts of Moses and of Isaiah describe an experience of extraordinary intensity. Nevertheless, I maintain that fundamental elements of this experience characteristically occur in the lives of many other individuals. *The personal address, the need for response, the awareness of self, the bestowing of a new orientation, the gaining of stability and above all the sense of a presence far beyond the ordinary and mundane – these elements are not at all unusual for the religious experience.* On the other hand, it must be admitted that such experiences may be less frequent in our highly technological society, and those readers who have no acquaintance with them will need to exercise their powers of empathy in order to appreciate the shift from Cicero to the Apostle Paul. Nota bene: such empathy should not be confused with agreement; it is simply a matter of the proper interpretative approach to religious texts.

Finally, we take a look at the conversion of the Apostle Paul as recorded in the 9th Chapter of the Book of Acts, verses 1–9:

> But Saul, still breathing threats and murder against the disciples of the Lord, went to the high priest and asked him for letters to the synagogues at Damascus, so that if he found any belonging to the Way, men or women, he might bring them bound to Jerusalem. Now as he journeyed he approached Damascus, and suddenly a light from heaven flashed about him. And he fell to the ground and heard a voice saying to him, "Saul, Saul, why do you persecute me?" And he said, "Who are you, Lord?" And he said, "I am Jesus, whom you are persecuting; but rise and enter the city, and you will be told what you are to do." The men who were traveling with him stood speechless, hearing the voice but seeing no one. Saul arose from the ground; and when his eyes were opened, he could see nothing; so they led him by the hand and brought him into Damascus. And for three days he was without sight, and neither ate nor drank.

As compared with the call experiences of Moses and Isaiah, the conversion experience of Paul contains some new elements. As far as we know, the call experiences of Moses and Isaiah were the beginning of a deep devotion to the God of Israel. In contrast, Paul – then known as Saul – was already an ardent follower and supporter of Pharisaic Judaism before his conversion. So his experience on the road to Damascus was not the beginning of a deep devotion to the God of Israel, but rather a complete reorientation of that devotion, hence a conversion. In comparison with the experiences of Moses and Isaiah, the experience of Paul had a strong *cognitive dimension* that involved a fundamental change in his thinking and beliefs. The radical change in Paul's thinking is symbolized by the physical changes in his body; his impaired eyesight made it impossible for him to continue his mission against the followers of Jesus. Furthermore, the account is not mythological in the strict sense if one defines mythology as the interaction of the gods or God with human beings. To the extent that one doubts the details of the account, one should classify it as legendary, not mythological. Paul hears not the voice of God speaking to him, but rather the voice of Jesus who was an historical person. Nevertheless, the conversion experience of Paul exhibits many characteristics in common with the call experiences of Moses and Isaiah. Paul is addressed personally by name and is required to give a response. In doing so, he acquires an immediate reorientation in his life and a new awareness of himself. Whereas Paul was formerly the mighty persecutor of the followers of Jesus, he is now being led by the hand into a future that has not yet unfolded before him in all clarity. The three-day fast that followed the conversion experience gives expression to the humility that filled him as the sacred broke into the everydayness of his life.

It must be emphasized that we have not presented the experiences of these three men with the intention of convincing the atheist of the reality of God. Rather, we have highlighted the character of the religious experience in contrast to the philosophical experience in an effort to establish a hermeneutical access to the texts of the Apostle Paul and Augustine. If one approaches the US Constitution as though it were a mathematical text, one will have great difficulty understanding the wisdom embodied in it. If one attempts to read Kurt Gödel's incompleteness proofs as though they were poetry written in iambic pentameter, one will be hopelessly confused. Likewise, it is impossible to gain insight from a religious text if one approaches the text as if it were strictly philosophical. And need it be said? If one insists that a religious text fit into the framework of modern science, one will completely miss the point.

Chapter 3

"The Message of the Apostle: Paul"

It is well known that Jesus during his lifetime directed his message to a Jewish audience that considered itself to be the descendants of Abraham and the recipients of the Mosaic Law. So when Jesus talked about the law, it was clear to his hearers that he was referring to the Law of Moses. In the Sermon on the Mount in Matthew, Chapters 5–7, we read these words that were reported of Jesus: "Think not that I have come to abolish the law and the prophets; I have come not to abolish them but to fulfil them. For truly, I say to you, till heaven and earth pass away, not an iota, not a dot, will pass from the law until all is accomplished. Whoever then relaxes one of the least of these commandments and teaches men so, shall be called least in the kingdom of heaven. ..." Following this fundamental statement about the law, Jesus proceeded to present a radical interpretation of the law that went well beyond that of his contemporaries. In his mind, adultery, for instance, was not simply a matter of physical intercourse, but rather a matter of the heart (5:27–30). The entire approach of Jesus in radicalizing the law assumed the validity of the Mosaic Law – an assumption that was quite unproblematic among his hearers.

If the Christian Church in the following decades had developed into a branch of Judaism, the theological ideas presented by the Apostle Paul in Romans 2:12–16 would have been completely unnecessary. As we can see quite clearly in Paul's letter to the Galatians, he arrived at an understanding of Christian faith that was based on the contrast between law and grace rather than simply on the fulfillment of the law. Being a Jew, Paul like Jesus assumed the validity of the Mosaic Law, but instead of emphasizing a radicalization of the law, he claimed that the attainment of righteousness was only possible through the recognition of the distinction between law and grace and the embrace of God's grace through faith. So whoever wants to live in peace and harmony with God must approach God not with works of the law, but rather through faith in the grace of Jesus Christ. We need not discuss at this point further differences between the teachings of Jesus and the theology of Paul. Central for our topic is simply this: Both assumed the validity of the Mosaic Law. That is, they could legitimately take the Mosaic Law as a starting point for proclaiming their teachings.

But the Christian Church did not remain within the boundaries of Judaism. On the contrary, it rapidly spread into the Gentile world of the first century and was confronted with other religious traditions as well as with Greek philosophy. This shift in context was of paramount importance for the development of Paul's theology. In addressing the Athenians, for example, he could no longer assume that his audience knew anything about the Mosaic Law. This law was not a part of their tradition, and therefore the Pauline contrast between law and grace was for them unintelligible. Had this been an insurmountable problem, then Christianity would have remained a branch of Judaism. But the message of Christian faith had from the outset a universal character, an openness for human beings as such. Thus it was incumbent upon the Apostle Paul to expand the understanding of law from the narrow bounds of the Mosaic tradition toward a universal understanding of law that made his message intelligible to Jews and Gentiles alike. Such a development in the theology of Paul forms the background of the verses in Romans that we will now examine. The critical text is Romans 2:12–16, which reads as follows:

> All who have sinned without the law will also perish without the law, and all who have sinned under the law will

> be judged by the law (vs. 12). For it is not the hearers of the law who are righteous before God, but the doers of the law will be justified (vs. 13). When the Gentiles who have not the law do by nature what the law requires, they are a law to themselves, even though they do not have the law (vs. 14). They show that what the law requires is written on their hearts, while their conscience also bears witness and their conflicting thoughts accuse or perhaps excuse them (vs. 15) – on that day when, according to my gospel, God judges the secrets of men by Christ Jesus (vs. 16).

These verses contain a number of interpretive difficulties that have been the subject of much discussion in the history of the Christian Church. Generally speaking, we sense in these verses the Jewish background of the Apostle Paul, but it is clear that he is appealing to a much broader audience than Jesus did. In verse 12, he states categorically that all human beings, Jews and Gentiles alike, will be required to render an account of their actions before God. In this regard, there is no distinction between Jews and Gentiles. With or without the Mosaic Law, sin is sin and will be punished. Gentile sinners who did not receive the law of Moses will simply perish, whereas Jewish sinners who were living under the Mosaic Law will be judged by the law. Therefore, the Jews should not suppose that they have a great advantage over the Gentiles simply because they received the law of Moses. As verse 13 states: It is not the *hearers* of the law that are justified before God, but rather the *doers*. If the Jews have not obeyed the law, they will be judged just as harshly as the Gentiles who have sinned without the Mosaic Law. So they await the same condemnation and ruin as the Gentiles.

However, verse 13 contains another thought. The principle that the doers of the law, not the hearers are justified raises the question about the possibility that the Gentiles themselves might obey some kind of law and thus be justified. At this point, there is a shift in the meaning of the word "law", and we begin to sense the influence of Stoicism on the theology of Paul. Then in the following verses 14 and 15 the marks of Stoic philosophy become very apparent. Finally, in verse 16 there is a return to ideas that reflect Paul's Jewish background.

Although the ideas in verses 14 and 15 are clearly Stoic, it is uncertain how Paul acquired these ideas. We know that there was considerable Stoic influence in the city of Tarsus where Paul was born. Strabo, the Greek geographer and historian who was born in Asia Minor around 64 B.C., tells us that Tarsus rivaled Athens and Alexandria as a center of philosophical study. In particular, he comments on the Stoic Athenodorus who was born in Tarsus in 74 B.C. and studied Stoicism under Posidonius. Yet even within Judaism itself Stoicism had already begun to make inroads as we see in the philosophy of Philo of Alexandria (circa 20 B.C.–A.D. 50). Living in the Jewish diaspora, Philo attempted to combine the Stoic concept of nature and natural law with the Jewish understanding of the Torah. The result was an innovative mixture of Greek and Jewish thought, whereby Philo always understood the natural law of Stoicism to be more or less identical with the Torah. Regardless of how Paul acquired his knowledge of Stoicism, it is indisputable that he understood the basic tenets of Stoic thought. Certainly Paul's knowledge of Stoic terminology and concepts was assumed by the author of the Book of Acts when he reported the celebrated speech of Paul on the Areopagus in Athens.[1]

Let us now take the verses 14 and 15 in succession. Verse 14 reads: "When the Gentiles who have not the law do *by nature* what the law requires, they are a law to themselves, even though they do not have the law." The key Stoic phrase in this verse is "by nature" (φύσει), and Paul employs it in order to explain how the Gentiles could possibly fulfill the law. Although the Gentiles did not receive the Mosaic Law, by virtue of nature itself they know the law and have the opportunity to obey it. Significantly, Paul does not write "If the Gentiles ...", but rather "When

---

[1] Acts 17:22–31.

the Gentiles ..." That is, the sentence is temporal, not conditional. So it is clear that he is actually reckoning with the occasional fulfillment of the law by the Gentiles, and the way in which Paul phrases verse 14 reveals the Stoic background of his thought. He does not say that the Gentiles are living *under* this law analogously to the way in which the Jews are living *under* the law of Moses, but rather he claims that the Gentiles *are* a law to themselves. This thought is only understandable from the standpoint of Stoic philosophy according to which *nature and law are inseparably connected.* Thus it seems very likely that Paul is appealing in this passage to the Stoic concept of natural law, i.e. to that divine law which permeates the universe. In virtue of nature, the Gentiles not only *fulfill* the law, but in some sense they *are* the law. That is, law is a part of nature to which they belong.

Interestingly enough, there is some precedent for this thought in the writings of Philo, where he addressed the problem of the patriarchs who lived before the Mosaic Law was given. In particular, Philo was at pains to demonstrate that Abraham was a model of obedience to the law, although the law of Moses was not given until much later. In his book *On Abraham*, Philo writes: "He [Abraham] did them [the divine law and the divine commands] not taught by written words, but unwritten nature gave him the zeal to follow where wholesome and untainted impulse led him. And when they have God's promises before them what should men do but trust in them most firmly? Such was the life of the first, the founder of the nation, one who obeyed the law, some will say, but rather, as our discourse has shown, *himself a law and an unwritten statute.*"[2] A more literal translation of the Greek phrase (νόμος αὐτὸς ὤν) in Philo's statement would be: "being himself a law", which brings us very close to the expression of Paul that the Gentiles "are a law to themselves". However, the differences between Philo and Paul are significant. Philo is referring to the patriarchs, i.e. to the founders of the Jewish nation, whereas Paul is referring to the Gentiles and by implication to all hu-

[2] PHILO, *On Abraham,* Ch. XLVI, Sec. 275 f. (italics added).

man beings. Secondly, Philo considers the law, which Abraham *was* and to which he was obedient, to be more or less identical with the Mosaic Law. On the other hand, Paul gives us no indication in verse 14 regarding the content of the law that the Gentiles *are* and to which they may be obedient.

Paul continues this line of thought in verse 15 where he gives more detail about the law that the Gentiles have, i.e. that the Gentiles *are*: "They show that what the law requires is written on their hearts, while their conscience also bears witness and their conflicting thoughts accuse or perhaps excuse them." Literally, the first half of this verse reads: "They show that the *work* (ἔργον) of the law is written in their hearts." This part of verse 15 is odd for two reasons. First of all, one would expect Paul to contrast the *unwritten* law of the Gentiles with the *written* law of Moses that the Jews had received. As we saw in Cicero, the idea of an unwritten law in nature that is eternal and that provides the foundation for the written laws of the state was a well-established tenet of Stoicism. Philo adopts this idea of an unwritten law, but associates it – unlike the Stoics – with the Mosaic Law. In contrast to both Cicero and Philo, Paul says that the Gentiles have indeed a *written* law, but it is written in their hearts, not on tables of stone. Of course, Paul is speaking here metaphorically, but the metaphor is very significant. The comparison between the law of Moses written on the tablets of stone and the natural law written in the hearts of the Gentiles suggests the use of the term "inscription" as an appropriate translation of the verse. In this case, the passage would read: "They show that what the law requires is *inscribed* on their hearts." But again, we do not yet know the content of this inscription.

Secondly, Paul's contrast between the written law of Moses and the inscription in the heart of the Gentiles is surprising because it reverses the Stoic order of priority between written and unwritten law. In Stoic thought, the unwritten law was primary inasmuch as it provided the measure for determining the justice of the written laws of the state. Therefore Cicero insists: "It is wrong to pass laws [i.e. laws of the state] obviating this law [the eternal natural law]; it is not permitted to abrogate any of it; it cannot be totally repealed. We cannot be released from this law by the senate or the people. … but all nations at all times will be bound by this one eternal and unchangeable law, and God will be the one common master and general (so to speak) of all people." So Cicero contrasts the eternal law of God with the temporal laws established by men, whereas Paul is thinking solely about the law of God, whether it be the Mosaic Law or the inscription in the hearts of the Gentiles. Both are equally the law of God. Or to put it another way: The inscription in the heart and the tablets of stone are simply two different ways in which God deals with human beings.

For the ancient Hebrews as well as for the Jews at the time of Paul, the heart was considered to be the innermost part of the individual's intellectual and volitional life. It was the core of the individual's personality and the point at which the individual came into contact with God. The heart speaks to God (Psalm 27:8), and the heart trusts in God (Psalm 28:7). In the heart, faith in Jesus Christ arises: "For man believes with his heart and so is justified, and he confesses with his lips and so is saved" (Romans 10:10). Given this understanding of the heart, Paul's statements in verse 15 mean that God has inscribed the law in the very core of the individual. *In that hidden region of the soul where God and man meet, there is an indelible inscription that obligates*. And yet, the content – if there indeed be a content – of this inscription remains a mystery.

Thus far we have been speaking of the law of nature written in the hearts of the Gentiles, but Paul actually formulates the matter differently. He says that the *work of the law* (τὸ ἔργον τοῦ νόμου) is written in their hearts. The singular "work" is puzzling. If he had intended to say that all of the various works of the law are written in the heart, he would have used the plural. Had he done so, one might argue that the inscription in the heart should be identified with the so-called Noahide commandments or laws. The seven laws of Noah or Noahide Laws comprise a list of commandments that the Jewish rabbis considered to be the minimum requirements for the sons of Noah, i.e. for all human beings. Whereas the Jews considered that they held a special place in God's plan for the world and were therefore subject to the entire Torah, they conceded that non-Jews could be considered righteous if they obeyed the Noachide Laws. These were as follows: Do not worship idols, Do not curse God, Do not commit murder, Do not engage in Incestuous, Adulterous or Homosexual Relationships, Do not steal, Do not eat of a live animal, Establish courts of justice. The first six are clearly prohibitions, whereas the seventh is a commandment.

A list of the Seven Noahide Laws is first attested in Jewish sources in the second half of the second century A.D.[3], but it is generally assumed that the list is much older and was perhaps known to the Apostle Paul. On this assumption, the comparison of the Mosaic Law to which the Jews were obligated with the Noahide Laws to which the Gentiles were obligated would have been quite understandable in the Jewish community of the first century A.D. However, there are two aspects of the Pauline text that speak against such an interpretation. Most obviously the occurrence of the singular "work" instead of "works" cannot be explained on the assumption that Paul is thinking of the Noahide Laws. Additionally, the contrast between the Noahide Laws and the Mosaic Law is based on an inequality between the Jews and the Gentiles, which is totally out of place in the context of Romans 2. In this text Paul is arguing against the supposed privileged position of the Jews over against the Gentiles. All human beings, Jews and Gentiles alike, are according to Paul in the same position before God.

Pursuing a second possible interpretation, it might be suggested that Paul is reducing the entire Mosaic Law to a *single* principle as he does in Romans 13:8 where he writes: "for he who loves his neighbor has fulfilled the law". Paul repeats this idea of the law in Galatians 5:14: "For the whole law is fulfilled in one word, 'You shall love your neighbor as

[3] David Flusser, "Noachitische Gebote", *Theologische Realenzyklopädie*, Studienausgabe, Teil II, S. 582.

yourself.'" Nevertheless, we must take into account that the commandment of love is always associated with the Mosaic Law, not with a law inherent in nature. Thus it seems unlikely that Paul was interpreting the inscription in the hearts of the Gentiles simply as a summary principle of the written law. Furthermore, it must be remembered that Paul refers to the fulfillment of the inscription in the heart "by nature": "When the Gentiles who have not the law do *by nature* what the law requires, they are a law to themselves. ..." In view of this, it is reasonable to interpret the law inscribed in the heart as a *dimension of human existence that binds us to God*, and in accordance with the appearing of nature (i.e. "by nature"), the Gentiles fulfill the obligation of the law. So the inscription in the heart is the inescapable necessity of being committed to the Other, and this requirement is fulfilled on the deepest level of human existence by holding firmly to this commitment. One can perhaps numb the conscience, but one cannot totally silence it. One can curse God and profess atheism with the lips, but one cannot erase the inscription in the heart.

This one commitment to God is the foundation of all other commitments in life. For example, the marriage commitment, i.e. the commitment to the other person, is founded on the commitment to the eternal Other. Commitment to the Other is not just an obligation in the moral or legal sense; it is an inherent necessity, the sine qua non of being human. Viewed from this perspective, same sex marriage is exposed as detrimental because it levels the differences involved in the commitment. A commitment to the qualitatively *same* is fundamentally different from a commitment to the significantly *other*, and thus it cannot serve as a symbol of the commitment to the radically Other – a symbol through which we have access to the transcendent. What the commitment to the Other entails is, of course, not self-evident, and in particular situations, interpretation of the inscription is necessary. This is the function of the conscience: to interpret the way in which we are committed to the Other.[4]

As we saw in our discussion of Cicero, the concept of conscience was developing in the first century B.C. from an awareness of something in general to an awareness of right and wrong. In the *Tusculan Disputations*, Cicero speaks of the pangs of conscience, thus associating a punishment for non-compliance with the demands of conscience. As we noted, Cicero's understanding of conscience should not be confused with the modern concept of individual conscience that is formed through the demands and restrictions of society. The Freudian idea of a superego would have been quite foreign to Cicero. For him conscience was grounded in universal, eternal law and therefore ultimately in God himself. Similarly the Apostle Paul was not thinking of our modern concept of conscience when he wrote: "They show that what the law requires is written on their hearts, while their conscience also bears witness and their conflicting thoughts accuse or perhaps excuse them." *Conscience*, which is a Greek concept, is very closely related to the *heart*, which is a Hebrew concept. The inscription of the law lies hidden in the heart, and the conscience is the voice that interprets this inscription and announces it to the individual. The conscience cannot be separated from the inscription in the heart without ceasing to be conscience as Paul understood it. We find a parallel construction using the word "conscience" in Romans 9:1 where Paul writes: "I am speaking the truth in Christ, I am not lying; my conscience bears me witness in the Holy Spirit. ..." For the one trusting in Jesus Christ, his conscience is rooted in the presence of the Holy Spirit. For the non-believers of Romans 2:15, however, the conscience is rooted in the inscription of the heart and "speaks" the truth about the necessary commitment to the Other and its meaning in particular situations. Out of this arises a conflict of thoughts in the individual,

[4] Those readers familiar with Scholastic Theology may detect here a parallel to the Thomistic understanding of the conscience and the synteresis. This is not, however, the place to explain the differences.

some thoughts accusing and others excusing him. It is as though a judicial process is being conducted in the recesses of the self, and in verse 16 we learn that this process is, as it were, a preview of the last judgment "when, according to my gospel, God judges the secrets of men by Christ Jesus".[5] The analogy between the judicial process in the individual and the last judgment underscores the seriousness of the conscience.

A vital question concerning Paul's statements in Romans 2:12–16 remains to be answered. When he asserts that the Gentiles "do by nature what the law requires", we are confronted once again with the problem of understanding the word "nature". The use of "nature" (φύσις) in connection with law is without doubt a Stoic idea since there is no Hebrew equivalent for the Greek word φύσις. So clearly, Paul is deviating from his Jewish background in employing the word "nature", but we cannot assume that he understood the word "nature" as Cicero did. More importantly, we should certainly not think that he understood the word "nature" as we do. To reduce the meaning of "nature" to observable biological, chemical and physical processes that can be investigated in the laboratory would totally miss the point. And any suggestion that the Gentiles did "by nature" what the law requires because of their genetic makeup would be absurd. However, eliminating what the word *does not mean* does not tell us what the word actually *does mean,* and the difficulty of interpreting the word in the writings of Paul is compounded by the fact that it occurs only rarely.

In Paul's letter to the Church at Rome, he uses the word "nature" in two quite different contexts. Taking a look at the overall structure of the epistle, we note the following. In addition to a salutation (1:1–7), a preamble (1:8–17) and a conclusion (15:14–16:27), the letter contains four major sections: *the revelation of the justice of God* (1:18–4:25), *the con-*

[5] The textual transition in Greek from verse 15 to verse 16 is awkward, and numerous suggestions have been set forth in order to solve the problem. I have inserted a hyphenation between the two verses, reading verse 16 as an elaboration of the thought in verse 15.

sequences of justification (5:1–8:39), *the mystery of Israel* (9:1–11:36) and *the Apostle's admonition* (12:1–15:13). Of these four sections the first and second are very closely related, and the fourth is an admonition that fits well with the first and second sections. In contrast, the third section seems to be loosely connected to the others and could almost be considered an excursus on the situation of Israel. A closer examination, however, discloses an interesting parallel between the first and the third sections. The revelation of the justice of God in the first section takes place in the present lives of the Jews and Gentiles, whereas the mystery of Israel in section four points toward an eschatological revelation at the end of time. Significantly, Paul employs the word "nature" in both sections, albeit in quite different contexts. In fact, the only occurrences of "nature" in the letter are found in these two sections: section one, 1:26 f and 2:14 and section three, 11:21 ff. Since we have already dealt with the occurrence in 2:14, we will focus now on 1:26 f and 11:21 ff.

In approaching the occurrence of the word "nature" in 1:26 f, we begin with Paul's statements in 1:18 f, where he opens the substantive part of his letter with this bold statement about wrath of God against the Gentiles who have fallen into sin: "For the wrath of God is revealed from heaven against all ungodliness and wickedness of men who by their wickedness suppress the truth." We note immediately that the revelation is expressed in the present tense. That is, the revelation under consideration in this passage is not a future eschatological event; the wrath of God is an event in the present. How the wrath of God is manifested remains to be seen, but it is the ungodliness and wickedness of human beings that have called it forth. The twofold reference to ungodliness and wickedness is reminiscent of the two tables of stone containing the Ten Commandments, the first table addressing the relationship between God and men, the second regulating the relationships among men. The "ungodliness" (ἀσέβεια) of verse 18 is not the neglect of the gods (ἀθεότης), nor is it atheism in the modern sense of denying the existence of God. Rather, "ungodliness" (ἀσέβεια) is impiety and its opposite is piety or reverence for God (εὐσέβεια). The impious are not antireligious in the broadest sense, but they engage in sacrilege by worshipping the creature instead of the Creator.

Employing Stoic terminology, Paul charges that the Gentiles knew that they should not have behaved in this manner. "For what can be known about God is clear to them, because God has shown it to them. Ever since the creation of the world his invisible reality, namely his eternal power and deity, has been clearly perceived in the things that have been made" (vss. 19 f.). At first blush, one might think that Paul is adopting Stoic theology as presented in the writings of Cicero, and indeed there are undeniable similarities. As we saw in our discussion of Cicero's *On the Nature of the Gods*, he thought that nature provided a proof of the existence of the gods: "If at the sight of a statue or painted picture you know that art has been employed, and from the distant view of the course of a ship feel sure that it is made to move by art and intelligence, and if you understand on looking at a horologe, whether one marked out with lines, or working by means of water, that the hours are indicated by art and not by chance, with what possible consistency can you suppose that the universe which contains these same products of art, and their constructors, and all things, is destitute of forethought and intelligence?"[6] Just as we can deduce from the appearance of a horologe that there was a creator of the instrument, we can deduce from the wonderful works of nature that there was a Creator of the whole universe. This was an early Stoic version of the so-called Watchmaker argument that was presented in the eighteenth century by the English clergyman William Paley and subsequently criticized by atheists from the time of Thomas Huxley down to the biologist Richard Dawkins.

In spite of the similarities between Cicero's argument and the words of Paul in Romans 1, there is a fundamental difference that we must take into account. The argument of the Stoics was based on logic; the pivotal point of the argument was the validity of deduction, which was highly

[6] CICERO, *On the Nature of the Gods* (De natura deorum), Bk. II, Ch. 57.

developed by the Stoics. From an observation of the visible, it is possible to deduce the reality of the invisible. In contrast, Paul's argument does not depend upon logic in any form, but rather it is grounded in the revelation of God to humankind. He writes: "For what can be known about God is clear (φανερόν) to them, because God *has shown* (ἐφανέρωσεν from φανερόω) it to them." The Greek word for "has shown" can be translated as "has made known" or "has revealed". What can be known about God is clear because God has made it clear. Paul continues: "Ever since the creation of the world his invisible reality, namely his eternal power and deity, has been perceived (καθορᾶται) contemplatively (νοούμενα from νοέω) in the things that have been made". We note that the invisible things of God are not conceptualized *analytically*, but rather they are perceived by the mind. The analytical mind has no access to the reality that Paul is describing. On the other hand, it would be a mistake to consider the perception of the invisible things of God as a mystical experience. Paul is describing a thinking perception, a meditative thinking, not a transition into an ecstatic state. Moreover, he does not indicate that faith is the basis of this experience; so no "leap of faith" is involved here, no *sacrificium intellectus*. The perceiving of the invisible things of God may not be possible for the analytical thought process of modern science, but it is definitely possible for the reflective understanding of the human mind. Thus Paul describes the experience in noetic terms; it is the mind (νοῦς) that perceives the invisible things of God. Paul claims that human beings in virtue of their intellectual capacities can perceive the invisible things of God. In the things that have been made we perceive through meditative thinking the invisible things of God.

Paul's appeal to the natural understanding of man *as* man comes as a surprise in view of the fact that his theology is based on religious, rather than philosophical experience. It should not be supposed, however, that he has temporally abandoned his theological perspective. Reflecting further upon his comments, we notice a significant difference between his views and those of Plato. Consider the contrast between the *invisible things* and the *made things* in Paul's text. In the writings of Plato the contrasting concepts of the *visible* (ὁρατός) and the *invisible* (ἀόρατος) became central as designations for the world of sense perception, on the one hand, and the world of ideas, on the other hand. This word pair is very rare in the Septuagint (i.e. the Greek translation of the Hebrew Bible), but it occurs frequently in the writings of Philo.[7] Assuming the Pauline authorship of the Epistle to the Colossians, we know that Paul was familiar with the contrast between invisible and visible as it appears in Philo[8], but in Romans 1:19 he chooses not to employ it. Instead he contrasts the *invisible* things of God with the things *made*, i.e. with the things *created*. Ever since the creation of the world, the invisible things of God have been known through the things that He created. The significance of this shift from "visible/invisible" to "created/invisible" can be easily overlooked.

The *visible* world does not necessarily appear as the *created* world. Nor does an argument such as that of William Paley guarantee that it will *appear* as a "created world". Either the visible things *appear* as created or they do not. We are reminded again of Heraclitus, the Obscure, whose understanding of nature went well beyond his contemporaries. In Fragment 123 he wrote: "Nature loves to hide herself." As we saw, Heraclitus did not understand nature simply as the sum total of all things living and non-living, but rather as the appearing of these things. Guided by the root meaning of the word "nature" in Greek (φύσις from φύω), Heraclitus conceived of nature as "a springing up" or as "a growing" of things, not in the biological sense, but rather in the sense of appearing. Yet this appearing always stands in tension with a concealing, which is indicated by the word "hiding". Nature loves to hide herself. The appearing of things loves to conceal itself. When nature occurs, there is

[7] "Invisible" occurs more than 100 times and "visible" over 70 times.

[8] In fact, the Colossians 1:16 passage is the only occurrence of the word pair in the New Testament.

a shining forth and there is a concealing. There is always a mystery in nature – a mystery that is hidden in the very appearing of nature.

Needless to say, Paul was not a Jewish Heraclitus, and we are not suggesting that he has adopted the thoughts of Heraclitus in the same way that he took over certain Stoic concepts. Nevertheless, there is a certain similarity between Heraclitus and Paul with regard to the appearing of things. Neither of them is focusing on the visible world as opposed to the invisible. Heraclitus does not anticipate the Platonic distinction between the *visible* (ὁρατός) and the *invisible* (ἀόρατος) nor does the Apostle Paul hark back to it. Both are describing the appearing of things, albeit in different ways. Unlike Heraclitus, Paul is not speaking in Romans 1:19 f about the *sheer* appearing of things, but rather about the appearing of things *as* created. A glimpse of the invisible power of God is disclosed when the things of the sensible world appear as created. This invisible power of God cannot be deduced; it can only be perceived by a meditative thinking free of distractions. As we have indicated, Paul's focus on the created things instead of the visible things grants us a new understanding of nature. As with Heraclitus, nature for Paul was not simply the sum total of the trees, the rivers, the mountains and the animals; it was the appearing of the trees, the rivers, the mountains and the animals as the *created things* of God. Nature for Paul is that which comes forth as created, and meditative, reflective thinking is the response to this appearing that allows us to perceive it.

Paul's understanding of nature as the "appearing of created things" is quite different from that of the modern scientific mind, which really does not understand *nature* at all. The analytical thinking of modern science understands only *abstracted segments* of nature that it categorizes as physics, biology, chemistry etc. Furthermore, science tends to see these segments of nature as obstacles to be overcome. So the basis of the scientific relationship to nature is one of control and manipulation, and scientific access to nature is made possible through analysis, not reflective thinking. Without doubt, the achievements of modern science have been very positive in many ways. Through the analysis of certain segments of nature, many discoveries have been made that are quite beneficial to the physical health and enjoyment of human beings. Such utilitarian success is crucial to the scientific enterprise and was already being discussed as the new science emerged.

Early proponents of the scientific method in the seventeenth century such as Francis Bacon were convinced that the scientific revolution would usher in an age, in which the suffering of humanity would be reduced and the living conditions of humankind would be greatly improved,[9] and in certain areas, it is undeniable that these hopes have indeed been fulfilled. Any cancer patient today who has been healed from this dreaded disease will gladly acknowledge the benefits of modern science. But at a deeper level, the benefits have come at a high cost. In the midst of the analysis of nature, we have lost sight of nature itself. We have forgotten what is being revealed in nature. We have become blind for that which cannot be analyzed, for that which escapes the grasp of technological thinking. As Paul writes in verse 22: "Claiming to be wise, they became fools, and exchanged the glory of the immortal God for images resembling mortal man. …" In our "wisdom", we no longer perceive the invisible things of God, i.e. the power of God. Instead our analysis of nature only increases our awareness of our own intellectual capacity and thus raises mortal man to the status of the immortal God. The power of the divine is replaced by the power of the human intellect. This is the distinguishing mark of humanism – to make man the measure of all things.

Pure humanism is eo ipso atheistic in the sense that it openly rejects the transcendent God. It is not, however, antireligious because its praise of human capacities transforms the human being into an idol of reverence. Humanists *believe* in the essential goodness of human nature, although the empirical evidence for this belief is almost totally lacking. This is the fundamental sin of humankind. It is not a sin against other human beings.

[9] BRUSH, *Naturwissenschaft als Herausforderung für die Theologie,* 2008, S. 34 f.

It is the sin against God, and from this *one theological sin* follow the *many moral sins* that Paul depicts in the first chapter of Romans. How these moral sins follow, Paul tells us in verses 24–32. Significantly, these verses, which themselves belong to section one (1:18–4:25), reflect a threefold structure, each subsection being introduced by the phrase "God gave them up" (παρέδωκεν αὐτοὺς ὁ θεός): 24 f., 26 f., and 28–32.

We begin with the first subsection (vss. 24 f.): "Therefore God *gave them up* in the lusts (ἐπιθυμίαι) of their hearts to impurity, to the dishonoring of their bodies among themselves, because they exchanged the truth about God for a lie and worshiped and served the creature rather than the Creator. ..." According to Paul, the *many* sins of humankind follow from the *one* sin against God, which is the rejection of his power as it appears in nature. The way in which these many sins follow is explicitly described by Paul: God gives them up. Paul uses the same Greek word (παραδίδωμι) three times in order to emphasize his point, and this word can be translated variously as "give up", "turn over", "hand over" or "deliver". God hands them over to their own passions, and without the moral compass of the divine, they fall into the most perverse practices. As Augustine once noted, the wrath of God is not revealed as *force*, but rather as *abandonment* (*non cogendo, sed deserendo*).[10] God simply lets them go their own way. They have not perceived nature as the appearing of created things, and their blindness for nature is now reflected outwardly through their actions. They can no longer control their own passions (ἐπιθυμίαι), but rather their selfish passions control them. Here we see that the wrath of God and the self-destruction of human beings are intertwined. The wrath of God is not an empirical event that could be observed, analyzed and recorded; rather it can only be "read" indirectly on the self-destruction of man and the disintegration of a society.

Subsection two (vss. 26 f.) reads: "For this reason God *gave them up* to dishonorable passions. Their women exchanged natural relations for unnatural, and the men likewise gave up natural relations with women and

[10] AUGUSTINE, *Sermon* 57 (Sermones ad populum), Ch. 9.

were consumed with passion for one another, men committing shameless acts with men and receiving in their own persons the due penalty for their error." These verses are often quoted as a proof text for the fact that the Bible considers homosexuality to be a sin. Aside from the problematic method of proof texting, this opinion does not yet grasp the depth of Paul's words. The eroticizing of public and private life, which the neo-Marxist atheist Herbert Marcuse urged in his *Eros and Civilization* (1955), is the hallmark of an atheistic society, i.e. a society that praises the creature rather than the Creator. The crucial words here are: creature and Creator, and if we take our lead from this fundamental contrast, subsection two cannot be understood in isolation from subsection one, where Paul says that they "serve the creature rather than the Creator". As a result, they have exchanged the natural relations (τὴν φυσικὴν χρῆσιν) for the unnatural (παρὰ φύσιν), i.e. for that which it is *against nature*. The phrase "against nature" (παρὰ φύσιν) was common in Stoicism and was contrasted with "according to nature" (κατὰ φύσιν). Chrysippus used these phrases in reference to moral acts as well as to the welfare of human beings in general. For Zeno, it was "against nature" (παρὰ φύσιν) for a man to live with a woman who was married to another and thereby to disturb the husband's household.[11]

Paul's contrast between "against nature" and "natural relations" is consistent with his frequent theological emphasis on relationships. Just as the blindness of man for the power of God in nature involves the relationship between God and man, the moral acts of human beings are exemplified on the fundamental relationship between a man and a woman. When the truth of nature is no longer perceived, it is no longer possible to distinguish between natural and unnatural relationships. Nature becomes nothing more than the sum total of living and non-living things, and actions are considered to be "natural" and therefore moral as long as they do not disturb the individual things unduly. But this line of reason-

[11] ZENO, Fragment 244, in: IOANNES ARNIM, *Stoicorum Veterum Fragmenta*, Vol. I, (1905), 1964, p. 58, l. 13–15.

ing is blind for nature *as* nature, and it is not possible to pass judgment on an action as unnatural unless one knows what nature is.

There have been attempts to explain away Paul's obvious criticism of homosexuality in verses 26–27 by suggesting that he was simply condemning pederasty, not a homosexual relationship between two consenting adults. In trying to make a case for this interpretation, proponents of homosexuality have noted that Paul uses the words "male" (ἄρσηv) and "female" (θῆλυς) in these verses instead of "man" (ὁ ἀvηρ) and "woman" (ἡ γυνή). From this, they conclude that he was referring to boys, not to adult men. Given the extremely weak linguistic and historical evidence for such an interpretation, it takes a considerable amount of imagination to make the view plausible, but Sarah Ruden has risen to the occasion in her little book *Paul among the People: The Apostle Reinterpreted and Reimagined in his own Time* (2010). This is not the place to discuss the hermeneutics of imagination, which involves the influence of French philosophers such as Paul Ricoeur on American thinking. Suffice it to say that Ms. Ruden has mastered the art of imagination as she understands it, if not the art of historical interpretation.[12] Where evidence fails, she imagines. Consider for instance the following: "I picture Paul, flushed and sweating in his rage as he writes that *everyone* is responsible for what pederasty has made of society…" And again: "I think that is because Paul was pioneering a general condemnation of pederasty in the West. …"[13] So in the mind of Ms. Ruden, Paul was only condemning pederasty, not homosexuality in general. In its modern form, she is convinced that the Apostle would have approved of gay relationships. Relying on her imagination, Ms. Ruden does not hesitate to quote Greek

[12] To be more direct, I see little evidence in her book that she understands the philosophical concept of imagination from KANT's *Critique of Judgment* down to the hermeneutics of PAUL RICOEUR. Philosophical imagination is quite different from undisciplined fantasizing.

[13] SARAH RUDEN, *Paul among the People: The Apostle Reinterpreted and Reimagined in his own Time*, 2010, p. 67 f.

poetic material as if it were providing reliable *historical* information, and she regularly cites material of the second century A.D. as though it were relevant for the Apostle Paul. Still, her most glaring deficiency in *reimaging* Paul is her total lack of understanding of Paul's theology. It was Paul's theology that provided the context for his condemnation of homosexuality as it appears in the first chapter of Romans.

On the linguistic side, it is important to note that Plato in his *Symposium* makes it quite clear that he is discussing pederasty by employing terms such as "boy" (ὁ παῖς) and "lad" (τὸ μειρακίον).[14] I see no reason to think that the Apostle Paul could not have used these words if he had indeed meant to say what Ms. Ruden imagines. Regarding the words "male" and "female", it is evident that Paul is emphasizing through the use of these expressions the sexual dimension of the transgression, but there is no association in the text of these terms with pederasty. Modern and postmodern interpreters may disagree with the views of Paul on homosexuality, but intellectual integrity demands that we acknowledge the content of his words.

There is, however, a more fundamental problem that is usually overlooked in considering Paul's comments on homosexuality. Perverse sexual practices are not just sins according to Paul; they are a punishment for the fundamental sin of worshipping the creature rather than the Creator. When nature is no longer perceived meditatively, when the appearing of nature is no longer experienced as a manifestation of the power of God, then human beings become the measure of all things; they adore themselves and worship their own bodies. In short, they fall prey to the sensuous and become dominated by the power of pleasure. For some, this will manifest itself in the form of homosexual and other perverse sexual practices. For others, it may take the form of an insatiable desire for pleasure in other areas including the consumption of food and drink. Then, those members of society who are heterosexual and refrain from perverse sexual practices are not necessarily innocent of the funda-

[14] PLATO, *Symposium*, 191e–192a.

mental sin of worshipping the creature rather than the Creator. One need only consider the enormous expenditure of energy and money in modern Western societies for the purpose of improving the health and beauty of the body. Such thoughts should give us pause to reflect on our own culture and its obsession with the physical body – its health, its beauty, its comfort and its pleasure.

Finally, we come to the third subsection (vss. 28–32) that contains a catalogue of vices: "And since they did not see fit to acknowledge God, God gave them up to a base mind and to improper conduct. They were filled with all manner of wickedness, evil, covetousness, malice. Full of envy, murder, strife, deceit, malignity, they are gossips, slanderers, haters of God, insolent, haughty, boastful, inventors of evil, disobedient to parents, foolish, faithless, heartless, ruthless. Though they know God's decree that those who do such things deserve to die, they not only do them but approve those who practice them."

Those who do not acknowledge God include not only the philosophical atheists who have considered the arguments for the existence of God and have arrived at a negative conclusion. Surprising as it may seem, the vast majority of those who do not acknowledge God are, what one might call, *practical* atheists who have simply excluded God from their daily lives. The penalty for both groups is the same: abandonment by God and self-destruction of the individual. Thus they not only fall deeper into perverse practices of all sorts, but also into covetousness, deceit, envy and so forth as Paul describes in these verses. To introduce this catalogue of morals sins, Paul employs for the third time the verb "to hand over" or "to give up". "And since they did not see fit to acknowledge God, God *gave them up* to a base mind and to improper conduct." The Greek phrase for "improper conduct" (τὰ μὴ καθήκοντα) is an allusion to the Stoic concept of duty (τὸ καθῆκον or *officium*), which designates the moral obligation according to nature. In the writings of Cicero, we have seen the importance of duty for the ethics of the Stoics. Now we see how the Apostle Paul interpreted "improper conduct". Having lost control of themselves, those who do not perceive the created things of nature now lose control of their relationships to others, thus becoming heartless and ruthless. As a direct result, the moral fabric of society disintegrates. The final sentence in this section is really a conclusion to the verses 24–32. Those who have become dominated by sensuous pleasure not only fall deeper and deeper into the spiral of self-destruction; they applaud others who do the same things that they do. In this way, the perversion of society acquires the veneer of normalcy.

According to Paul, all of this takes place because people worship the creature rather than the Creator. They become blind for the power of God appearing in nature. But what does it mean to say that nature appears as created? The past participle "created" indicates that the event is completed, but in reality it is happening continuously. So it would be more accurate to say the nature is being created. If this were not the case, then the "perception" of the power of God would rest upon a deduction, whereas in truth *the power of God is made known in the appearing of nature as being created in the moment.* This event of appearing can be further characterized as a *gift*. Nature does not simply appear; it comes to us as a gift that can only be received, not demanded. We may demand our rights in society, but we cannot attain the gift of nature by demanding it. The gift is not a gift if it is not received, and receiving requires an openness to the divine Other. Thus, we discover that receiving is the most fundamental natural action because it corresponds to nature itself. Acting according to nature is the same as responding appropriately to the appearing of nature as a gift, and this appearing includes one's own body. That is, the way in which we experience nature in general is crucial for our understanding of our own bodies. Do we possess our bodies as we possess other objects? Is it our right to do with our bodies as we desire? Or is the body a gift from God? The Apostle Paul was totally clear on this matter, and in addressing the Christians at the Church in Corinth, he admonishes them to shun immorality, i.e. sins against their own bodies. He writes: "Shun immorality. Every other sin which a man commits is outside the body; but the immoral man sins against his own body. Do you not know that your body is a temple of the Holy Spirit within you, which you have from God?" The city of Corinth was known in antiquity for its licentiousness. The libertines of the city argued that satisfying sexual desires was in principle no different from satisfying one's hunger by taking food. Paul rejected their analogy – not because he condemned sexual relationships in general, but because licentiousness is no more necessary for satisfying sexual desires than gluttony is for satisfying hunger. In making decisions about our own bodies, we should never lose sight of the relationship of God to our bodies. For Christians, the body is the temple of the Holy Spirit, and for all humankind, the body is a gift from the divine Other just as nature is a gift. With this, we complete our treatment of the first passage in which the word "nature" occurs.

The second passage in which Paul uses the word "nature" is found in Romans Chapter 11, where he takes up the relationship between the Jewish nation and the Gentiles and then addresses the fate of Israel. The literary device that Paul employs in these passages is the allegory of the olive tree. In the allegory, the cultivated olive tree symbolizes the Jews, whereas the wild olive shoot symbolizes the Gentiles who have been grafted into the tree. Paul writes: "Now I am speaking to you Gentiles. … But if some of the branches were broken off, and you, a wild olive shoot, were grafted in their place to share the richness of the olive tree, do not boast over the branches. … For if God did not spare the natural (κατὰ φύσιν) branches, neither will he spare you. … For if you have been cut from what is by nature (κατὰ φύσιν) a wild olive tree, and grafted, contrary to nature (παρὰ φύσιν), into a cultivated olive tree, how much more will these natural branches be grafted back into their own olive tree."[15] Once again Paul's usage of Stoic terminology is apparent in the phrases "by nature" and "contrary to nature", but this time he uses the Stoic terminology in a much different sense than in Chapter 1. Whereas "nature" in Chapter 1 had the basic meaning of "things appearing as cre-

[15] Romans 11:13, 17, and 24.

ated" through which the power of God was made known, the word now refers to the "revelation of God's favor" (i.e. election) through which human beings attain fulfillment (i.e. salvation).

As we saw earlier, the appearing of things as created can be further characterized as a gift, and now we see that the gift assumes the meaning of a *healing, saving event*. When nature in its fullest sense appears as a gift, it bestows a renewing power on human beings. By the phrase "nature in its fullest sense", we mean the appearing of things through which both the *power* and the *loving favor* of God are revealed. Significantly, this revelation has an inner history. That is, "nature in its fullest sense" refers to the revelation of the history of salvation. Therefore, "according to nature" means in accordance with the history that began with the promise to Abraham and continued through the revelation of the Torah at Sinai down to postexilic Judaism, and "against nature" means an interruption of this inner history of the appearing of the power and loving favor of God. So the allegory of the olive tree points to the history of God's self-manifestation, the history of a promise that he made. The Israelites were *by nature* the *cultivated* olive tree since they had received the promise, whereas the Gentiles were *by nature* a *wild* olive tree because they were not included in this promise. But suddenly and surprisingly, God acted "against nature", i.e. against his previous self-manifestation, and revealed the primacy of faith over obedience to the Torah. This interruption in the inner history of the promise was so paradoxical that most of the Jews did not respond with faith, but rather with disbelieve and even hostility. Thus, they were cut off, and the Gentiles who did believe were grafted in the olive tree. In this passage, the *historical dimension* of nature becomes very apparent. It is not history in the modern sense, but rather the inner history of the appearing of God's power and love, the history of God's self-manifestation. Through God's act *against nature*, the Torah was replaced by faith. Or perhaps better: The promise to Abraham was disclosed in its universal dimension and in its inseparable relationship to faith. We are reminded of Paul's comments in Chapter 2, where he maintains that a person "is a Jew who is one inwardly, and [that] real circumcision is a matter of the heart, spiritual and not literal" (2:29). So the promise is fulfilled in faith.

With the possible exception of Ephesians 2:11–22, Paul's statements in Romans 11 concerning the relationship between Christian Gentiles and Jews are unique within the entire corpus of New Testament writings and present the interpreter with multiple problems. For our purposes, we have ignored most of the exegetical difficulties in Chapter 11 and focused on Paul's use of the word "nature" in the allegory of the olive tree. For in Paul's discussion of the allegory, we gain additional insight into his understanding of nature. Before leaving this allegory, there is one further point to be made. Consider the contrast between the phrase "against nature" in Chapter 1 and in Chapter 11. In Chapter 1, we read that human beings have acted against nature, whereas in Chapter 11, it is God who has acted against nature. When man acts against nature, he abandons God and in so doing he destroys himself and his society. In acting against nature, man refuses to acknowledge God as God. As Luther wrote in Thesis 17 of the "Disputation against scholastic theology", man does not want God to be God (*deum esse deum*), but rather he wants himself to be God and God not to be God (*se esse deum et deum non esse deum*).[16] So he worships the creature, rather than the Creator. But when *God* acts against nature, he paradoxically brings forth good to the benefit of all. There is a hidden lesson in this for us. Only God can produce good by acting against nature, and it is sheer hubris for human beings to think that they possess this capacity. As Paul vividly describes, the results of their arrogance are always the same: self-destruction and the disintegration of society.

[16] LUTHER's usage of the words *naturaliter* and *natura* must be understood in the context of his reaction to Scholastic Theology.

Chapter 4

"The Doctrine of the Theologian: Augustine"

Augustine was born in November, A.D. 354 in Roman North Africa. He attended school in Thagaste where he received instruction in reading, writing, and arithmetic, and learned Greek as well as Latin. He was particularly fond of rhetoric, and the classical Latin instruction led him to read Virgil's *Aeneid*. When Augustine was 16 years old, he moved to Carthage where he continued his study of rhetoric and read with great interest Cicero's *Hortensius* (i.e. the anonymous work attributed to Cicero). As Augustine himself reports, reading Cicero became a turning point in his life, and he later described the experience as a conversion to philosophy.[1] It is fair to say that Augustine's interest in philosophy never waned throughout his entire life, although he later viewed philosophy as subordinate to Christian thought.[2]

Soon after his "conversion" to philosophy, Augustine became interested in Manichaeism, which considered itself to be a higher form of Christian thought with strong philosophical leanings, and he remained active within the group for nine years. Eventually, however, he became dissatisfied with the inability of the Manichaeans to answer his probing questions about philosophy and religion, and so he moved from Carthage to Rome where he became interested in the scepticism of the

---

[1] AUGUSTINE, *Confessions* (Confessionum libri tredecim), Bk. III, Ch. 4.

[2] AUGUSTINE, *On Christian Doctrine* (De doctrina christiana), Bk. II, Ch. 41.

New Academy. Thereafter he moved to Milan in order to accept a position as *magister rhetoricae*, and it was in Milan that he came into contact with the theologian Ambrosius, whose rhetorical skill and knowledge of Christianity left a lasting impression on Augustine. Augustine's reading of the works of Plato in the Latin translation of Marius Victorinus introduced him to Neoplatonism, which he enthusiastically embraced and supplemented through his study of the letters of the Apostle Paul.

In August A.D. 386, Augustine experienced a burst of insight as he was walking outside his house in Milan that he describes as a conversion experience to an ascetic Christian life.[3] From this decision he never wavered. A year later he was baptized into the Catholic Church and embarked upon his chosen lifestyle. But the quiet life of an ascetic was not to be his. During a visit to Hippo, Augustine attended a worship service where the resident Bishop Valerius publicly encouraged Augustine to enter the priesthood, and the congregation supported the ordination unanimously. So in late A.D. 390, Augustine was ordained into the priesthood. In spite of his new responsibilities, Augustine never gave up his ascetic lifestyle, and Bishop Valerius assisted him by making a plot of land available on which a monastery could be erected. Sometime around A.D. 395, Valerius ordained Augustine as co-Bishop of Hippo, and following the death of Valerius in A.D. 396, Augustine became the sole bishop of the city with responsibilities that he had never envisioned or wanted. In this position, he remained until his death in A.D. 430. As bishop he was involved in conflicts with numerous groups: the Manichaeans, the Donatists, the Pelagians and the Arians. He penned an enormous corpus of Christian writings that extend over a period of 35 years. He experienced the invasion of the Vandals as they crossed the straits of Gibraltar in 429 and besieged Hippo in the summer of 430. In August of 430, Augustine died, leaving behind one of the largest collection of writings from late antiquity that we possess.

[3] AUGUSTINE, *Confessions*, Bk. VIII.

In the following discussion, no attempt will be made to present the "theology" of Augustine. The breadth of Augustine's thought is so great that both Catholics and Protestants alike have appealed to his writings on various topics. Our aim is much more modest. We will simply be investigating some of his writings in an effort to ascertain how he understood nature. Obviously such a procedure brings with it certain limitations, but boundaries must be set.

In the broadest sense, Augustine understood the word "nature" as a reference to the defining characteristic of a thing. In philosophical terms, the nature of a thing is its essence. "Nature" refers to what something actually is. In this sense, both God and the world fall under the category of nature. Nevertheless, Augustine's thought is dominated by the fundamental distinction between God and the world so that a tension is immediately introduced into the idea of nature. It is the nature of God to be *absolute* both in power and in goodness, whereas it is the nature of the world to be *relatively* powerful and good. It is the nature of God to be *unchanging*; it is the nature of the world to be *changing*. The changeable world is subject to time and space, whereas God as unchangeable is not subject to these structures. God is *eternal*, the world is *temporal*. At this point, we already observe an important difference between Augustine and the Stoics. Whereas the Stoics conceived of Zeus as *immanent* in nature, Augustine maintained the *transcendence* of God over the natural world. Furthermore, Augustine maintained that the world, being temporal, had a beginning and will have an end, and therefore the question about the origin of the world became foremost in his thought. In this context, the transcendence of the absolute God over the relative world becomes a distinction between the *creating nature* of God and the *created nature* of the world, whereby the latter is fundamentally dependent on the former.[4] Significantly, this dependence of the world on God is in

[4] AUGUSTINE, *On the Nature of the Good* (De natura boni), Sec. 19; *On true Religion* (De vera religione), Ch. XVIII, Sec. 35 and Ch. XX, Sec. 38; *On Genesis against the Manicheans* (De Genesi contra Manichaeos), Bk. II, Ch. 29, Sec. 43.

the thought of Augustine twofold; it includes both the first creation of the world by God as recorded in Genesis, Chapters 1–3 and the sustaining power of God in the world following the initial creation.

Finally, the fundamental distinction between God and the world is reflected within created nature itself in the form of the distinction between *corporal* and *spiritual*. Bodies are spatially and temporally mutable natures, whereas the soul is subject to time, but not space. Thus the soul is only temporally mutable. Since God is subject to neither time nor space and is immutable, we observe a hierarchy of natures from physical bodies at the lower end of the scale extending upward to God as the absolute pinnacle. The soul and other spiritual beings occupy a range in the middle of this hierarchy.

Thus far, we have been considering nature in the theology of Augustine in the sense of essence. The nature of something describes what something really is. But Augustine's understanding of nature went much deeper than this static definitional meaning. Nature for him was not only the essence of something; it was an activity, a dynamic process, a force. Two of Augustine's main sources for thinking about nature were Stoicism and the Bible. To be sure, the concept of *nature* is not central to the biblical tradition. In fact as we have seen, classical Hebrew had no linguistic equivalent for the Greek φύσις or the Latin *natura*. However, the idea of *creation* did become central to biblical thinking, and it included not only the *result* of divine activity, but also the *activity* itself. So in combining Greek philosophical thought with biblical theology, Augustine joined together nature and creation to form a dynamic understanding of process in the world.

The creator-nature and the creation-nature are correlative concepts. If there is a Creator, there must be a creation, and if there is a creation, there must be a Creator. So in considering the creation-nature, we are implicitly dealing with the creator-nature as well. Nevertheless, it is instructive to focus on the creation itself in the twofold sense mentioned above: the *original creation* and the *sustaining creation*.

We begin with the account of the original creation (*conditio prima*). Augustine wrote several works on creation as well as extended sections on creation in other works.[5] In the following, we will concentrate on his most complete interpretation of creation as it appears in *The Literal Commentary on Genesis in Twelve Books* (*De Genesi ad litteram libri XII*). Contrary to what one might think, Augustine's understanding of the creation account in Genesis 1–3 differs significantly from the literalistic interpretation that is held today by many conservatives. Augustine understood the original creation not as a progression over six days (the so-called Hexaemeron), but rather as a single event.[6] That is, he believed that the entire creation was created simultaneously. To be sure, the first chapter of Genesis presents the creation of the world as though it occurred over a period of six days, beginning with the creation of light and culminating in the creation of human beings. However, Augustine did not think that this account should be understood literally. Rather, he believed that it was intended for those who could not grasp the complexities of simultaneous creation. Augustine's reasons for interpreting the "events" of Genesis 1 as a simultaneous act come in part from the difficulty of reconciling the account of creation in Genesis 1 with that in Genesis 2.[7] Furthermore, he saw in passages such as Ecclesiasticus (Sirach) 18:1 a confirmation of the simultaneity of creation.[8] Here we read: "He who lives forever created all things at the same time" (*qui uiuit in aeternum, creauit omnia simul*). For the uneducated, Genesis 1 presented the cre-

---

[5] AUGUSTINE, *On Genesis against the Manicheans* (De Genesi contra Manichaeos, around A.D. 388), *Unfinished literal commentary on Genesis* (De Genesi ad litteram inperfectus, A.D. 393), the last three books of the *Confessions* (A.D. 400), *The literal Commentary on Genesis* (De Genesi ad litteram libri XII, written in the first two decades of the fifth century), and Books XI and XII of *The City of God* (De civitate dei, between A.D. 416–418).

[6] AUGUSTINE, *The literal Commentary on Genesis* (De Genesi ad litteram), Bk. IV, Ch. 33, Sec. 51–Ch. 34, Sec. 55, in: MIGNE, *Patrologia Latina*, Vol. 34.

[7] AUGUSTINE, Bk. V, Ch. 23, Sec. 46.

[8] AUGUSTINE, Bk. IV, Ch. 33, Sec. 52.

ation in a form that could be easily grasped[9], but behind this simple form of expression lay for Augustine the mystery of the instantaneous origination of the world out of nothing, the *creatio ex nihilo*.

Augustine's doctrine of creation out of nothing set him apart from the Greek philosophical tradition that had held to the idea of the eternality of matter, and it introduced an understanding of existence as the situation of the world between God and nothingness. Thus, Augustine can say that the creation is both *ex deo* (from God) and *ex nihilo* (out of nothing). Not that the world *proceeds* from God, but rather that the world was *made* by God. As Augustine says: "not born from God, but ... made by God out of nothing" (*non de deo nata, sed a deo ... facta de nihilo*).[10] So human beings exist in the tension between the absolute goodness of God and absolute nothingness. It is the absolute goodness of God that prevents man from falling into absolute nothingness, and it is the absolute nothingness that limits the goodness of man. That is, it is the nothingness out of which man arises that makes corruption possible.

As we mentioned above, the distinction of natures between immutable and mutable, absolute and relative also involves levels of goodness, and Augustine addressed the problem of good and evil during his controversy with the adherents of Manichaeism. This system of religious thought originated in Persia during the third century A.D. and was founded by Mani who maintained a "consistent dualism which rejects any possibility of tracing the origins of good and evil to one and the same source".[11] According to Mani, evil and good are independent principles. Matter is evil, whereas God is good. According to the Manichaean myth, the two primal principles of Light and Darkness dwelled originally in their own realms, coeternal but independent. In the course of creation, however,

[9] AUGUSTINE, Bk. IV, Ch. 33, Sec. 52; Bk. V, Ch. 3, Sec. 6; Bk. VI, Ch. 6, Sec. 9.

[10] AUGUSTINE, *Unfinished literal Commentary on Genesis* (De Genesi ad litteram inperfectus), Ch. 1, Sec. 2.

[11] R. MCL. WILSON, "Mani and Manichaeism", *The Encyclopedia of Philosophy*, (1967), 1972, Vol. 5, p. 149.

these principles became mixed in human beings, whereby the soul was identified with Light and the body with evil.

In his early life, Augustine was attracted to Manichaeism, but as time passed, he became more and more dissatisfied with the failure of its adherents to answer fundamental questions. A turning point in Augustine's thinking came when he realized that the Manichaeans were focusing entirely on the *source* of evil in the world without raising the question about the *essence* of evil. In *On the Nature of Good* Augustine writes: "When we ask *whence* comes evil, we should first ask *what* evil is and what good is" (*cum quaeritur, unde sit malum, prius quaerendum est, quid sit malum…*).[12] When he replaced the question *unde sit malum* (*whence* is evil?) with the question *quid sit malum* (*what* is evil?), his thinking was directed toward Neoplatonism where he found an answer in the concept of privation. This new insight led him to reject the Manichaean duality of good and evil and to assert that evil does not really exist. Everything that exists is good inasmuch as it exists.[13] Certainly nature is not absolutely good, but what we call "evil" is not an independent principle alongside the good. Evil is simply the *privation* of good. "Through the diminishing of good corruption increases" (*bonum minuendo crescit corruptio*).[14] Augustine exemplifies this through a physical phenomenon: "Take festering, which men call specifically a corruption of the body. Now if there is still something deep in the wound which it can consume, the corruption grows as good is diminished. But if there is nothing left to consume, there will be no festering since there is no good left. There will be nothing for corruption to corrupt. …"[15] Such an interpretation allowed Augustine to maintain the essential goodness of the entire creation.

In discussing the simultaneity of creation, we have not yet explained the way in which development occurred after the instant of creation. Just

---

[12] AUGUSTINE, *On the Nature of the Good* (De natura boni), Sec. 4 (italics added).
[13] AUGUSTINE, Sec. 1.
[14] AUGUSTINE, Sec. 20.
[15] AUGUSTINE, Sec. 20.

as the modern cosmologist tries to explain the development of the universe after the "Big Bang" and the evolutionary biologist provides an explanation for the development of organic forms, Augustine introduced principles of development that were consonant with his doctrine of creation. When Augustine maintains that the entire creation arose in an instant, he does not mean that everything was immediately present in its proper form, but rather that the *potentiality* for everything was immediately present. In explaining this aspect of creation, he appeals to the concept of seminal reasons (*seminales rationales*) that originated with the Stoics (λόγοι σπερματικοί). According to this doctrine, certain seeds of reason were implanted in matter at creation – seeds that would latter grow and develop into the visible world as we know it. The Neoplatonist Plotinus had already adopted the Stoic view of seminal reasons in order to explain the inherent ordering principles of the universe, and likewise Augustine took over this Stoic concept, combining it with his own biblical understanding of creation. In Genesis, Chapter 1, we read that God created through his word: "And God said, 'Let there be light'; and there was light." Augustine interpreted the creation through the word of God to be a sowing of rational principles that would develop in time.[16] In Greek Augustine's line of thought is much more apparent than it is in English. For, the Greek *logos* includes both meanings: "reason" and "word". So the creation through the divine *word* (*logos*) could easily be identified with the Stoic concept of the seminal *reasons* (*logoi*). Following the Stoics, Augustine held further that these seminal reasons or active principles were inherent forces in nature that would produce both the organic and inorganic forms of the world when the conditions were favorable (*acceptis opportunitatibus prodeunt*).[17] At times, Augustine

---

[16] Augustine, *The literal Commentary on Genesis* (De Genesi ad litteram), Bk. IV, Ch. 33.

[17] Augustine, *On the Trinity* (De trinitate), Bk. III, Ch. 9, Sec. 16, in: Migne, *Patrologia Latina*, Vol. 42.

referred to these principles as "natural laws" (*naturales leges*)[18], but of course he was not thinking of natural laws in the modern sense. Rather, these are rational structures of the universe that set determinate boundaries for development.

It should be apparent that Augustine's understanding of development in nature is quite different from the Darwinian theory of evolution. Yet in the course of the raging debate between the evolutionists and the creationists, there have been numerous attempts by creationists to bring Augustine's view of creation into the discussion, as though he had developed a theological concept of evolution that can rival the Darwinian theory. In my opinion this attempt is both historically absurd and theologically misguided. The context in which Augustine thought – the issues that concerned him, the questions that he raised, the presuppositions of his theology – was so totally different from those of the modern world that a direct comparison of Augustine and Darwin is quite meaningless. For Augustine, all of the species were "planted" in matter at the instant of creation, and the development of nature cannot go beyond these bounds. He writes: "Just as mothers are pregnant with their offspring, so the world itself is pregnant with the causes of things coming forth."[19] These comments bear the marks of a world where Stoicism and Neoplatonism filled the air. This is not to say that they have no relevance for our world. On the contrary, the thoughts and ideas of past philosophers and theologians offer at times very valuable insights, but their words must be interpreted historically and a "bridge of understanding" to the present must be constructed. Since a general theory of interpretation is not our main topic, we must break off these sketchy reflections and return to the doctrine of Augustine.

---

[18] AUGUSTINE, *The literal Commentary on Genesis* (De Genesi ad litteram), Bk. IX, Ch. 17, Sec. 10.

[19] AUGUSTINE, *On the Trinity* (De trinitate), Bk. III, Ch. 9, Sec. 16.

In the thought of Augustine, God is not only the *Creator* of the world, but also the *sustainer* of the world.[20] That is to say, God's creative activity never ends. It is just as active at the present moment as it was at the instant of creation. In the later theological tradition, one spoke of the continuing creation (*creatio continua*) of God as opposed to the initial act of creation. Although Augustine never employed the phrase *creatio continua*, he developed a clear understanding of the sustaining creative power of God and based his arguments on biblical passages where such an activity seemed to be indicated. For instance, when the Jews accused Jesus of breaking the law by healing a man on the sabbath, Jesus answered: "My father is working still, and I am working." (John 5:17).[21] In the statement: "My father is working still", Augustine saw a reference to the sustaining activity of God in the world. A more explicit reference he found in Psalm 104:30: "When thou sendest forth thy Spirit, they are created; and thou renewest the face of the ground."[22] When Augustine wrote about the initial creation of the world out of nothing, he was going against the stream of Greek philosophical thought that had maintained the eternality of matter. But the situation was quite different regarding the sustaining power of God in the world. On this point, Augustine was much more in line with the philosophical tradition and could quote the Stoic poet to whom the author of Acts referred in 17:28. Here we read: "In him (God) we live and move and have our being."

Already in the fragments of Heraclitus, the thunderbolt of Zeus emerged as an ordering power, creative and sustaining. Adopting this understanding, Cleanthes portrayed Zeus as an immanent, creative, rational, and providential presence in all things. The sustaining power of

---

[20] This aspect of AUGUSTINE's thought is reminiscent of the Stoics, and as a matter of fact, we know that AUGUSTINE had read CICERO's *De natura deorum*. See AUGUSTINE, *The City of God* (De civitate Dei), Bk. IV, Ch. 30.

[21] AUGUSTINE, *The literal Commentary on Genesis* (De Genesi ad litteram), Bk. IV, Ch. 11, Sec. 21.

[22] AUGUSTINE, Bk. X, Ch. 8, Sec. 13.

nature or Zeus was a fundamental tenet of Stoic thought, and so it was very easy for Augustine to combine this tradition with biblical references that seemed to point in the same direction. The necessity of God's creative power at each moment Augustine found expressed in Psalm 104:29: "When thou hidest thy face, they are dismayed; when thou takest away their breath, they die and return to the dust." Without the continuing creative activity of God in the world, the entire universe would sink into nothingness.[23] The relationship between Creator and creation is not that of a sculptor to his work of art, whereby the sculpture stands independent of the artist as soon as it is completed. Or if one prefers an analogy from the performing arts, consider a composition of music. The great musical compositions of the classical period fall into silence if they are not performed. It is ultimately the performance that counts, the dynamic sound. Similarly the creation would fall into nothingness without the continual performance of God's creative activity. Does this mean that the physical world would disappear? Does this mean that there would be no matter, no force fields? Not at all. What it does mean is this: The world would no longer appear as creation. Like a forgotten sheet of music that falls into silence, the world would fall into nothingness, into the void of meaninglessness.

That God is continually active in nature suggests the possibility of attaining a certain knowledge of God from the observation of nature, and in fact Augustine pursues this line of thought in a very original manner. As we saw in our discussion of Paul's letter to the church at Rome, nature itself makes the reality of God known to us: "For what can be known about God is plain to them, because God has shown it to them. Ever since the creation of the world his invisible nature, namely, his eternal power and deity, has been clearly perceived in the things that have been made" (vss. 19 f.). And in connection with the law in Chapter 2, Paul wrote: "When the Gentiles who have not the law do by nature what the law requires, they are a law to themselves, even though they do not have

---

[23] AUGUSTINE, Bk. V, Ch. 20, Sec. 40.

the law. They show that what the law requires is written on their hearts. ..." (vss. 14 f.). Expanding on the ideas of Paul, Augustine maintained that God not only has *written the law in the hearts of men*, but that He has also *written about His presence in nature as a whole*. In accordance with the Apostle Paul, Augustine states that a certain knowledge of God can be obtained from the appearance of nature, but he goes beyond the original idea of Paul by asserting that such knowledge is possible because God has *written* it in nature.

Thus, Augustine could speak of the "Book of Nature" (*liber naturae*) alongside the "Book of Scripture". In fact, it appears that Augustine coined the phrase "Book of Nature" in the course of his controversy with Faustus who was a staunch adherent of Manichaeism. In rejecting the Manichaean dualism of good and evil as well as the concomitant valuation of matter as evil, Augustine insisted that the creation, i.e. matter, is essentially good and furthermore that it bears the marks of its Creator. He writes: "But if you [i.e. Faustus] had first looked at the whole creation so that you attributed it to God its author as if you were reading a certain great book of nature (*liber naturae*) about things ... you would not have been led into these impious follies and blasphemous fancies with which, in your ignorance of what evil really is, you heap all evils upon God."[24] To my knowledge, this is the only occurrence of the exact phrase "Book of Nature" in the writings of Augustine, but he refers to the idea in various ways in many other works. In his commentary on Psalm 45, he writes: "The divine page is the book that you must hear; it is the book of the universe that you must observe. The pages of Scripture can only be read by those who know how to read and write, while everyone, even the illiterate, can read the book of the universe."[25] Or again in a sermon on Matthew 11, Augustine writes: "Some people, in order to dis-

[24] AUGUSTINE, *Against Faustus the Manichean* (Contra Faustum Manicheum), Bk. XXXII, Ch. 20.

[25] AUGUSTINE, *Expositions on the Psalms,* Psalm 45:7 (Enarrationes in Psalmos, 45, 7), in: MIGNE, *Patrologia Latina*, Vol. 36, p. 518.

cover God, read a book. But there is a great book: the very appearance of created things. Look above and below, note, read. God whom you want to discover, did not make the letters with ink; he put in front of your eyes the very things that he made. Can you ask for a louder voice than that? Heaven and earth cry out: God made me."[26]

Augustine's distinction between the Book of Scripture and the Book of Nature was the beginning of a tradition that continued down to the time of Johannes Kepler, the great astronomer of the late sixteenth century.[27] Johannes Kepler was born in 1571 to Lutheran parents in Weil der Stadt (today Württemberg). After completing his study of the humanities at the University of Tübingen, he entered the theological school in Tübingen with the intention of becoming a theologian. However, his study was cut short when he was offered and accepted a teaching position in Graz where he was to teach mathematics. Kepler's decision to switch from theology to mathematics and science was motivated in part by an experience that he understood as a divine revelation. In his early work on astronomy entitled *Mysterium Cosmographicum* (1596), Kepler explained how he discovered that the five regular bodies of Plato can be arranged so that they describe the paths of the six planets (only six planets were known at that time).[28] The discovery of the correspondence between the movement of the planets and the five unique solids (Tetrahedron, Octahedron etc.), which form the basis of Plato's understanding of the universe in the *Timaeus*, confirmed Kepler's decision to devote himself to the study of astronomy. We know today that this correspondence was based on a geometrical coincidence, and as soon as other planets besides those visible to the naked eye were discovered, Kepler's geometrical model no longer fit. Nevertheless, Kepler's discovery was a

---

[26] AUGUSTINE, *Sermons, No. 126* (Sermones, 126), ed. by A. MAI in: MIGNE, *Patrologia Latina Supplementa*, p. 505.

[27] In the following discussion, I am indebted to JÜRGEN HÜBNER's fine study in: *Die Theologie Johannes Keplers zwischen Orthodoxie und Naturwissenschaft,* 1975.

[28] JOHANNES KEPLER, *Mysterium Cosmographicum*, Gesammelte Werke, Vol. I, p. 15.

life-changing experience for him. As a Lutheran and a theology student at Tübingen, he was familiar with Augustine's distinction between the Book of the Scripture and the Book of Nature, and after his discovery about the movement of the planets, he was convinced that his God-given task in life was to decipher the "second revelation" of God in nature. In Kepler's mind, astronomers were the high priests of God who dealt with the Book of Nature[29], and following Plato, he believed that God was always concerned with geometry (Θεὸν ἀεὶ γεωμετρεῖν).

The impact of the concept "Book of Nature" on the young astronomer of the sixteenth century testifies to the importance of Augustine's thought on Western civilization. Of course, Augustine's approach to nature was quite different from that of Kepler. Whereas Kepler proceeded in a scientific manner in order to analyse and quantify nature, Augustine approached nature meditatively and interpretively. In the Latin text of Psalm 144:10 (English translation is 145:10), we read: "All your works, O Lord, confess you, and all your saints bless you."[30] In interpreting this passage, Augustine points out that there are two types of confession, namely the confession of sin and the confession of praise, and that the psalmist in 144:10 is thinking of the confession of praise. So the meaning of the passage is this: "All your works praise you" (*Laudent te omnia opera tua*). Still the question remains as to how nature can praise God, and Augustine answers this question in the following way: "Because when you meditate (Latin: *considerare*) upon it [i.e. nature] and see its beauty, you praise God in it. A certain voice belongs to the silent earth, the splendour of the earth. When you pay attention and see its splendour, when you see its fertility and its power … when you look and in your meditation you, as it were, interrogate it – the seeking itself is an interrogation – when in a state of wonderment you have sought and

---

29 Johannes Kepler, *Briefe 1590–1599,* Gesammelte Werke, Vol. XIII, Number 91, pp. 182 ff.

30 Augustine, *Expositions on the Psalms,* Psalm 144:10 (Enarrationes in Psalmos, 144:10), in: Migne, *Patrologia Latina*, Vol. 37, p. 13.

investigated, and you have discovered the great power, the great beauty and the magnificent excellence, since by itself and from itself, it is not able to have this excellence, immediately it comes into your mind, that it was not able to exist out of itself, unless from a Creator. That which you have found in it is the voice of confession itself, as you praise the Creator. When one meditates on the whole beauty of this world, does not the splendour itself, as it were, with one voice respond: 'Not I, but God has made me'."[31]

Clearly, Augustine is not simply referring in this passage to a casual observation of nature as, for instance, when one enjoys the landscape of the countryside while traveling through an unfamiliar area. A casual looking at this or that does not lead to the knowledge of God about which Augustine wrote. More is required. Nor is Augustine anticipating the modern concept of the scientific analysis of nature – an intense focusing on a small segment of nature in order to dissect it into its component parts, to quantify them and to propose an explanation of their interaction. Rather, Augustine is describing a much more holistic view of nature. The key words in his description are: meditation, wonderment, and interrogation. It is as though the person enters into a conversation with nature and probes the mystery of existence. Then in a state of absolute wonderment, the individual meditates on this mystery and watches carefully that which appears. The Latin word for "meditate" in this passage is *considerare*, which one might be tempted to translate as "consider" or "reflect upon". However, in the writings of Cicero, *considerare* is often paired with *contemplari* (to contemplate) without any apparent distinction in meaning.[32] So it would seem that the Latin *considerare* is closer in meaning to the English "contemplate" than it is to "consider". On the other hand, Augustine's usage of *considerare* and *contemplari* differs from that of Cicero and bears the marks of the mystical tradition stem-

---

[31] AUGUSTINE, Vol. 37, p. 13.

[32] See for example: CICERO, *Academics* (Academica), Bk. I, p. 127 and *On Duties* (De officiis), Bk. I, Ch. XLIII, Sec. 153.

ming from Plotinus. In the mystical tradition, meditation was one of the stages in the movement toward the contemplation of the Absolute. That is, meditation was not identical with contemplation, but rather it was a necessary step toward the contemplation of the beatific vision.[33] So in order to grasp Augustine's meaning, we must understand "meditation" first of all in its relationship to "contemplation".

The word "contemplation" is derived from the Latin word *templum*, which was a space marked out by the augur with his staff. The *templum* was an open space for observation, a cleared and open space, and the verb *contemplor* meant "to look at attentively", "to gaze upon" or "to contemplate". The augur is fully concentrated on watching the open space and looking for signs that he can interpret. So the word "contemplation" played a central role in the writings of the mystics. Plotinus describes the mysterious coming and going of the vision of the One (Absolute) in this way: "But one should not inquire whence it comes, for there is no 'whence': for it does not really come or go away anywhere, but appears or does not appear. So one must not chase after it, but wait quietly till it appears, preparing oneself to contemplate it, as the eye awaits the rising of the sun. … For the intellect will stand still facing toward the vision, looking at nothing other than the Beautiful, totally turning and giving itself up there, standing still and somehow filled with strength. … But it did not come as one expected, but it came as not coming. For it was seen, not as having come, but as being there before all things."[34]

As we have said, meditation is not yet contemplation, but it is certainly moving in that direction. Meditation involves a giving of oneself to that which appears, a forfeiting of the hubris that dominates everyday life,

---

[33] For an example of AUGUSTINE's use of the word *contemplatio* or *contemplator*, see *Expositions on the Psalms,* Psalm 26 (Enarrationes in Psalmos, 26), in: MIGNE, *Patrologia Latina*, Vol. 36, where he speaks of contemplation of the immutable, eternal Good. See also *Expositions on the Psalms*, Psalm 75 (Enarrationes in Psalmos, 75), in: MIGNE, *PL*, Vol. 36.

[34] PLOTINUS, *Enneads*, V. 5, Ch. 8. The English translation is a modified version of the Loeb Classical text.

and an openness to the experience of wonderment. He who is arrogant about his acquired knowledge cannot meditate.[35] He who thinks that he has "all the answers" cannot meditate. He who considers himself to be self-sufficient cannot meditate. Augustine invites the reader to approach nature meditatively. Instead of exercising constant control over nature, he asks us to engage nature in a conversation and to listen to that which nature has to say. We are invited to open ourselves to the mystery of existence and to perceive the ineffable power that grounds nature. Of course, Augustine knew quite well that many people are not prepared to open themselves for experiences of the divine. Just as Paul charged the Gentiles in Romans 1:25 that "they exchanged the truth about God for a lie and worshiped and served the *creature* rather than the *Creator*", Augustine wrote in his work *On Free Will*: "Woe to those who abandon you [i.e. God] as leader and wander among your vestiges, who love your nods rather than you yourself and forget that which you intimate thereby. … You do not cease to intimate to us what and how great you are."[36] Both the "vestiges" and the "nods" are metaphors for nature inasmuch as nature signifies that which lies beyond.

From these passages, we can observe the way in which Augustine's doctrine of creation intersects with his understanding of *language* and *interpretation*. In his work on interpretation entitled *On Christian Doctrine* (*De doctrina christiana*), Augustine draws a fundamental distinction between sign and reality (*signa et res*) and develops thereupon a theory of signification. With regard to language, the signs are words and expressions that signify things, but the sign/reality relationship is not limited to language. A linguistic sign can signify a thing that itself becomes a sign for something else. The word "smoke" signifies a gas produced by burning material, but smoke itself can be a sign of fire. That is, not only

[35] In his *Confessions*, AUGUSTINE mentions the threefold temptation of pleasure, inquisitiveness, and pride as the primary hinderance to approaching God (see his introductory remarks to Book X).

[36] AUGUSTINE, *On Free Will* (De libero arbitrio), Bk. II, Ch. XVI, Sec. 43.

words, but also *things* can be signs, and therefore the interpretation of signs applies not only to the Book of Scripture, but also to the Book of Nature. The Book of Nature is full of signs that point to the presence of God, but those who are absorbed in the signs never perceive the reality to which they bear witness.

In the course of his controversy with the Manichaeans, Augustine rebuked them for not paying attention and not meditating upon the unity of the universe. "The force and power of integrity and unity are so great that many good things are pleasing only when they come together and form a whole (Latin: *universum*). The universe takes its name from unity. If the Manichaeans would meditate (*considerare*) upon this, they would praise God, the author and Creator of the universe."[37] This is an interesting passage because it shifts the focus from the individual vestiges and signs of divine power to a meditation upon the whole.

So far we have dealt with the Book of Nature inasmuch as it testifies to the reality of God, but the content of the Book of Nature is twofold. It not only discloses the *creative power of God* in nature; it also reveals the *moral standard* contained in nature, i.e. the *lex naturae* (law of nature). As we saw in Chapter 2, the idea of natural law seems to have originated with the Stoics, and the phrase *lex naturae* or *lex naturalis* became very common in the writings of Cicero. In *On the Laws* he writes: "The most learned men have taken their starting point from law; and they are probably right to do so if, as these same people define it, law is the highest reason, innate in nature, which commands things that must be done and prohibits the opposite. When this same reason is secured and established in the human mind, it is law."[38] The law that is innate in nature is the highest reason and is to be distinguished from Roman law (*ius civile*) which is written and specific. Although the highest law is everywhere in nature, human beings have a privileged position in the search

---

[37] AUGUSTINE, *On Genesis against the Manicheans* (De Genesi contra Manichaeos), Bk. I, Ch. 21.

[38] CICERO, *On the Laws* (De legibus), Bk. I, Ch. VI, Sec. 18.

for it, and therefore an understanding of natural law is inseparable from an understanding of human nature. By nature, the individual has a certain knowledge of God, even if it is inadequate, and the acknowledgment of the reality of God is at the same time an acknowledgment of one's own nature, including an acknowledgment of natural law. So in *On Duties* we read: "Furthermore, if nature prescribes that one man should want to consider the interests of another, whoever he may be, for the very reason that he is a man, it is necessary, according to the same nature, that what is beneficial to all is something common. If that is so, then we are all constrained by one and the same law of nature (*lex naturae*)."[39] The parallels between Cicero and Augustine on the matter of natural law are striking. In both cases, natural law is considered to be innate in human beings, and it is thought to convey a certain knowledge of God as well as the knowledge of right and wrong. Nevertheless, there are significant differences that distinguish the two thinkers. The transcendence of God in the thinking of Augustine and his commitment to the Christian tradition led to a different classification of law and to a different understanding of natural law in the human mind.

Fundamental for Augustine were the distinctions between four types of law: *eternal law* (*lex aeterna*), *natural law* (*lex naturalis*), *divine law* (*lex divina*) and *temporal law* (*lex temporalis*). In his controversy with the Manicheans, Augustine discusses at some length his views on *eternal law*. Consider his polemical work *Against Faustus* where he rejects the Manichean doctrine of law and defines the eternal law as "divine reason or the will of God, which commands us to preserve the natural order and forbids us to disturb it". Accordingly, he defines sin as "anything done or said or desired against the eternal law".[40] At this point in his theological development, Augustine insisted that human beings are in

[39] CICERO, *On Duties* (De officiis), Bk. III, Ch. VI, Sec. 27.

[40] AUGUSTINE, *Against Faustus the Manichean* (Contra Faustum Manicheum), Bk. XXII, Ch. 27, in: MIGNE, *Patrologia Latina*, Vol. 42.

virtue of their will capable of following and fulfilling the eternal law.[41] Faustus, the defender of Manichaeism, had charged that Abraham had committed a sin by turning to the handmaiden Hagar in order to have a son. The story of Abraham, his wife Sarah, and her handmaiden Hagar is recorded in Genesis Chapter 16. The account begins as follows: "Now Sarai, Abram's wife, bore him no children. She had an Egyptian maid whose name was Hagar; and Sarai said to Abram, 'Behold now, the Lord has prevented me from bearing children; go in to my maid; it may be that I shall obtain children by her'. And Abram hearkened to the voice of Sarai. So, after Abram had dwelt ten years in the land of Canaan, Sarai, Abram's wife, took Hagar the Egyptian, her maid, and gave her to Abram her husband as a wife. And he went in to Hagar, and she conceived. … And Hagar bore Abram a son; and Abram called the name of his son, whom Hagar bore, Ishmael."[42]

In responding to the charge of Faustus, Augustine maintained that Abraham not only had not sinned, but that he had fulfilled the eternal law of God by taking Hagar as his wife. He writes: "Referring, then, to the eternal law which enjoins the preservation of natural order and forbids the breach of it, let us see how our father Abraham sinned, that is, how he broke this law, in the things which Faustus has charged him with as highly criminal. In his irrational craving to have children, says Faustus, and not believing God, who promised that his wife Sara should have a son, he defiled himself with a mistress. But here Faustus, in his irrational desire to find fault, both discloses the impiety of his heresy, and in his error and ignorance praises Abraham's intercourse with the handmaid. For as the eternal law – that is, the will of God the Creator of all – for the preservation of the natural order, permits the indulgence of the bodily appetite under the guidance of reason in sexual intercourse, not for the gratification of passion, but for the continuance of the race through the procreation of children; so, on the contrary, the unrighteous

[41] AUGUSTINE, *On Free Will* (De libero arbitrio), Bk. I, Ch. XVI, Sec. 34.
[42] Genesis 16:1–4 and 15.

law of the Manichaeans, in order to prevent their god, whom they bewail as confined in all seeds, from suffering still closer confinement in the womb, requires married people not on any account to have children, their great desire being to liberate their god."[43] So according to Augustine, Abraham "preserved the natural order by seeking in intercourse only the production of a child. ..."[44] and thereby fulfilled the eternal law.

The modern reader may question the morality of Abraham's action, but in actual fact, polygamy was widely practiced in the ancient Near East. Within the cultural setting at the time of Abraham, his action was not only acceptable, but quite rational. In a seminomadic life, the offspring of parents were particularly important for tending the flocks and the fields. Since Abraham's wife Sarai had born no children, it was reasonable for him to take Sarai's Egyptian maid Hagar as a second wife. Thus Augustine's defense of Abraham is that he was following the eternal law and preserving the natural order of the universe by lying with Hagar.

Preserving the natural order of the created world does not yet exhaust, however, the meaning of the eternal law. When the eternal law appears in the human heart, Augustine calls it the *natural law* (*lex naturalis*). The distinction in terminology was apparently motivated by Augustine's reading of Romans 2:14. In his exposition *On the Sermon on the Mount,* Book II, Augustine writes concerning the enemies of Christianity: "For when will they be able to understand that there is no soul, however perverse, which nevertheless in some way is able to reason, in whose conscience God does not speak? For who but God has written the law of nature in the hearts of men? That law concerning which the Apostle says: 'For when the Gentiles who do not have the law do naturally the things contained in the law, these, having not the law, are a law unto them-

[43] AUGUSTINE, *Against Faustus the Manichean* (Contra Faustum Manicheum), Bk. XXII, Ch. 30, in: MIGNE, *Patrologia Latina*, Vol. 42.
[44] AUGUSTINE, Bk. XXII, Ch. 30.

selves, and these show the work of the law written in their hearts…'"[45] In *Diverse Questions* number 53, Augustine emphasizes again that the lex naturalis is written in the rational soul in order to morally guide human beings in their interactions with each other.[46]

In contrast to both eternal law and natural law, Augustine comments in various contexts on *divine law.* In his exposition of Psalm 118: 25, for instance, he quotes Romans 2:14 and distinguishes the natural law (*lex naturalis*) from the divine law of Moses (*lex divina*). Whereas the divine law was given through Moses to the people of Israel, the natural law is a part of human nature and cannot be absent in a mature individual unless that person ceases to be fully human. Furthermore, Augustine identifies the content of the natural law with the so-called Golden Rule, which appears in Matthew 7:12: "So whatever you wish that men would do to you, do so to them."[47] Regarding the relationship between the natural law and the divine law – the one written in the rational soul, the other written on the tables of stone –, Augustine maintains that the divine law augmented and strengthened the natural law among the people of Israel.

Finally, Augustine explains in *On Free Will* the necessity of *temporal law* (*lex temporalis*), which is simply man-made law for the purpose of organizing social life and promoting the common good. He writes: "If a people, then, is well balanced and serious-minded, a careful guardian of the common good; if everyone in it thinks less of his private interests than of the public interests, it would be right to pass a law allowing that people

---

[45] AUGUSTINE, *On the Sermon on the Mount* (De sermone Domini in monte), Bk. II, Ch. 32, in: MIGNE, *Patrologia Latina*, Vol. 34.

[46] AUGUSTINE, *Diverse Questions* (De diversis questionibus liber unus), Question 53, Sec. 1, in: MIGNE, *Patrologia Latina*, Vol. 40.

[47] AUGUSTINE, *Expositions on the Psalms*, Psalm 118:25 (Enarrationes in Psalmos, 118:25), in: MIGNE, *Patrologia Latina*, Vol. 37. Cf. *Treatise on the Gospel of John* (In Joannis Evangelium tractatus, CXXIV), Tractatus XLIX, Ch. XI, Sec. 12, in: MIGNE, *Patrologia Latina*, Vol. 35. It should be noted that Augustine quotes the Golden Rule in its more common negative formulation rather than attending to the uniqueness of the phrasing by Jesus.

to appoint its own magistrates to administer its affairs, that is, its public affairs. ... Let us, then, if you please, call that a temporal law, which, though it be just, may be justly changed to suit altered circumstances."[48]

Returning to Augustine's understanding of natural law, we must distinguish somewhat between his early writings in which he argued against the Manichaeans for the goodness of nature and his later writings during his controversy with the Pelagians. Both the controversy with the Manicheans and the Pelagian controversy were formative for Augustine's theological views. Pelagius was a Christian monk of Celtic origin who stressed the essential goodness of human nature and the freedom of the human will. In fact, he emphasized the freedom of the will to obey and fulfill the commandments of God to the point that the grace of God seemed unnecessary for the performance of good works and the attainment of righteousness. So in his controversy with the Pelagians, Augustine was obliged to temper his original position on the goodness of human nature. Simply stated, he claimed that human nature is – as he had insisted against the Manichaeans – fundamentally good, but that it has been corrupted or damaged through sin. Augustine employed both terms: corrupted (*corrupta*) and damaged (*vitiata*), but we need not inquire about the possible differences of nuance between the terms. For our purposes, the crucial question concerns the extent of the damage.

In order to answer this question, we must take a closer look at the transition in Augustine's thought regarding free will. As we know, he had previously interpreted evil to be the privation of good, and from this standpoint, damaged nature is still good inasmuch as it is nature. In *On Free Will* he writes: "Nature is perfect. Not only is it free from blame but it deserves praise in its own order. If you see anything lacking in the perfection of nature you call it a vice or a fault. By the very fact that you blame its imperfection you bear witness that you would be pleased with it if only it were perfect."[49] At this point in Augustine's thinking, human

[48] AUGUSTINE, *On Free Will* (De libero arbitrio), Bk. I, Ch. VI, Sec. 14.

[49] AUGUSTINE, Bk. III, Ch. XIV, Sec. 41.

nature appears to be intact; the will of man is still free and the law of nature informs him about proper moral conduct. But the controversy with the Pelagians brought about a significant shift in Augustine's thought. As a result of his intensive study of the writings of the Apostle Paul, Augustine came to the conclusion that the original state of man had been lost through the sin of Adam and that this change affected both the stability of the soul and the clarity with which the law of nature could be perceived. In the original state, there was a harmony of body and soul because the soul was in control of the desires (*concupiscentiae*) of the body. In man's present state, however, the desires of the body overwhelm the soul and impair its stability. This does not mean that the soul no longer possesses free will, but rather that the damaged will is very limited in its ability to perform good.

In his anti-Pelagian writing *On the Spirit and the Letter*, Augustine takes up once again the statement of the Apostle Paul in Romans 2:14 f: "When Gentiles who have not the law do by nature what the law requires, they are a law to themselves, even though they do not have the law. They show that what the law requires is written on their hearts. ..." In Chapters 46–48 of this work, Augustine offers two possible interpretations of the Pauline passage, both of which he considers consistent with other teachings of the gospel. The more plausible of the two is presented in Chapter 48 where he recognizes that non-Christians often perform works that must be considered praiseworthy. He writes: "they who do by nature the things contained in the law must not be regarded as yet in the number of those whom Christ's grace justifies, but rather as among those some of whose actions (although they are those of ungodly men, who do not truly and rightly worship the true God) we not only cannot blame, but even justly and rightly praise, since they have been done ... according to the rule of righteousness; though at the same time, were we to discuss the question concerning the end for which they are done, they would hardly be found to be such as deserve the praise and defence which are due to righteous conduct. Nevertheless, since God's image has not been so completely destroyed in the soul of man by the blemish of earthly affections, as to have left remaining there not even its outermost features, thus it might be justly said that man, even in the ungodliness of his life, does, or appreciates, some things contained in the law." So regarding the Gentiles, Augustine concludes: "*what was impressed on their hearts when they were created in the image of God has not been wholly blotted out*".[50]

Let us retrace our steps for a moment. We have established that the eternal law of God is termed the natural law when it appears in the human heart. Regarding the content of the natural law, we have seen that Augustine identifies it with the Golden Rule of Matthew 7:12. This identification is very helpful, but unfortunately inadequate as a general rule for moral conduct. That is, there are many situations in which the application of the rule leads to consequences that do not seem moral at all. Ernest Fortin discusses this problem in his essay "Augustine, Thomas Aquinas, and the Problem of Natural Law". Concerning Augustine's understanding of natural law, Fortin writes: "The difficulty arises when one begins to inquire into the nature of that law. A first intimation as to what its content might be is provided by the maxim that enjoins us to avoid doing to others what we would not have them do to us. Still, it is hard to see how such a rule could serve any but the most general purposes."[51]

Augustine himself was very much aware of the limitations of the Golden Rule, and in his literary dialogue with Evodius in *On Free Will*, he gives us the following example:

> *Augustine* – Tell me now why you think adultery is evil. Is it because it is forbidden by law?

---

[50] AUGUSTINE, *On the Spirit and the Letter* (De spiritu et littera), Ch. XXVII–XXVIII, Sec. 48 (italics added).

[51] ERNEST L. FORTIN, "Augustine, Thomas Aquinas, and the Problem of Natural Law", *Classical Christianity and the Political Order, Collected Essays of Ernest Fortin*, Vol. 2, ed. J. BRIAN BENESTAD, 1996, p. 206.

Evodius – It is not evil because it is forbidden by law. It is forbidden by law because it is evil.

Augustine – Suppose someone were to press us, stressing the delights of adultery and asking why it is evil and why we think it is worthy of condemnation. Do you think that people who wanted not only to believe that adultery is evil but also to know the reason why it is so, would be driven to appeal to the authority of the law? You and I believe without the slightest hesitation that adultery is evil, and I declare that all peoples and nations must believe that too. But our present endeavour is to obtain intelligent knowledge and assurance of what we have accepted in faith. Give this matter your best consideration and tell me the reason why you know that adultery is evil.

Evodius – I know it is evil because I should not wish it to be committed with my own wife. Whoever does to another what he would not have done to himself does evil.

Augustine – Suppose someone offered his wife to another, being willing that she should be corrupted by him in return for a similar license allowed him with the other's wife. Would he have done no evil?

Evodius – Far from that. He would have done great evil.

Augustine – And yet his sin does not come under your general rule, for he does not do what he would not have done to him. You must find another reason to prove that adultery is evil.

So Augustine demands in this dialogue an additional reason for condemning adultery, and he finds it in the more comprehensive understanding of eternal law that we have already encountered in *Against Faustus*.

Here Augustine defines the eternal law as "divine reason or the will of God, which commands us to preserve the natural order and forbids us to disturb it". In view of this, evil is defined as "anything done or said or desired against the eternal law".[52] In the dialogue with Evodius, Augustine returns to the idea of eternal law: "Briefly to express in words as best I can the idea of eternal law as it is stamped upon our minds I should say this: it is just that all things should be in perfect order."[53] Since the eternal law "stamped upon our minds" is precisely the natural law, it is apparent that Augustine is assuming an essential connection between an understanding of *natural law* and *human nature*. For what it means for a human being to be in perfect order depends on his nature.

In approaching an answer to the question of human nature, Augustine inquires first of all about that aspect of human nature which sets man apart from other animals. "Whatever it is that puts man above the beasts, mind or spirit ... if it dominates and rules the other parts of which man is composed, then a man is most perfectly ordered."[54] Admittedly, there are numerous aspects of human nature such as the love of glory that seem to set man apart from the beasts, but above all, it is mind or spirit or reason that most clearly distinguishes man. So when this part dominates, the whole is perfectly ordered. Augustine continues: "When reason or mind or spirit rules the irrational emotions, then the part dominates in a man which ought to dominate according to what we have discovered to be the eternal law."[55] So the case of adultery is deemed to be evil because the irrational emotions are allowed to overwhelm reason, and this in turn eventually leads to unhappiness because the best part of man is weakened.

---

[52] AUGUSTINE, *Against Faustus the Manichean* (Contra Faustum Manicheum), Bk. XXII, Ch. 27, in: MIGNE, *Patrologia Latina*, Vol. 42.

[53] AUGUSTINE, *On Free Will* (De libero arbitrio), Bk. I, Ch. VI, Sec. 15.

[54] AUGUSTINE, Bk. I, Ch. VIII, Sec. 18.

[55] AUGUSTINE, Bk. I, Ch. VIII, Sec. 18.

In reviewing our comments on Augustine's understanding of nature, it is apparent that the initial idea of nature as the essence of a thing plays only a secondary role. More central to his theology is created nature, which he considers to be both good and rational. However, created nature is not self-sustaining because it stands in constant tension with the nothingness out of which it arises. This means that creation is not simply a single event in past time, but also an occurrence at each moment of time – an occurrence that can be perceived meditatively. Accordingly, belief in the creation of nature is not solely a matter of deduction, as in the case of William Paley; rather, the belief arises out of an immediate experience that involves meditative interpretation. Ultimately, both the creative power of God and the moral law are manifested through such interpretation. These reflections lead us back to the Apostle Paul and his message about the appearing of nature as created. Still, there is a difference to be noted. For Augustine, nature appears as created through interpretation, albeit meditative interpretation, but nonetheless interpretation. On the matter of conscience, Augustine is certainly following the Apostle, but he goes beyond Paul in his attempt to clarify the meaning of the natural law to which the conscience harkens. In addition to associating the natural law with the Golden Rule, Augustine emphasizes the rationality of natural law in a manner uncharacteristic of Paul.

In concluding our discussion of Augustine, we want to set his understanding of nature in relief by contrasting it with the ideas of several other thinkers. To begin, we focus on the primacy of interpretation in Augustine's understanding of nature. Then we take up the contrast between the natural and the supernatural, and finally we consider human nature itself.

First of all, it is apparent that Augustine was not interested in laying the foundation for a physics, either in the Aristotelian sense or in the sense of modern science. The detailed analysis of motion that we find in Aristotle's *Physics* is completely missing in the works of Augustine. As we have noted, he is not primarily concerned with the essence of individual things nor does he lay stress on the categorization of the objects of nature. Rather, Augustine is interested in uncovering the *religious and moral message of nature*. This focus on the religious and moral dimensions of nature was based on his belief that nature is fundamentally good. To be sure, he expressed this belief in a philosophical language that is foreign to the modern mind, as we can see in his idea of privation. The notion that evil is simply the privation of good is not convincing to those in the modern era who are troubled by the apparent violence and destruction often exhibited in natural phenomena. Nevertheless, a valuation of nature as fundamentally evil is equally problematic and unconvincing.

The scientific mind prefers to avoid the question of good and evil altogether by insisting that a valuation of nature is unnecessary for its purposes. That may be true. An estimation of good and/or evil in nature would not seem to be relevant for research in the area of particle physics or for a classification of biological forms. Before one praises this "objectivity" of science, however, one should consider the possibility that the attitude of science only reflects its inherent limitations, i.e. its blindness for nature itself. The scientific reduction of nature to objects of investigation obscures the question of good and evil in nature. For Augustine, this question was unavoidable, and based on his study of philosophy and the Christian scriptures, he concluded that nature as a whole is fundamentally good.

Augustine's valuation of nature led him to search for the religious and moral message of nature. Clearly, the very suggestion that nature proclaims a message involves a reversal of the scientific obsession with control. If nature does indeed have a message for human beings, then *listening and interpreting* must take precedence over *analyzing and controlling*. The interpreting of messages reaches as far back in time as some of the oldest extant documents of Western civilization. In a sense, interpretation is always involved in listening to messages, but the process of interpretation becomes very apparent when the message is not immediately understandable. This is a very familiar phenomenon to those who are trying to learn a foreign language. At first, one must learn individual words and phrases, and then one must grasp some of the basic grammatical structures. Additionally, there is the task of interpreting a flow of sounds as meaningful within the language in question. Only within a flow of sounds can individual words be properly interpreted because the meaning of sounds can vary from one language to another. Take, for example, the sound represented in English by the letters "g, i, f, t". Although German and English are both Germanic languages and the sounds represented by these letters share the same etymology, they have a completely different meaning in the two languages. In a German sentence, the sound means "poison", i.e. a harmful or lethal substance, whereas in an English sentence, it means "present", i.e. something freely given by one person to another. Of course, problems of interpretation also arise within one's native language as, for instance, when one attempts to understand a document such as the US Constitution. The suggestion that a historical document out of the eighteenth century does not require interpretation is simply naive. The very act of trying to understand words and linguistic expressions of the late eighteenth century as well as the attempt to place them in their proper historical context are part and parcel of the process of interpretation.

But not all interpretation is directed toward specific languages, historical or contemporary. Some of the oldest examples of interpretation involve dreams or natural phenomena. In Chapters 40–41 of the Book of Genesis, we find recorded the way in which Joseph interpreted the dreams of his fellow prisoners and even of the Pharoah himself. In modern times, the interpretation of dreams has been proposed as a therapeutic method for treating particular psychological disturbances. Notably, one of Sigmund Freud's earliest works was entitled *The Interpretation of Dreams* (*Die Traumdeutung*). In attempting to interpret the dreams of his patients, Freud was aware that interpretations are difficult to attain and that they can never claim the mathematical certainty desired by Descartes. Nevertheless, he was convinced that the interpretation of dreams yielded a privileged access to the unconscious. In his words: "The dream interpretation is the *Via regia* to the knowledge of the unconscious in the life of the soul."[56] Freud's statement is often misquoted as though it read: "The *dream* is the Via regia. ..." It is not the dream itself, but rather the *interpretation* of the dream to which Freud was referring. Furthermore, the phrase *Via regia* is usually translated as "Royal Road"; this is not incorrect, but it conceals the meaning that Freud wanted to convey. The *Via regia* was an ancient trade route running East-West through central Europe. It was essential for conveying valuable goods, but it was also inherently fraught with dangers.

Whereas Freud's interpretation of dreams involved the use of tedious analytical procedures and required extended periods of time, Augustine's interpretation of nature was accomplished in a sudden moment of insight, or not at all. It is true that Augustine speaks of meditation as the path to the interpretation of nature. But meditation is not a method in the modern sense; meditation is an openness to that which appears in nature. As we have seen, Augustine refers to the vestiges of nature that point to the reality of God that lies beyond them. Such passages are a part of Augustine's doctrine of signification that applied to both the written scripture and nature, i.e. the Book of Scripture and the Book of Nature. The analogy is not intended to suggest that the *same principles of interpretation* apply to both; instead, it simply underscores the *need for interpretation* in both cases. For, the presence of God in nature is not apparent to the casual observer any more that the meaning of a historical document is apparent to the casual reader. In the latter case, a method of investigation is necessary; in the former case, a meditative openness is required. As Augustine writes: "When one meditates on the whole beauty of this world, does not the splendour itself, as it were, with one voice respond: Not

[56] SIGMUND FREUD, *Die Traumdeutung*, 1900. The German text reads: "Die Traumdeutung aber ist die Via regia zur Kenntnis des Unbewußten im Seelenleben" (p. 613). The English text is my translation.

I, but God made me."[57] This interpretation of nature is fundamentally different from the analytical-logical approach employed by the ancient Stoics as well as by the Anglican theologian William Paley.

Our second point, which concerns the distinction between the *natural* and the *supernatural,* brings to light a further difference between Paley and Augustine. In order to grasp the significance of Augustine's position, we must investigate first of all the history of the natural/supernatural distinction. At the outset, it must be admitted that the distinction is not a part of our everyday discourse. In fact, scientists generally consider the supernatural to be esoteric and unrealistic. For the scientific mind, the supernatural implies a blind belief that, so to speak, short-circuits the rational faculty of the human mind. One speaks here of a *sacrificium intellectus*, a sacrificing of the intellect, in order to believe the unbelievable. On the other hand, many contemporary scientists including Richard Dawkins seem to think that nature is perfectly rational and understandable. Of course, Dawkins will admit that there is much about nature and life forms in particular which is still unknown, but he maintains that nature is in principle knowable by means of methodological reduction and careful analysis.

However, such optimism is not shared by all scientists. Particularly in the area of quantum physics, scientists tend to be much more cautious about making statements of such sweeping optimism. Consider, for instance, the Nobel Laureate physicist Richard Feynman who found nature to be very baffling. In the early 1960s, Feynman held a famous lecture entitled "Probability and Uncertainty – the quantum mechanical view of nature" in which he presented a thought-experiment demonstrating the wave-particle duality of the electron. Since the time of Feynman's lecture, numerous actual experiments have been constructed in order to verify his conclusions, and the results have shown that the electron does indeed sometimes behave like a particle, sometimes like a wave. Far

[57] AUGUSTINE, *Expositions on the Psalms,* Psalm 144:10 (Enarrationes in Psalmos, 144:10), in: MIGNE, *Patrologia Latina*, Vol. 37, p. 13.

from voicing Dawkins' optimism, Feynman described the behavior of nature in the case of the electron as – in his words – "screwy".

In view of this, we can begin to see the complexity of the alleged distinction between the natural and the supernatural. Whereas a leading physicist of the twentieth century described *nature* as "screwy", a significant segment of our society believes that the *supernatural* is "screwy". So what is the supernatural? Is it simply nature showing itself to be very "screwy"? Or is the supernatural distinct from nature? There is a wide range of opinions on this topic, spanning a spectrum from atheistic scientists to religious fanatics. To gain some clarity on the matter, it behoves us to take a closer look at the word pair "natural/supernatural". If we investigate the meaning of these terms over a period of time, we discover that the same words are used in considerably different ways by different authors. Even in science, words are used in different ways at different periods of time, but the scientific formulation of concepts in terms of symbols and numbers makes it easier to detect the different meanings. Take, for example, the concept of mass. In classical physics, there were two different concepts of mass. There was inertial mass given by the well-known formula $F=ma$, and there was gravitational mass defined in the formula $F=Gm_1m_2/R^2$. As Albert Einstein noted, these two formulae present us with two different definitions of mass, and classical physics had no explanation for the equivalence of inertial mass and gravitational mass. This dilemma was the starting point for Einstein's development of the General Theory of Relativity.

In the case of our word pair natural/supernatural, the situation is more difficult to assess because the words are not defined in unequivocal symbols and numbers. Thus, one must pore over the writings of philosophers and theologians who represent different historical periods in an attempt to ascertain the shift in meaning that is important for our understanding. In the following, the reader should bear in mind that I am suppressing a lot of details in order to offer a readily understandable presentation of the topic. In general, we can speak of three separate periods in which the words "natural" and "supernatural" were defined. *In the first period, the relationship between the natural and the supernatural was understood to be complementary and for that reason the relationship appeared to be plausible.* That is not to say that it was correct, but only that it was plausible. And because it was plausible, it was worth debating. *In the second period, the contrast between the natural and the supernatural became very problematic.* In this period, beginning in the seventeenth century with the work of Galileo and Newton, the relationship between the natural and the supernatural was dominated by the discoveries of the new empirical sciences, and from that point forward, the conflict between science and religion became intense. As the scientists offered causal explanations and empirical evidence for one phenomenon after another, the theologians retreated and searched for an available "space" for their talk about the supernatural. So in this period, the relationship between the natural and the supernatural was no longer *complementary*, but rather *contrary*. Finally, we come to the period in which we are still living today. *In this third period, the relationship between the natural and the supernatural has become totally incoherent and therefore completely meaningless.* So what was once plausible and then problematic has become totally meaningless. The reader should keep these ideas in mind: the complementary relationship was plausible, the contrary relationship was problematic, and the incoherent relationship is meaningless.

When, one might ask, was the relationship between the natural and the supernatural ever *plausible*? To answer this question, we must turn our thoughts to a prescientific period of European culture when the great intellectuals were theologians, not scientists. The Roman Catholic theologian Thomas Aquinas, born in 1225, developed a philosophical-theological system in which the natural and the supernatural were indeed complementary. Aquinas did not think of the natural and the supernatural as complementary in the sense that the two supply each other's deficiencies, but rather in the sense that the one completes and perfects the other. So the relationship was not based on mutual dependence or equality. Instead, the natural and the supernatural formed a hierarchy, whereby the supernatural perfected the natural.

Based on the philosophy of Aristotle, Aquinas built a system of thought in which the natural formed the *substructure* of reality, and the supernatural formed the *superstructure* that completed and perfected the substructure. This relationship of substructure and superstructure can be exemplified by a consideration of ethics. The ability of human beings to develop the classical ethical virtues of justice, wisdom, temperance and courage was thought to be an essential element in the substructure of the world. Nevertheless, human beings were by nature not able to bring these virtues to a state of perfection, and at this point, the supernatural came into play as a complement to the natural. Specifically, the theological virtues of faith, hope, and charity were thought to be necessary in order to perfect the classical virtues of justice, wisdom, temperance, and courage, and the ability to develop faith, hope, and charity was considered to be a supernatural gift. So in this context, the supernatural did not in any way contradict the natural, but rather it perfected the natural. In the context of the thirteenth century, the idea of a substructure and a superstructure, i.e. of the natural and the supernatural in a complementary relationship, seemed very plausible and certainly worthy of debate.

We must turn now to a later historical period in which the relationship between the natural and the supernatural became very problematic. Whereas the complementary relationship between the natural and the supernatural was plausible in the thirteenth century, the rise of science in the seventeenth century rendered the complementary view of Thomas Aquinas completely untenable. As we know particularly from the conflict between Galileo and the Roman Catholic Church, the new science rejected Aristotle's understanding of nature, and when this substructure crumbled, the superstructure became very problematic. William Paley's supernaturalism, which dominated British theology in the late eighteenth and nineteenth centuries, provides a prime example of this problematic relationship. Significantly, Paley's version of supernaturalism did not reject the new science of the day. Rather, it attempted to demonstrate that the supernatural was not logically excluded from the scientific worldview. How did Paley do this?

It must be remembered that the classical physics of Isaac Newton offered a scientific explanation of the *inorganic* world, but said nothing about the *organic* world. That is, the physicists of the seventeenth and eighteenth centuries could not explain the phenomenon of life, and therefore theologians like Paley could appeal to living organisms in order to argue for the reality of the supernatural. So in his famous work *Natural Theology* (1802), Paley cited the well-known watchmaker argument and maintained that the human eye in particular indicates intelligent design of the world. In the pre-Darwinian world of the eighteenth and early nineteenth centuries, Paley could propose arguments from the biological realm without openly contradicting the laws of physics.

Similarly, Paley had argued in his earlier work *Evidences of Christianity* (1794) that miracle accounts such as the raising of Lazarus from the dead could be accepted as supernatural events because they did not violate the laws of physics at that time. To be sure, not all miracle accounts could be handled so easily. Take, for instance, the miracle account of Jesus walking on water. Here we have a clear case where Newton's law of gravity would seem to render the event impossible. So Paley's argument in such cases drew on the new mathematical science of probability that was developing in the eighteenth century. From the standpoint of probability, the law of gravity does not mean that in every conceivable case it is impossible to walk on water. Natural laws allow for variations even if these are very rare. So the question becomes one of evaluating probabilities. There is a certain probability that the authors of the New Testament falsely reported the event, and there is a certain contrary probability that the event actually happened. So in *Evidences of Christianity*, Paley attempts to demonstrate the moral integrity of the New Testament authors as a means of bolstering the probability that the supernatural miracles actually occurred. If the individuals who reported the miracles were upstanding and honest, then the probability of the miracle increases proportionally. Note that Paley does not attempt to *prove* the truth of the miracles. Nor does he appeal to a *leap of faith* in order to believe the miracles. He simply argues that it is *highly probable* that they took place. The supernatural in this case may not contradict the natural, but it certainly does stand in a contrary relationship. Walking on water is contrary to our everyday experience, and therefore the relationship between the natural and the supernatural became very problematic.

The third period in the history of the relationship between the natural and the supernatural was clearly signaled by a transition in the scientific community from *consensus* to *crisis* – a transition that is associated with two names: Albert Abraham Michelson and Albert Einstein. As we saw in Chapter 1, Michelson expressed in his book entitled *Light Waves and their Uses,* published 1903, the optimistic consensus around the turn of the century that all of the fundamental laws of physics had already been discovered: "The more important fundamental laws and the facts of physical science have all been discovered, and these are now so firmly established that the possibility of their ever being supplanted in consequence of new discoveries is exceedingly remote".[58] Few statements in the history of science have been so emphatically stated and so patently wrong as this one. Then two years later, Albert Einstein published his revolutionary article entitled "On the Electrodynamics of Moving Bodies" (*Zur Elektrodynamik bewegter Körper*), in which he placed the fundamental laws of classical physics in question and developed the "Special Theory of Relativity". In the same year, 1905, Einstein published another article entitled "A Heuristic Point of View concerning the Emission and Transformation of Light" (*Über einen die Erzeugung und Umwandlung des Lichts betreffenden heuristischen Standpunkt*), in which he explained the photoelectric effect by assuming that light is composed of packets or particles. From this point onward, physics was characterized more by crisis than by consensus, and the particle nature of light eventu-

[58] ALBERT ABRAHAM MICHELSON, *Light Waves and their Uses*, 1903, p. 23 f.

ally became a cornerstone in quantum physics in spite of the enigmatic character of this phenomenon.

Based on James Clerk Maxwell's equations for electromagnetic radiation, the energy of a light wave should depend on its *amplitude*, not its *frequency*. This prediction was not, however, confirmed by the experimental results of the photoelectric effect. If we shine an intense light on a metal sheet such as cesium, the energy of the light is transmitted to electrons in the cesium, and consequently, these electrons are emitted from the surface of the cesium. With the appropriate apparatus, we can measure the energy of each emitted electron as it leaves the surface. Let us assume that each electron has an energy level of 4 eV. If we now reduce the intensity of the light, we would expect the emitted electrons to have a lower energy level – perhaps 3 eV. But to our surprise, the electrons still have an energy level of 4 eV. We can reduce the amplitude of the "light wave", i.e. its intensity, to the point that it is hardly visible, but the energy of the emitted electrons will remain the same as before. At low intensity levels, fewer electrons will be emitted, but the energy level of each electron will remain 4 eV. These results led to the conclusion that light is composed of discrete packets of energy and that the energy level is solely dependent upon the frequency of the light. So in quantum physics, we define the energy of a packet of light or a photon as the product of its frequency and Planck's constant ($E = hv$). Nevertheless, there are many situations in which we observe an interference pattern of light – a phenomenon that leads us back to the conclusion that light is indeed a wave.

So where do we stand today after four hundred years of experimental and theoretical physics? To be sure, many advances have been made, but when we try to grasp nature in a comprehensive theory, we are reminded once again of Richard Feynman's statement that nature is just plain "screwy"! According to traditional thinking about the natural and the supernatural, it was always assumed that we understood the natural well enough. Or at least, it was assumed that we could in principle understand the natural. This is, I think, the position of Richard Dawkins. In the absence of this certainty, however, the contrast between the natural and the supernatural becomes meaningless. How can we compare the supernatural with something that is fundamentally obscure?

The impossibility of any meaningful contrast between the natural and the supernatural can be illustrated from the scientific as well as from the religious side, but for the sake of clarity, we shall approach the problem solely from the perspective of physics. Frank Tipler, professor for mathematical physics at Tulane University, has attempted in several publications to demonstrate that modern physics is totally consistent with Christian doctrines. Tipler became generally known for this position in his book *The Physics of Immortality*, which was published in 1994. More recently, he has published *The Physics of Christianity* in which we find statements such as this: "According to Christians, Jesus rose from the dead in a 'resurrected body,' a body that we will all have at the Universal Resurrection in the future. This 'Glorified Body' was capable of 'de-materializing' at one location and 'materializing in another." Tipler then proceeds to explain how we can account for this process in the context of our current knowledge of quantum physics. For our purposes, the importance of Tipler's views lies not so much in his attempts to render Christianity scientific, but rather in his transformation of the natural/supernatural distinction. By exploiting the enigmatic character of nature as it is manifested in quantum physics, Tipler effectively reduces religion to science. What was once considered to be supernatural is now explained in terms of natural interactions. Such an interpretation eliminates any meaningful contrast between the natural and the supernatural.

Since we have moved from the plausible to the problematic and finally to the meaningless, the question arises as to whether we can revive this traditional structure in any way. In the writings of Thomas Aquinas, the relationship between the natural and the supernatural was thought to be complementary. William Paley changed this relationship of complementarity to one of contrariety, and religious conservatives such as

Frank Tipler have rendered the relationship completely meaningless. If it were possible to revive the relationship between the natural and the supernatural, we would certainly prefer a relationship of complementarity to one of contrariety, but there is little reason at present to think that the distinction can be revived in any meaningful sense. This state of affairs may seem distressing to many religious leaders, but in my view, it should motivate the Christian church to search for more profound theological solutions. It cannot be emphasized enough that the natural/supernatural distinction has not always been an element of Christian theology.

Let us consider again the doctrine of Augustine. In my opinion, it presents us with an alternative that is theologically more sound than any of the historical versions of the natural/supernatural distinction. Since Augustine thought that the whole of nature signified the presence of God, he never made a formal distinction between the natural and the supernatural. In fact, Augustine's holistic view of nature, according to which nature is sustained by the continual activity of God, precludes a distinction that limits God's activity to the realm of the supernatural. Before the revival of Aristotelian thought during the Middle Ages, there was no need to distinguish between nature as an object of physics and the supernatural as a separate realm of phenomena. In view of this, it is understandable why Augustine held to the belief that God manifested himself in nature as a whole. For Augustine, it would be wrong to say that God interfered with the laws of nature in performing "miracles". Such an assertion would mean that God acted against himself since the whole of nature is sustained by his power. Theologically, Augustine's holistic understanding of nature is much more promising than the natural/supernatural distinction of William Paley. If one perceives meditatively the presence of God in nature, one need not dispute the theories and hypotheses of scientists concerning this or that aspect of nature.

Finally, we come to our third point of comparison where we consider Augustine's understanding of human nature in contrast to predominate views of contemporary society. For our purposes, it will suffice to present the ideas of Sigmund Freud and Noam Chomsky. The significance of Freud's views on human nature can be understood most clearly against the background of Aristotelian thought. Aristotle had defined a human being as the "rational animal" (Latin: *animal rationale*). In his famous work *On the Soul*, Aristotle claimed that every living being has a soul (ψυχή), whereby he was not employing the word "soul" in a religious, but rather in a purely philosophical sense. When Aristotle wrote about the soul, he was referring to a principle of life that animates the organic world. Plants have the lowest form of soul, namely the vegetative soul, which provides the drive to obtain nourishment and to reproduce, in short, the drive of self-preservation. Animals, too, have this vegetative capacity, but in addition, their souls possess sensibility, which grants them the possibility of sense perception. Finally, the soul of a human being possesses not only the vegetative and the sensible faculties, but also the rational, and it is precisely the rational faculty, the capability of rational thought, that distinguishes human beings from all other living creatures. Thus, the adherents of Aristotle's philosophy defined human beings as the *rational animal* (Greek: ζῷον λογιστικόν, Latin: *animal rationale*).

In the depth psychology of Sigmund Freud, a revolutionary development took place that we might call an inversion of the traditional structure of the soul. For Aristotle, the rational faculty of the soul was primary, and one of its chief duties was to keep the vegetative part, i.e. the irrational part, under control. This understanding of the relationship between reason and desire became a central element of Christian thought in the Middle Ages and found its classical formulation in the theology of Thomas Aquinas. One of the major contributions of Freud was the realization that the vegetative faculty of the soul, i.e. the irrational desires of the lowest part of the psyche, plays a much larger role in the development of the personality and in the daily conduct of the individual than thinkers from Aristotle to Aquinas had recognized. By placing sexuality at the forefront of the psychoanalytic understanding of human nature,

Freud was able to demonstrate that the vegetative faculty cannot be controlled as easily as one had thought and that the attempt of the rational part of the soul to control it may lead to severe psychological disorders. In light of this, the traditional structure of human nature appeared untenable. Whereas Aristotle emphasized the rational part of the soul, Freud gave much more weight to desires, specifically to sexual desires, than any thinker before his time.

The so-called Cognitive Revolution that emanated from MIT in the mid-1950s and that was enthusiastically promoted by Noam Chomsky deviated from both Aristotle and Freud in its understanding of human beings. Taking as their starting point the mind/body duality of Descartes, the proponents of the Cognitive Revolution pursued a thoroughgoing materialism by eliminating the mind portion of the duality. Since the inception of the Cognitive Revolution, many variations of its basic tenets have been proposed, but it is generally accepted by all of its adherents that "mind" is a meaningless term and should be replaced by "brain". That is, human beings have brains, but not minds. Therefore, the human experience of consciousness can be adequately explained through the concepts of neural science. The supporters of this view include both Richard Dawkins and Daniel Dennett, as we have mentioned earlier. For both of these men, any appeal to the traditional concept of mind is tantamount to introducing the supernatural into a rational discussion about nature. In addition to this reductionistic understanding of mind as brain, there is another element of the Cognitive Revolution that was promoted by Chomsky and others. Just as the mind was reduced to the brain, the rational was reduced to the computational so that the similarity between the brain and the computer could be maintained. If the brain functions in the same manner as a computer, then it should be possible to develop "artificial intelligence". The impressive successes of computer programs in playing games have been hailed as conclusive evidence of human-like intelligence. Still, the question remains as to whether all human thinking is really computational, and on this issue, there are divergent opinions among professionals.

In summary, Freud emphasized the irrational impulses in human nature over the rational, whereas Chomsky retained the classical emphasis on rationality, but identified it with computational processes. Needless to say, both of these understandings of human nature are atheistic, and therefore, both are fundamentally different from Augustine's doctrine. Based on his reading of Stoicism and Neoplatonism, Augustine asserted unequivocally the rationality of the human soul, but in a sense quite different from the proponents of neural science. For Augustine, reason included not only the capability of performing logical operations; more fundamentally, it made possible a knowledge of God, and it endowed human beings with a moral compass. Although Augustine adopted the focus on rationality from the philosophical tradition, he went well beyond philosophy in describing the soul as the *image of God* in accordance with Genesis 1:27. In the end, the biblical, theological orientation was decisive for the formation of Augustine's thinking. On the one hand, Augustine maintained that human beings are fundamentally good – a valuation that is impossible for either Freud or Chomsky. On the other hand, he recognized the fault lines in human nature that limit the performance of good. The former, i.e. the goodness of human nature, was associated with the image of God, while the latter, i.e. the fault lines in human nature, was described as the outcome of original sin. The balance between these two is lacking in both the Freudian and the Chomskian understanding of human nature. Freud's emphasis on the libidinal element in the psyche resulted in a rather pessimistic view of human nature because any possible improvement in society could only be achieved at the expense of the individual. This was the major theme of Freud's *Civilization and its Discontents* (*Das Unbehagen in der Kultur*, 1930). At the other extreme, Chomsky's view of humans as computational machines with flesh and blood led to an overestimation of the capacities and possibilities of human beings. In contrast to both of these atheistic views,

Augustine's understanding of human nature as fundamentally good, but existentially damaged presents a realistic view of human beings that can guide our personal endeavors and temper our expectations of others.

Finally, Augustine's belief that human beings were created in the image of God provides the basis for his understanding of the human conscience. Because of the image of God in humans, they are able to distinguish between good and evil. In the depth psychology of Freud, the traditional understanding of conscience was reduced to the superego, which has no relationship to God and is simply formed by the influence of society. Given this understanding, it would be impossible for an individual to rise above the values of his surroundings in order to critique the status quo. Without the dimension of transcendence in human nature, human beings are condemned to the "moral values" of their contemporaries. The Chomskian view of human nature as analogous to a computer fares no better than the Freudian when we are seeking a foundation for conscience. In spite of Chomsky's decade-long criticism of American foreign policy and his adoption of a well-known philosophical phrase in the title of his little publication *The Common Good* (1998), he is unable to explain how a computational brain can develop ethical values that go beyond an established ideology. In contrast to both Freud and Chomsky, Augustine's insistence on the divinely endowed conscience opens the possibility of real moral progress because the eternal "ought" remains always the measure of the temporal "is".

Chapter 5

"On Thinking"

The Tragedy of the Blind Watch

The failure of the weak is never tragic. It may evoke in us sympathy or pity, but it is never viewed as tragic because tragedy presupposes greatness. Only the great can fall into tragic failure through their hubris. This was the insight of the Greek tragedian Sophocles when he wrote Oedipus Rex. Before the time of Sophocles (496–406 B.C.), the story of Oedipus was a well-known fable among the Greeks and is attested in several sources including Homer's *Odyssey*.[1] From Homer, we learn that Oedipus' mother Jocasta did a terrible thing in her ignorance. She married her son Oedipus who had killed his father, i.e. her husband, the King of Thebes, but the gods let the truth come out and punished their evil deeds. When Jocasta learned what had happened, she hanged herself in anguish, and Oedipus suffered the horrors that the avenging Furies can inflict. In the hands Sophocles, this ancient fable was transformed into a classic tragedy that exhibited both the greatness of Oedipus and his arrogance (hubris) as well.

As the play begins, the slaying of Laios, the King of Thebes, the ascension of Oedipus to the throne, and his marriage to Jocasta have already occurred. These events are the background, not the substance of the play. Sophocles' play begins with the lamentation of the people of Thebes who are being plagued by the gods because the murder of Laios has not yet

[1] HOMER, *Odyssey*, Bk. IX, lines 271–280.

been avenged. Oedipus does not know at this point that he himself is the guilty party, that it was he who had slain the King of Thebes. Having been abandoned by Laios and Jocasta at birth, he had been reared by other parents in Corinth.

Soon after the play begins, Oedipus initiates an inquiry into the events that led to the death of Laios. It is an earnest quest for truth and therein lies the greatness of Oedipus. He is determined to find the truth and to save Thebes from total destruction. The murderer must be found; the old defilement must be uncovered; the penalty must be paid. But then hubris or arrogance sets in, and Oedipus begins to distrust the oracles delivered to him by the prophets and seers of the gods. His determination to discover the truth through his own investigation becomes stronger with each passing day. In a choral response, Sophocles writes of Oedipus: "The tyrant is a child of hubris. … Haughtiness and the high hand of disdain/ Tempt and outrage god's holy law;/ And any mortal who dares hold/ No immoral Power in awe/ Will be caught up in a net of pain. … Our masters [i.e. Oedipus and Jocasta] call the oracle/ Words on the wind, and the Delphic vision blind!/ Their hearts no longer know Apollo,/ And reverence for the gods has died away."[2] Hybris, which is a characteristic of Greek tragedies, is sometimes translated as arrogance or pride. This is not wrong, but it is incomplete. Hybris is fundamentally an affront to the gods; it is a refusal to accept the inherent limitations of human nature; it is a denial of one's own finitude. Wolfgang Schadewaldt, the classical philologist, saw in the figure of Oedipus a point of contact with modern Europeans, especially with the scientists.[3] The scientific drive to attain new knowledge at any cost is indeed similar to the drive of Oedipus. In the end, Oedipus' arrogance was his ruin. When the truth came out, Jocasta committed suicide. Agonized by the death of Jocasta, who was

[2] SOPHOCLES, *The Oedipus Cycle*, Ch. 1, "Oedipus Rex", line 873 and line 885 to the end, transl. by DUDLEY FITTS and ROBERT FITZGERALD, (1939), 1977.
[3] WOLFGANG SCHADEWALDT, *Hellas und Herperien*, Vol. I, (1960), 1970, p. 471.

both his mother and his wife, Oedipus inflicted blindness upon himself and was led out of Thebes in disgrace.

The historical circumstances surrounding Sophocles' writing of the tragedy are not unimportant. It was soon after the death of Pericles (429 B.C.) and the great plague in Athens when he began work on this tragedy. The war with Sparta, the death of Pericles, the apparent inability of the Athenian democracy to provide effective leadership – viewing these events, Sophocles sensed the coming destruction of the world in which he had lived. He saw with foreboding the decay of moral values and faith in the gods which had been characteristic of the Athenians. It was as though a defilement was being concealed in the city-state; so the truth had to come out, the defilement had to be disclosed. The tragedy of disclosing the truth was that the morally corrupt elements of society turned out to be the greatest and most noble.

There is without doubt a greatness in the scientific mind, but this greatness has led to a debilitating blindness. As Heraclitus said: "Present, they do not see." Or as Jesus preached: "Seeing they do not see." A narrowing of vision has left them blind for anything outside the confines of analysis and quantification. This is tragic indeed because what the scientific mind has accomplished could not have been accomplished without this narrowing of vision. The analysis was necessary; the quantification was inevitable; the narrow focusing was unavoidable. And all of this has produced incredible results for the benefit of human life and society, but it has also produced a blindness for the very foundation of the search for truth.

Contrasting Modes of Thought

In searching for a way out of the narrowness of scientific thinking, it is instructive to contrast various modes of thought. Perhaps the simplest contrasts are those between active and passive thinking or between intellectual and emotional, but neither of these pairs really leads to any new insights. Particularly, the intellectual vs. emotional contrast is unproductive because the rational and the affective aspects are always present in any mode of thinking, albeit in varying proportions. The most intense analytical scientist is often very passionate about his work, and the passionate artist is always guided in some way by the "logic" of his art. The contrast between active and passive thinking, which is currently in popular parlance, is equally unproductive. Essentially, it is only a psychological distinction based on a more or less vague notion of conscious and unconscious processes. Active thinking is identified with focused, critical thinking similar to that of the scientist, whereas passive thinking is much less focused and aimless, drifting easily into the area of subconscious or unconscious thoughts. In contradistinction to the active vs. passive mode of thought, it is interesting to note that the classical distinction of Thomas Aquinas was not between active and passive *thinking*, but rather between active and contemplative *life*.[4] Both the active and the contemplative life are directed to an end, and both involve the intellect. The end of the contemplative life is the knowledge of truth; the end of the active life is some external activity, often one with moral consequences. This contrast might be worth pursuing in connection with the blindness of scientific thinking. Specifically, one could raise the question concerning the scientist's desire for truth in the event that the truth has no bearing on external activities. We will return to the matter of truth shortly.

Perhaps the most obvious contrast would be between faith and reason, i.e. between believing and reasoning. It is a favourite contrast maintained by the atheist who considers himself to be the paradigm of intellectualism and the Christian to be a rigid adherent of unreasonable, unverified beliefs. On the one hand stands the brilliant activity of the enlightened intellect, on the other hand the *sacrificium intellectus* of the believer who is straining to believe the unbelievable. This is a complicated topic and exceeds the scope of our present discussion, but several observations are in order. Firstly, as in the case of the intellectual vs. emo-

[4] THOMAS AQUINAS, *Summa Theologiae*, Secunda Secundae, Question 179.

tional contrast, there is always a mixture of reason and belief in every mode of thinking. In the history of science, there are numerous examples of highly respected scientists whose belief in a traditional concept outweighed their reasoning about the empirical evidence. Likewise, there were theologians whose reasoning about religious matters provided the starting point for developing their beliefs. Thomas Aquinas, for instance, did not consider assent to the existence of God to be an article of faith, but rather a rational conclusion. For our present purposes, however, the critical problem with the faith/reason contrast is this: None of our investigated sources, that is, neither Heraclitus, Cicero, the Apostle Paul, nor Augustine, tell us that faith is necessary for a proper understanding of nature. This is unequivocally the case with Heraclitus and Cicero, but even Paul and Augustine acknowledge the possibility of understanding nature as creation outside of Christian faith. So the critical question is not: Are we willing to sacrifice our rational thinking in order to believe?, but rather: What sort of thinking grants us access to the experience of nature to which our sources testify?

More fruitful than the contrast between faith and reason is the contrast between scientific thinking and theological thinking. In my work entitled *Naturwissenschaft als Herausforderung für die Theologie: Eine historisch-systematische Darstellung (Natural Science as a Challenge for Theology: A historical-systematic Presentation,* 2008), I described the scientific mode of thinking in this way: it is empirical, mathematical, causal-analytical, practical, imaginative, but historically uprooted and temporally segmented.[5] This characterization may not be adequate

[5] BRUSH, *Naturwissenschaft als Herausforderung für die Theologie: Eine historisch-systematische Darstellung*, 2008, p. 208. Some readers may be troubled by the fact that I use the terms "scientific" and "technological" more or less synonymously. Although there may have been some justification in the early days of scientific development for the distinction between "pure" science and technology, the distinction seems to have lost any real meaning. If one understands "pure" science as science for its own sake, i.e. scientific research that holds no prospect of ever being applied practically, it is difficult to imagine that such research would be funded in today's economically driven society.

for every branch of contemporary science, but in viewing the history of natural science from the seventeenth century down to the present, it captures quite well the type of thinking which is dominant in scientific circles. In contrast, I described the theological mode of thinking as fundamental, linguistic, existential, at the same time committed to tradition and oriented to the future in hope and therefore temporally integrated.[6] An elaboration of two points in these descriptions will assist us in our present search for an appropriate mode of thinking: the contrast between mathematics and language, and the contrast between temporally segmented and temporally integrated.

Let us start with the role of mathematics in science. It has been said that natural science originated with the transition from the Middle Ages to the modern world, whereas theology belongs to a prescientific world, characterized by myth and superstition. It is true that the beginnings of *modern* science are identifiable in the sixteenth and seventeenth centuries when Europe was experiencing a renaissance of thought and a transition into modernity. Nevertheless, natural science did not appear for the first time during this period. Already in ancient Egypt and in Greece, we can observe the inception of a mode of thought that later blossomed in the modern era – a mode of thought that combined technological expertise with mathematical knowledge. One of the most impressive examples of this is the construction of the Egyptian pyramids. In the famous Moscow Mathematical Papyrus (circa 2000–1800 B.C.), we find the calculations for the volume of pyramids as well as the solution of other mathematical problems. From the outset of its development, science has been interwoven with mathematics and in some ways dependent on new mathematical insights.

Although some advances in science were made by the ancient Greeks – one thinks immediately of Archimedes (285–212 B.C.) –, the devel-

More fundamentally, the technological control of nature was from the seventeenth century onward the foundation on which the scientific enterprise was built.

[6] BRUSH, p. 210.

opment of Greek science was hindered by the numbering system that was employed. The Greeks used their letters as designations for numbers and did not have our positional notation. For instance, the letter "ρ" designated one hundred, and it retained this meaning regardless of its position in a string of numbers. Equally awkward were the numbers of the Romans; complex calculations with Roman numerals are almost impossible. When Fibonacci introduced into Europe at the beginning of the thirteenth century the so-called Arabic numbers (actually developed by the mathematicians of India) as well as the system of positional notation, science gained an invaluable tool necessary for its further progress. From the seventeenth century onward, it became apparent that quantification and mathematical formulation were the hallmark of modern science. In the broadest sense, applying numbers to a segment of nature is what constituted the new science. Consider, for example, the concept of the aether. The ancient Greeks had developed the idea of the aether in the universe, and the idea was initially retained by modern scientists because it provided a hypothetical medium for the propagation of light waves. However, the concept was no longer acceptable within the framework of modern science after the Michelson-Morley experiment demonstrated that it could not be measured and quantified.

In contrast, theological thinking depends on language, not numbers. From the myth of creation in the first chapter of Genesis, where we read that the world was created through the *Word* of God, to the prophetic formula "Thus *says* the Lord", down to the *sayings* and parables of Jesus and the *Logos* of the Gospel of John, language has stood at the center of thinking in the Hebraic-Christian tradition. Furthermore, the Protestant Reformation of the sixteenth century was based on the primacy of the proclaimed word, and the traditional educational requirement for Protestant theologians to learn Hebrew, Greek and Latin testifies to the centrality of language in the process of formulating the Christian message. In comparison with numbers, which have a universal character, words are essentially dependent on context. They are conditioned by the syntax of the sentence, by the culture in which they are spoken and by the historical circumstances in which they occur.

Proponents of the Cognitive Revolution such as Noam Chomsky have attempted to reduce language to a universal structure and to separate it from the actual historical and cultural context in which it is found. From a scientific point of view, the attempt makes sense; that is, it makes sense if one views human beings as computers with flesh and blood who perform computational operations. But all human thinking is not computational thinking, and accordingly, language as a whole cannot be reduced to an object of scientific analysis. In reading Chomsky's *Cartesian Linguistics* as well as his later writings, one wonders how he would account for classical Hebrew, which has a quite different grammatical structure than the Indo-European languages. Moreover, the uniqueness of language families and of particular languages resists the logical categorization typical of modern science. Consider, for instance, the Basque language that is spoken in Northern Spain and that is not related to any other known language, living or dead. Even the individual words within a particular language lack the constancy characteristic of numbers. Whether in New York, London or Sidney, the number 3 has a universal meaning that does not change. Of course, we may speak of 3 trees or 3 electrons, but the *concept* of 3 remains the same. Words are different. The meaning of a word is dependent upon a particular context. A road sign at an intersection in London that read "Yield" would seem very odd to the Londoner because the word carries connotations in British culture that do not fit the situation. However, in New York this sign would disturb no one. This cultural dependence of words renders the translation from one language into another complicated, if not completely impossible. It is well known that the German word *Geist* cannot be translated accurately into English. Under the necessity of translation, we use the English word "mind" or "spirit", but neither really captures the meaning of the German. As we have seen in previous chapters, the Greek word *logos* defies translation into Latin and certainly into English. Therefore, it should be apparent that these characteristics of language limit considerably the value of a scientific analysis such as that of Chomsky.

In addition to its contextual character, language has an undeniable *event character* that is irreducible to a logical structure. Particularly in the last half of the twentieth century, this event character of language was investigated philosophically by John Searle and theologically by Gerhard Ebeling. Although Searle and Ebeling approached the problem of language from different perspectives and hence arrived at different conclusions about the event character of linguistic expressions, we need not delve into these differences at the moment.

For the sake of clarity, we will follow Searle first of all in distinguishing between statements that do not qualify as linguistic events and those that do. The statement: "It is cold in this room" conveys information, but it is not an event. "I have lived in this house for ten years" also simply conveys information. Many statements in everyday conversation are of this type. They communicate a certain content, they give information about a thing or a situation and so forth. There is, however, a different class of statements that we call linguistic events because the *content* of the statement is *actualized in the speaking* of the statement. That is, what the statement *says* actually *occurs* when it is spoken. A prime example of this occurs between two people when the words are spoken: "I love you." Imagine that a young couple is celebrating its first wedding anniversary over a romantic dinner by candlelight and as they lift their wine glasses to toast, the words are spoken: "I love you." Nobody will understand this statement as purely a matter of information. In the very speaking of the words, the love is communicated. What the statement *says* actually *occurs* in the speaking. That is a linguistic event. There are, of course, other types of linguistic events that are less romantic. In general, this category includes commands, decrees, promises, insults and others. If I say to my neighbor: "I promise to return your lawn tools tomorrow ", the sentence does not simply convey information. The promise occurs in the statement itself. Or if I say to someone: "You're an absolute idiot", I am not simply providing an opinion or communicating information. I am insulting the person, and the insult occurs in the act of speaking. Verdicts in a courtroom are similar. When the judge pronounces the verdict, something occurs in the speaking that alters the life of the person charged. Linguistic events have a wide range of importance in interpersonal relationships. Some are relatively insignificant; others literally change the course of our lives.

The linguistic events of religious significance are those that change our lives most fundamentally, and the historical record of the New Testament indicates that the words of Jesus were of this type. It was the depth and power of Jesus' words that created the aura around him. Some linguistic events that occurred in his speaking involved very few words, others were extended into a story. When he said, for example: "Your sins are forgiven", and the hearer actually experienced the release from guilt in the act of Jesus' speaking, the occurrence was what one might call a simple linguistic event. The parables, on the other hand, built complex events going beyond the simple one-sentence events that we have been discussing. When Jesus told the parable of the "Good Samaritan", something happened to the listeners. The power of the parable did not lie in the fact that it was an interesting moral story, but rather in its transforming effect on the hearers. If only for a moment, they experienced what the parable said – a world, in which there is a spontaneous and unreflective concern of one human being for another, in which ethnic differences becomes unimportant, and in which proper papers and credentials do not matter.

In concluding our consideration of mathematics and language, we maintain that the above delineated characteristics of language enable it to have a more fundamental access to nature than is possible through the application of numbers. To be sure, numbers are a *legitimate* response to certain segments of nature, but they are not the most *fundamental* response to nature itself. To anticipate a bit, it is the event character of language that *responds* or better *corresponds* to the event character of nature.

We turn our attention now to the contrast between segmented and integrated time. As we will discover, the contrast between words and numbers and the one between segmented and integrated time are very closely interwoven with each other. In Book XI of his *Confessions*, Augustine writes: *quid est ergo tempus? si nemo ex me quaerat, scio; si quaerenti explicare velim, nescio* ("So what is time? If no one inquires of me, I know; if I want to explain it to an inquirer, I do not know") .[7] Not only theologians such as Augustine, but also philosophers from the time of Plato and Aristotle have struggled with the notion of time. The difficulty of understanding time was one of the chief problems that Martin Heidegger addressed in his monumental work *Being and Time* (German: *Sein und Zeit*). Certainly we will not resolve the problem of time in the following paragraphs, but we do hope to gain some insight into the temporal element of a mode of thinking that goes beyond the purview of the scientist. From the standpoint of method, it is instructive to investigate the way in which time intersects with numbers and language.

If we were to ask someone the question: "What time is it?", we would probably receive an answer involving numbers, for instance: "It is 12:30 p.m." Such an answer is so common in our everyday lives that we rarely reflect upon the connection between *time* and *numbers*. Every household has at least one clock; public buildings have clocks; many town squares have clocks; and many individuals wear a wrist watch daily. All of these devises are provided with numbers so that we can determine the "correct time". If we have only two hours to perform a certain task, we need to know how much time has elapsed since we began. From this, we can draw a further conclusion. Time not only has something to do with *numbers*, but the passage of time is *measurable*. Yet, what seems quite obvious to us was foreign to people living in other historical periods and other cultures. If we were to pose the same question: "What time

[7] AUGUSTINE, *Confessions* (Confessionum libri tredecim), Bk. XI, Ch. 17.

is it?" to a person living in first-century Jerusalem, we might receive the answer: "Oh, it's about the sixth hour." Since there were no clocks in the modern sense, time was measured on the assumption that there were 12 hours between dawn and dusk. That is, the hour was a twelfth of the time between dawn and dusk, but clearly this traditional "hour" varied in length as the daylight period changed during the year. Thus halfway between dawn and dusk was always the sixth hour.

The first clocks in the modern sense were developed in the fourteenth century, and these were cathedral clocks. At first, they had no face and were designed only to strike the hours. In fact, the word "clock" is related to the German word *Glocke*, which means "bell". As the clocks became more accurate, numbers were added for the hours and eventually the minutes were included. Today, we have atomic clocks of extremely high precision that are accurate to 10^{-9} second per day. Such accuracy in the measurement of time is one of the great achievements of modern science. It is, however, one of the oddities of modern science that – in spite of its accuracy in measuring time and designating it numerically – it had difficulty determining the *direction* in which time is moving. Is time moving forward or backward? As Stephen Hawking discussed in his famous little book *A Brief History of Time*, classical physics had no way to determine the direction of time. If we consider Newton's second law of force (F=ma), the units are kilograms · meters / seconds squared. Whether the change in time is positive or negative, it is positive after it is squared, and so Newton's law is valid even if we are moving backward in time. The first real indication of a scientific "arrow of time" came when thermodynamics discovered the law of entropy. The second law of thermodynamics gives us a direction of time because it states that the world is moving from a state of *order* to a state of *disorder*. We observe a coffee cup falling from a table and breaking into pieces, but we never observe the pieces of the cup reassembling themselves and springing back onto the table. Time moves from order to disorder.

Reading Hawking’s discussion, one is struck by the fact that it took the scientific community so long to discover a theoretical basis for the obvious. Young people get older, but older people do not get younger. We already knew that time has a direction before the second law of thermodynamics was discovered! Perhaps, one finds it reassuring that science has found an explanation for the obvious, but at the same time, one wonders if the scientific mind has overlooked something else. All of this leads to the following question: “Is there something basically missing in the scientific understanding of time?” If we adopt scientific “clock-time” as fundamental, we arrive at an understanding of a person’s life as a series of points, each of which follows the one before it and all of which can be counted. Adding the second law of thermodynamics, we find that life is a one-way street that leads from birth to death, with no possibility of turning back and with no possibility of continuing indefinitely. But is this really the only way in which we experience time? As a series of points that can be counted and measured by a clock?

Trying to think about time without numbers will strike us at first as an odd endeavor because the linear view of time as a series of points was the basis of classical physics in the seventeenth and eighteenth centuries and is still dominant today in our technological world. Nevertheless, the grammatical structure of our *language* points us immediately in a different direction by distinguishing three tenses of time: past, present and future. Events that have already occurred belong to the past; events that are taking place now belong to the present; and events that have not yet occurred belong to the future. One notes that we can discuss these tenses of time without reference to numbers. Still, it may seem at first glance that the tenses of times represent a series of points like our clock-time, albeit a series that begins with past and ends with future. But this apparent similarity with clock-time is only an illusion, and as soon as we introduce the other tenses, namely present perfect, past perfect and future perfect as well as the progressive present, we realize that the tenses of times describe *events* and their relevance, not *points* in a series. Both the past tense and the present perfect tense refer to an event that occurred before the present, but they refer to it differently. The present perfect tense indicates relevance for the present that is not expressed in the past tense. "I have lived here for three years" does not have the same meaning as "I lived here for three years." The latter sentence refers to an event in the past that does not extend into the present, whereas the former includes the idea of extending into the present either as an actual event or as the event's immediate relevance for the present. Or consider the present tense. "He eats cereal for breakfast" does not mean that he did this at *one* point in a series, but rather that he does it habitually, i.e. at *many* points in time. Finally, the progressive tense in English indicates an ongoing event that "occupies" the "now" of time through some duration. It is very common in English to say, for instance: "I am writing a letter." But what does this sentence mean? Grammatically, we would say that it refers to something happening in the present. But which present? The "present" in which the letter was started is not the "present" in which the letter is completed. As these examples indicate, the attempt to correlate the tenses of time with points in a series is frustrated at every turn for the following reason. *Time as a series of points has an essential connection with numbers, whereas time as a description of events is inherently related to language.*

Just as the words in a sentence hang together and convey a meaning, the tenses of time are interrelated and enable unified experiences. The interrelatedness of past, present and future is apparent in the experience of promise and fulfillment; what was promised in the past and anticipated in the future is fulfilled in the present. Past, present and future are not three *points* in a series, but a *unified experience.* Time as an integrated whole is relatively unimportant for scientific research, but it is essential for making political and moral decisions. More importantly, it is our most fundamental experience of time and permeates our daily lives. Stated metaphorically, *time is a woven cloth, not a string of beads.* This can be illustrated clearly on the historical level. History is not simply a timeline of events, a chronical of what happened where and when. History is interrelatedness. History is a woven fabric of connections and meanings. Americans celebrate annually the 4th of July, and in the minds of many citizens, the event is associated with the founding of the country. Indeed, it can be understood in retrospect as a first step toward the founding of the country, but more accurately, the day commemorates the declaration of independence from England. The Declaration of Independence of 1776 speaks of "life, liberty and the pursuit of happiness", whereas the US Constitution of 1787 speaks of "life, liberty and property". A chronical simply records these facts, but history raises questions about the connections and the meanings. Why was there a shift from "pursuit of happiness" to "protection of property"? Did Shays' Rebellion in Massachusetts play a role? And who were these men who called themselves "We, the people"? History is a fabric of connections and meanings that can only be understood from the experience of unified time.

Before we proceed, let us evaluate where we stand. We are seeking a mode of thinking that is different from the usual scientific mode – a mode of thinking that will grant us access to nature as a whole. After considering briefly the notion of passive thinking, emotional thinking and believing (as a substitute for thinking), we settled upon the contrast between scientific and theological thinking in order to point us in the right direction. However, it should be stressed that theological thinking, as we have described it, is not the answer that we are seeking. Nevertheless, this mode of thinking does contain certain elements that we can incorporate. *Specifically, we have discovered that we are looking for a mode of thinking that is deeply linguistic and that is based on a unified experience of time. We will call this type of thinking "natural" because it is a mode of thinking that broadens our vision of nature.* Our next step involves a return to the question of truth.

As we saw in Chapter 1, Richard Dawkins uses the word "truth" repeatedly in his book *The Blind Watchmaker*, but he never defines the term, not even when he wanders into philosophical discussions. In the area of philosophy, an understanding of the concept of truth is a central issue, and numerous philosophers have proposed various ideas about the meaning of truth. In the literature, the primary concepts discussed are the correspondence theory, the coherence theory and the pragmatic theory of truth. The views of the postmodernists according to which there is no truth are blatantly nihilistic and are not capable of making any positive contribution to the present discussion. Based on Dawkins' usage, he seems to be assuming a *correspondence theory of truth* – a theory that has deep roots in the literature of Western civilization and that is still the predominant theory underlying the thinking of most individuals in their daily lives.

Although Thomas Aquinas gave the correspondence theory its classical formulation, a version of it had appeared previously in the writings of Aristotle. In Book 3 of his *Metaphysics*, Aristotle writes: "What is more, there cannot be anything between two contradictories, but of any one subject, one thing must either be asserted or denied. This is clear if we first define what is truth and what is falsehood. A falsity is a statement of that which is that it is not, or of that which is not that it is; and a truth is a statement of that which is that it is, or of that which is not that it is not. Hence, he who states of anything that it is, or that it is not, will either speak truly or speak falsely."[8] In this definition of truth, it is clear that Aristotle is considering truth to be a predication of sentences or statements. If someone says that Mr. Smith is a teacher, although Mr. Smith is *not* a teacher, then he combines two things, "Smith" and "being a teacher", that are not really connected. If, however, someone says that the flower is red and it *is* red, then he combines two things that are connected and therefore belong together. If the professor tells the students in a classroom that it is raining outside, and looking outside, they observe that it is *not* raining, they will consider the statement to be false.

Simple as this theory of truth seems at first blush, it encountered difficulties shortly after it was formulated. A member of the school of Megara

[8] ARISTOTLE, *Metaphysics*, transl. by HIPPOCRATES APOSTLE, (1966), 1975, p. 70.

pointed out a difficulty that has become known as the "liar paradox". Consider the statement: "What I am now saying is false". The statement is true if what the person is saying *is* false, and it is false if what he is saying is true. Solutions to the liar paradox have been sought by philosophers from ancient times down to the present, but this logical difficulty was not the only problem that arose in connection with Aristotle's theory. There were also metaphysical presuppositions of the definition that could be questioned. For instance, it must be explained what it means for "red" and "flower" to be "connected". Aristotle's answer would involve the concepts of substance and accidents, whereby it was assumed that an accident (or attribute) such as "red" could inhere in a substance such as "flower". In order for this to make sense, one must accept Aristotle's metaphysical classifications.

In the thirteenth century, Thomas Aquinas gave Aristotle's definition its classical formulation and, at the same time, shifted the focus of the definition significantly. Whereas Aristotle was concerned about the relationship between *sentences* and *objects*, Thomas considered truth to be a relationship between *thoughts* and *objects*. In his *On Truth* (*De veritate*), Thomas writes: "The second division [i.e. of truth] is based on the correspondence (Latin: *convenientia*) which one being has with another. This is possible only if there is something which is such that it agrees with every being. Such a being is the soul, which, as is said in *The Soul (De anima)*, 'in some way is all things'. ... True expresses the correspondence (*convenientia*) of being to the knowing power, for all knowing is produced by an assimilation (*assimilatio*) of the knower to the thing known, so that assimilation is said to be the cause of knowledge. ... The first reference of being to the intellect, therefore, consists in its agreement with the intellect. This agreement is called the equalization of thing and intellect (*adaequatio intellectus et rei*). In this conformity is fulfilled the formal constituent of the true, and this is what the true adds to being, namely, *the conformity (conformitas) or equalization of thing and intellect.*"[9]

The key phrase in this passage is: *adaequatio rei et intellectus*, which I have translated as "equalization of thing and intellect". The more common translation is the "correspondence of thing and intellect"; hence it has become known as the correspondence theory of truth. It has been suggested that Thomas Aquinas himself coined the word *correspondentia*. That may be true, but I know of no occurrence of the word in a context in which Thomas discusses truth. Regarding the phrase *adaequatio intellectus et rei*, Thomas tells us that it had already been used by Isaac Israeli, a ninth century Jewish Neoplatonist. In any case, Thomas employs various terms in order to express his understanding of the relationship between the *thing* and the *intellect*: agreement (*convenientia*), assimilation (*assimilatio*), conformity (*conformitas*) as well as equalization (*adaequatio*), and based on his discussion in *On Truth*, it is clear that the idea of agreement or conformity capture his concept of truth most clearly. Simply stated, there are things in the world, and there is the intellect of the individual. When the thinking intellect conforms to a particular thing, it attains knowledge and truth.

Straightforward as this definition of truth may seem, it is far from unproblematic. Assuming a world where there is an ontological difference between the intellect and things, how could the intellect possibly *conform* to the thing? Or assuming a totally materialistic world as Richard Dawkins and the cognitive scientists do, how is it possible for one thing (the brain) to conform to another thing (the object of investigation)? Substituting the word "correspondence" or "equalization" for "conformity" does not solve the problem. Still, the word "equalization" does shed further light on the matter at hand. We know that two things can never be totally equal, but rather only equal in some respect. Two individuals may be equal in intelligence, but quite different in other respects. So when we say that the intellect is made equal to the thing, we mean that it is made

[9] THOMAS AQUINAS, *On Truth* (De veritate), Question 1, Article 1 (italics added).

equal in some respect. This assertion does not clarify all of the difficulties, but it does indicate the relative character of truth claims based on correspondence or conformity. When Dawkins claims that Darwin's theory of evolution (in its contemporary form) is true, he can only mean that the theory is equal in *some respect* or conforms in *some respect* to the object under consideration. There are two problems with this claim. Firstly, in what respect the theory conforms remains in Dawkins' *The Blind Watchmaker* somewhat unclear. Perhaps, he only means that the theory conforms with regard to "adaptive complexity", but as we have seen, the weight that he places on adaptive complexity for his argument turns out to be very problematic. Secondly, his tacit assumption that the object under consideration is indeed "nature" is simply an unscientific and unverified assumption. It should be clear to any reader that the object under consideration is the "evidence" gathered by the scientific community, not "nature itself". This evidence may be very interesting and pragmatically very valuable, but it has no legitimate claim to represent nature as a whole. Scientific evidence is not nature. It is merely "nature" seen through the lens of a particular set of assumptions, and these assumptions include the bias that nature can be dissected, quantified and controlled.

As we have seen, the correspondence theory of truth can be understood as the agreement of a sentence to a thing or as the agreement of a concept to a thing. In either case, an agreement or an equalization of two heterogeneous elements is tacitly assumed to be possible. The difficulties that we have encountered in considering the correspondence theory suggest that there may be a more fundamental and therefore more satisfactory theory. Indeed, there was an alternative theory of truth that predated the writings of Aristotle and that can still be seen in the cave analogy of Plato in his *The Republic*. At the beginning of Book VII of *The Republic*, Plato asked Glaucon to imagine that human beings lived in an underground cave with a long entrance open to the light. Since childhood, these people were sitting facing away from the light, and their necks and legs were fettered so that they could not turn their heads toward the light. The only light in the cave came from a burning fire behind them at a distance. Between this fire and the prisoners, there was a road, and on the road was a wall behind which bearers of artificial objects moved to and fro. Since the prisoners only see the shadows of these objects projected onto the wall of the cave in front of them, they believe that these shadows are the only *reality*. The Greek word for "reality" in Plato's description is very important.[10] The word is ἀληθές – an adjective that Plato uses substantivally – , and it can mean either the "real" as opposed to the "apparent" or the "true" as opposed to the "false". The noun form is ἀλήθεια and means "truth". The inseparable connection between the "true" and the "real" reflects an understanding of truth that is quite different from the correspondence theory. In English, we have a remnant of this connection in expressions such as "true friend" or "true love", whereby the word "true" is taken to mean "genuine". Truth in this sense is not a predication of a sentence or a concept, but rather it is the thing itself that is true. In the cave analogy Plato tells us that the prisoners believe that the shadows are true, and this situation cannot change until they are released from their fetters and led into the light of day. Should one of the prisoners indeed be freed and led first of all toward the fire, he would consider the artificial objects to be truer than the shadows that he had seen earlier. Finally, if he were led through the passageway into the daylight, he would eventually recognize that the sun is the source of all truth and reason – the sun being a symbol of the idea of the good.

According to Heidegger, Plato obscures at this point in the cave analogy the connection between the real and the true that he had established in the first part. It is now the idea of the good that *confers* truth, whereas truth had been identical with the real or with being. Heidegger also insists that the more fundamental understanding of truth is discernible from the etymology of the word ἀλήθεια. The root of ἀλήθεια (truth) is ληθ-, which also occurs in other word combinations and has the meaning "to

[10] Plato, *The Republic*, 515c2.

conceal" or "to hide". By adding the privative "α" (equivalent to "un" in English), the meaning becomes "unconcealment" or "uncovering". So something is true when it is uncovered for what it really is, and it is precisely *the event of uncovering* that constitutes its truth. That is, the *truth* of the thing cannot be separated from the *event* in which it appears as what it really is.

We have now moved from the truth of the *sentence* to the truth of the *concept* to the truth of the *thing* and finally to the truth of the *event* in which the thing appears. If the bedrock of truth is an event, then the linguistic events that we considered earlier must play a foundational role in the discovery of truth. But how? We said that it is the event character of language that *responds* or better *corresponds* to the event character of nature. It should now be apparent that we are introducing the notion of correspondence in a way quite different from the correspondence theory of truth. We are not concerned with a correspondence between concept and thing, but rather with the correspondence between the event of language and the event in which things appear. Such correspondence cannot be manufactured through an act of the intellect, but rather it must be discovered. It is the event of disclosing in which language and nature merge. The event in which things appear occurs as a linguistic event. *Thus truth events are linguistic events.*

We have arrived now at a natural mode of thinking that is based on an integrated understanding of time and that is fundamentally linguistic. These two traits combine to yield a twofold focus in our investigation of nature. On the one hand, we will give attention to written historical documents in which nature is disclosed. On the other hand, we will observe the way in which language discloses nature in our everyday experience. In practice, this twofold focus of our investigation involves the interpretation of language in its historical as well as contemporary form, but it is important to realize that the two elements of interpretation can never be completely separated from each other. Take the case of Heraclitus, for instance. In interpreting one of his fragments, we are interpreting *his*

Greek and *our* English at the same time. Likewise, we are interpreting *his* world and *our* world at the same time. The contemporary and the historical cannot be neatly separated. A mode of thinking based on integrated time cannot be otherwise.

Still, a further question remains. Granted that we are employing a mode of thinking that requires the interpretation of historical documents interwoven with contemporary experiences, there would seem to be a bias in the selection of historical witnesses to be considered. Such a bias is not only undeniable, it is inevitable. We have chosen as witnesses for nature two philosophical and two theological texts: Heraclitus, the Stoics, the Apostle Paul, and Augustine. Had we chosen Democritus and Epicurus instead of Heraclitus and the Stoics, the outcome of the investigation would certainly be different. So the question is: How does one justify the choice of sources? The answer is as simple and it is unsatisfying. One doesn't. One simply acknowledges a commitment to a particular linguistic tradition just as the scientist in his everyday work acknowledges – tacitly or openly – a commitment to a particular conceptual framework. Neither the scientist, nor the philosopher, nor the theologian can claim to have arrived at an absolute starting point. How such commitments are formed is an interesting aspect of human thinking, but a lengthy discussion of the process would go beyond the scope of our investigation. Suffice it to say that personal temperament, life experiences, cultural milieu and education play a role in the formation of basic commitments. However, more important than the process of formation is the willingness of the interpreter or investigator to alter a previous commitment if it does not lead to truth or, in the case of nature, to the event of truth. A final cautionary note: It should be obvious that truth cannot be manufactured. Not even the syllogistic logic of Aristotle could manufacture truth. Logical arguments establish validity, not truth. If the premises are false, the conclusion will be false even if the argument form is valid. In the search for truth, one must adopt the attitude of patient watchfulness. Truth as event cannot be forced into view.

Chapter 6

"On Nature"

Silently a flower blooms,
In silence it falls away;
Yet here now, at this moment, at this place,
the whole of the flower, the whole of
the world is blooming.
This is the talk of the flower, the truth
of the blossom;
The glory of eternal life is fully shining here.

(from *A Flower Does Not Talk*)

Around the time of Heraclitus of Ephesus, another remarkable individual lived in India; his name was Shakyamuni Buddha, and he has become known all over the world as the founder of Buddhism. In the course of its long history, Buddhism has spread to many countries and has taken on various forms. The above poem was written by Zenkei Shibayama, a twentieth century adherent of Zen Buddhism and the former Abbot of the Nanzenji Monastery in Kyoto, Japan.[1] The contrast between the fourth line of the poem: "This is the talk of the flower, the truth of the

[1] Zenkei Shibayama, *A Flower Does Not Talk*, (1970), 1988, p. 205.

blossom", and the title of the book in which it appears: *A Flower Does Not Talk*, is both striking and thought provoking. In silence, the flower speaks. One is reminded of the following lines out of Psalm 19: "The heavens are declaring the glory of God; and the firmament proclaims his handiwork./ Day to day pours forth speech, and night to night declares knowledge./ There is no speech, nor are there words; their voice is not heard;/ yet their voice goes out through all the earth, and their words to the end of the world" (vss. 2–4).

In its present form, Psalm 19 probably belongs to the group of postexilic literature dating from the third or fourth century B.C., although the psalm itself could be much older. In any case, we encounter a similarity of thought between this psalm and the poem of Shibayama that raises the question concerning their fundamental understanding of nature. Of course, it would be a mistake to think that the two sources are conveying the same thought. Nevertheless, there seems to be a commonality when viewed against the background of modern scientific thinking about nature. In both the psalm and the poem, there is speech and yet no speech; there are words and yet no words. In silence a message is being communicated in language, and yet there is no audible expression. Even more remarkable is the association of language with nature. Whereas we usually strive to *control* nature to our benefit, we are invited here to *listen* to nature. Something is being said, but it is not man who is saying it. So we are urged to set aside our analytical thinking and to listen to the message of nature.

These thoughts lead us back to Heraclitus who had quite a bit to say about language and nature. Heraclitus tells us that all things are in constant flux and that nature exhibits a uniqueness from moment to moment. He writes: "The sun is new everyday" and "It is not possible to step in the same river twice". Nevertheless, those who harken to the *logos* will confess that all things are one. In our discussion of Heraclitus' fragments, we have seen wherein this oneness lies. It is not the oneness of a universal idea, of a generic concept or of an equation for everything. The oneness of which Heraclitus speaks is an event: the appearing and hiding of nature. When we think about nature, we usually analyse it, dissect it, and categorize it. "This flower is a geranium robertianum", we might say. It is native to Europe, parts of Asia, North America and North Africa. We have learned that it is a species of cranesbill, etc. etc. But in the end, we no longer have nature before us as the flower of Shibayama. We have our own concepts, categories, and theories about it. We may understand the cells in the flower. We may have a theory about how it grows. We may have an abstract structure in which we can assign it to a particular category. We have these products of our own thinking, but the flower itself is no longer present in our thinking. Almost unnoticed, our natural thinking has been overshadowed by the scientific mode of thinking.

For Heraclitus, it was otherwise. He understood nature as the appearing and hiding, the disclosing and concealing of that which is. Nature is not a *thing*, it is an *event*. Since it is not a thing, it cannot be categorized, and since it is an event, it is always unique and unrepeatable. Furthermore, this event occurs in the medium of language (*logos*). *So nature is a linguistic event.* In the last chapter, we discussed linguistic events of various types; some of these were relatively simple, others were complex and dramatic. We pointed out that the pronouncing of a verdict by a presiding judge in the courtroom is a linguistic event because it effects what it says. Other examples of linguistic events that we mentioned were expressions of love and promises. In the context of Heraclitus' fragments, we discover that there is one unique linguistic event that provides the foundation for humans to be truly human. It is the linguistic event of disclosing and concealing, and precisely this event *is* nature. We could say the nature is disclosed in this event, but it must be remembered that nature *is* the event. The matter could be expressed paradoxically in this way: *nature is both the event and that which is disclosed and concealed in the event.*

Heraclitus' understanding of nature is profound and in many ways foundational for our experiences as human beings. However, it is incomplete and must be expanded in several ways. Returning to Psalm 19, we discover immediately other aspects of nature that complement the understanding of Heraclitus. Let us consider the psalm text again. "The heavens are declaring the glory of God; and the firmament proclaims his handiwork./ Day to day pours forth speech, and night to night declares knowledge./ There is no speech, nor are there words; their voice is not heard;/ yet their voice goes out through all the earth, and their words to the end of the world" (vss. 2–4). The first sentence of this passage clearly introduces the idea of creation: "The heavens are declaring the glory of God; and the firmament proclaims his handiwork." The disclosing and concealing event of nature shows itself here as *creativity* in a double sense: it is the ultimate creative power of language, and it is the creation itself that is brought into existence through the disclosing and concealing. There is no reason to think that the "handiwork" or creation in this passage is static, as though it had been created at a certain time in the past and has remained always the same until the present. On the contrary, Psalm 104, which is also a psalm about creation, indicates an ongoing process as Augustine noted: "When thou hidest thy face, they are dismayed;/ when thou takest away their breath, they die and return to the dust./ When thou sendest forth thy Spirit, they are created;/ and thou renewest the face of the ground" (vss. 29–30).

As we have seen, the sustaining power of nature or Zeus was a basic tenet of Stoic thought from the time of Cleanthes, and in the thought of Augustine, this tenet was combined with Psalm 104:29 in order to arrive at an understanding of creation as the continual activity of God to sustain the world. Without the continuing creative activity of God, the world would sink into nothingness.[2] At this point, we must guard against a crassly materialistic understanding of the world. We are not suggesting that the physical entities such as trees, rivers, and mountains would fall into nothingness if the sustaining power of creativity were

---

[2] See discussion above on AUGUSTINE where he deals with the tension between God and nothingness.

removed. The trees, rivers, and mountains comprise our *environment*, but our *world* is constituted through the disclosing and concealing power of creativity. The way in which the flower discloses and conceals itself is the event of nature and constitutes a world. Reflect again upon the words of Shibayama: "Yet here now, at this moment, at this place, the whole of the *flower*, the whole of the *world* is blooming." As far as we know, animals are limited to an environment, but humans have a world constituted through language.

The most obvious indication of the event of nature in society is the establishment of relationships that transcend the moment. Such relationships can vary from the very personal ones within a family to the relationship between a scientist and his object of investigation. Without doubt, personal relationships provide the easiest access to the activity of disclosing and concealing that underlies all relationships. It is a truism to say that we can never fully understand another person. Whether we consider the intimate relationship between two persons within a marriage or the relationship between very close friends, we know that it is never possible to fully grasp the personality and spirit of the other person. Even after a lifetime together, sharing the joys and heartaches of life, we will still confess that there were aspects of the other person that we never really understood. A part of the other person's being was disclosed to us, but some part remained always concealed. Yet, the primordial creative activity of disclosing and concealing lies on a still deeper level. We must consider those moments in which something significant in the being of the other person was disclosed to us, and yet at that very moment, we sensed something withdrawing and concealing itself. Something was revealed and hidden at the same time. We experienced a clarifying burst of light like Heraclitus' thunderbolt and an unfathomable mystery at the same time. This is the creative activity of disclosing and concealing that lies at the heart of human relationships and that constitutes for us a world. Should this sustaining process ever cease, our world would fall into oblivion.

As we have noted, relationships vary from the interpersonal ones just described to the more formal ones of everyday commerce and finally to the so-called "objective" ones of the scientific community. So the question arises concerning the difference between an intimate relationship to another person and the relationship of the scientist to his object of investigation. Proponents of the Cognitive Revolution are fond of ridiculing the notion of mystery in nature as a relic of primitive thinking. For Dan Dennett, for instance, the human mind is no longer a mystery because – well, apparently because he decided that it isn't. Similarly Richard Dawkins claims that the organic world is no longer a mystery because he firmly believes in the capacity of Darwinism to answer all of the yet unanswered questions about nature. Sadly, their refusal to recognize the element of mystery in nature is not only unfounded, but ultimately disastrous from the standpoint of science. The scientist may not recognize that the disclosing of nature is always at the same time a concealing of nature, but it is precisely the concealing, the hiding of nature that sparks his interest and motivates him to spend countless hours in search of new answers. At the beginning of modern science, the astronomer Johannes Kepler was very clear on this point as indicated in his early work entitled *Mysterium Cosmographicum*. To be sure, Kepler modified his earlier views as he continued his investigation of the planets, but he never lost a sense of wonderment about that which he discovered. The mystery always remained. Were one to adopt a rather pessimistic view of our current situation, one might well come to the following conclusion. The fact that the mysterious is no longer recognized by many contemporary scientists may be an indication that our *world* really is falling into nothingness.

Our discussion to this point has modified or, perhaps better, articulated the disclosing and concealing of nature as expressed in the fragments of Heraclitus. *We have reflected upon the disclosing in the context of creation and found that the disclosing shows itself as "creating and sustaining", whereas the concealing has the character of an "unfathomable mystery”*. Moreover, the unfathomable mystery of nature can occur as the nothingness of an abyss into which the world could actually descend. The event of nature is always unique, sometimes occurring as joyful or beautiful, sometimes as terrifying and threatening.

Yet, there is another aspect of Psalm 19 that deserves consideration. A careful reading of the psalm shows that it is really composed of two parts. The first part, which we have just discussed, is probably the older section of the psalm. It is concerned with creation and ends with the following praise of the sun: “Its [the sun] rising is from the ends of the heavens,/ and its circuit to the end of them;/ and there is nothing hid from its heat.” In the second part, a connection is established between *creation* and the *law*. It reads: “The law of the Lord is perfect, reviving the soul;/ the testimony of the Lord is sure, making wise the simple;/ the precepts of the Lord are right, rejoicing the heart;/ the commandment of the Lord is pure, enlightening the eyes” (vss. 7–8). The juxtaposition of the section on creation and the section on law was a later, but very important development. Just as the sun illuminates the heavens from one end to the other, so the law illuminates the lives of human beings and guides their conduct. Just as nothing on earth is hidden from the rays of the sun, so also no human being can escape the light of the law.[3] The connection between creation and law implies that the law is considered to be inherent in man. That is, the law under consideration in this psalm is not one that is imposed from the outside on human beings, but rather it is, so to speak, built into the structure of the world as world and into human nature. Thus, the law is necessary for the well-being of humanity.

The distinction between an *imposed* law and an *immanent* law is of fundamental importance. In discussing the Stoic understanding of nature, we discovered that the Stoics thought of natural law as comprehensive. That is, they believed that natural law permeates the entire universe and regulates not only natural occurrences, but also moral conduct. In

[3] Cf. HERACLITUS, Frag. 16: “How can one escape that which never sets?” We observe also in this passage a connection between the sun and law.

describing the natural law, however, the Stoics were often unclear as to whether the law is imposed or immanent. In some passages, we read that the natural law *permeates* the universe like an extremely fine material substance called the "aether", and this reference to the aether suggests that the law is indeed immanent in nature. But in other passages, the natural law is said to be *dictated* to nature in the same way that a god would impose his commands on human beings. This wavering between an understanding of natural law as *immanent* or as *imposed* was probably not recognized by the Stoics themselves. On the one hand, we have a law that is *in* nature itself and cannot be separated from nature. Nature without this law would no longer be nature. That is, the law is constitutive for nature as such. If we consider the relationships expressed in a particular law, then these relations would be internal to nature itself. On the other hand, natural law as imposed is external to nature, and all of the relationships expressed in the law are external to the natural occurrences themselves. Without the imposed natural law, nature would remain unchanged because the relationships under consideration are external to nature and thus in no way constitutive for it. In the moral realm, natural law dictates right and wrong conduct, and so the question of imposition or immanence arises in the following way: Is the natural moral law immanent in human nature or is it imposed on humans by God? In the context of Stoic thought, the question cannot really be answered because of the near identity of nature and Zeus. For Zeus to impose the moral law would not be very different from the immanence of moral law in nature.

In the Hebrew thought reflected in Psalm 19, the matter is quite different because of the transcendence of God over nature. For God to impose a moral law on human beings from the outside would mean that something is required from them that is not constitutive for human nature in the first place. Consider the well-known prohibition against murder. Is this prohibition an imposed law that could be changed without any fundamental change to human nature? Or is it immanent in the notion of being human so that we would no longer be fully human without this prohibition? If we assume for the moment that human nature is essentially social, that is, if interpersonal relationships are constitutive for human nature, then the question can be transposed to a societal level. In this context the question becomes: Can the prohibition against murder be nullified without any fundamental change to society? One can raise a similar question with regard to the prohibition against incest or about the rules of marriage. Are such moral laws inherent in the structure of society as such or have they simply been imposed upon society by prior generations? If all such moral laws are thought to have been imposed in former times by other human beings, then they might well seem to be arbitrary and unnecessary in a modern society. So if there is no convincing reason for retaining them, we would be at liberty to change them as we please.

On the other hand, the immanence of such laws in society would mean that society itself would dissolve if these laws were removed. In the case of murder, the prohibition clearly appears to be essential for communal living and therefore immanent in the structure of society as such. For it is difficult to imagine a society in which murder was not only tolerated, but also accepted as normal. Although the case of marriage has been very controversial in recent decades, there are no historical grounds for thinking that a society can survive once the concept of gender has been hopelessly blurred and variant forms of marriage are considered normal. This is for the postmodern mind a very disconcerting thought, but nonetheless irrefutable. When we employ a mode of thinking that is deeply linguistic and temporally integrated, no other conclusion presents itself. Unfortunately, our contemporary world is dominated by a different mode of thinking – one that is analytical and temporally fragmented. In Western societies today, there is little sense that our present society is inexorably tied to the tradition out of which it grew, and there is almost universal agreement that all moral laws are imposed, not immanent. From an empirical, scientific viewpoint, there is no way to establish the validity of this modern assumption without removing the laws and observing the consequences. In the physical realm, no physicist would want to remove the Higgs field from the universe in order to observe the consequences, but in the moral realm, we have glibly removed moral restraints decade after decade as though no consequences would follow. If the prohibition against incest is inherent in human nature or if the intimate relationship between a man and a woman is immanent in human nature, then we disregard these immanent natural laws at our own peril.

The ambiguity between imposed law and immanent law in Stoic thought was resolved in Paul's Letter to the Church at Rome as well as in Augustine's writings on creation. According to both authors, the written Torah was clearly imposed on human beings from the outside, whereas the natural law in the hearts of men was considered to be constitutive for human nature. In his letter to the Romans, Paul writes: "When the Gentiles who have not the law do *by nature* what the law requires, they are a law to themselves, even though they do not have the law." In this verse, Paul employs the Stoic phrase "by nature" (φύσει) in order to explain how the Gentiles could possibly fulfill the law. Although the Gentiles did not receive the Mosaic Law, by virtue of nature itself they know what the law requires and therefore have the opportunity to obey it. The natural law is, as it were, inscribed in the hearts of all men. As we have seen, however, the content of this immanent law remains unclear in the writings of Paul. In contrast, Augustine identified the natural law written in the hearts of all human beings with the so-called Golden Rule in Matthew 7:12, but at the same time, he recognized that the Golden Rule is inadequate in many situations as a guide to moral conduct. Although neither Paul nor Augustine give us a clear understanding of the content of natural law in the hearts of men, we can ascertain from their comments that there is an inherent connection between the written law of tradition and the natural law of the heart.

The dialectic between traditional moral law and natural moral law precludes a strictly legalistic approach to morality since we cannot simply assume that traditional moral law is a codified form of natural law. At the same time, the dialectic between the two renders a modern disregard for traditional moral law not only irresponsible, but also detrimental to society. The argument that a traditional moral law does not fit into a modern or postmodern society does not in any way justify the nullification of the law. It would be naive to ignore the possibility that the structure of modern society and its newly found "values" simply stand in contradiction to the natural law in the hearts of men. Otherwise stated, it is certainly possible that we have developed a society that is detrimental to human nature. The dialectic between traditional moral law and natural moral law is not a Hegelian dialectic, which could be resolved in a new synthesis. Rather, it is a dialectic that leads us into the realm of interpretation where the truth of the outcome must be established through a disclosing and concealing linguistic event. The mark of the truth in this case will be *the resonance between the written and the unwritten law*.

As we have seen, natural thinking is the search for truth, whereby truth is understood as the event of disclosing and concealing. When natural thinking speaks of nature as creation, we should not be distracted by scientific theories about the origin of the universe, nor should we be confused by the abstract religious claim that the Bible teaches the doctrine of creation. Oddly enough, the scientific claim about the origin of the world and the fundamentalist claim about its origin share much in common. Both operate more or less with the same mode of thinking, and both utilize concepts – admittedly divergent – that are abstracted from nature. When natural thinking perceives nature as creation, it is because nature has been disclosed and concealed as the sustaining power of God. Precisely in this event of disclosing and concealing lies the possibility that the traditional written law resonate with the unwritten natural law in the heart. In this way, the written moral law is verified and its truth is established. Against this type of verification, no modern theory built upon psychological or sociological concepts can stand its ground.

Nevertheless, it is crucial to recognize that such verification of traditional moral law does not and cannot occur once for all time. The deeply linguistic and historical character of natural thinking precludes a static transmission of written law from one generation to another. Such a slavish adherence to written moral law would amount to a rigid legalism that had lost any trace of vibrancy. On the other hand, the linguistic and historical character of natural thinking prevents us from severing ourselves from our past. Both our collective, historical past and our individual, personal past are constitutive for us since we are as human beings a part of a process moving through integrated time. The modern or postmodern ideology that we can and should disregard tradition when it does not comport with our wishes and desires is rooted in a fragmented understanding of time and threatens to lead us into an absolute nihilism, both epistemologically and ethically. Because of our belongingness to the past, there will always be aspects of traditional written law that do indeed resonate with the natural law inscribed in our hearts, and it is in this context that the question of moral truth must be answered.

If the truth of the traditional written moral code lies in its resonance with the unwritten natural law of the heart, the question arises regarding the possibility of eradicating the inscribed law of the heart and therefore squelching the resonance. Expressed in quite different terms, this issue was vigorously disputed at the time of Augustine as well as later during the Protestant Reformation. In the context of traditional Christian theological terminology, the question revolves around the doctrine of sin and the extent to which original sin has damaged the human soul.

In our discussion of Augustine, we have seen how he changed his views during the controversy with the Pelagians. In his earlier writings, Augustine had interpreted evil to be the privation of good, and from this standpoint, damaged nature must still be considered good inasmuch as it is nature. In *On Free Will* he writes: "Nature is perfect. Not only is it free from blame but it deserves praise in its own order."[4] At this point,

[4] AUGUSTINE, *On Free Will* (De libero arbitrio), Bk. III , Ch. XIV, Sec. 41.

human nature appears to be intact; the will of man is still free and the law of nature informs him about the moral law. But in his controversy with the Pelagians, Augustine reflected more profoundly on the problem of sin and altered his original position on the goodness of human nature. He continued to insist that human nature is fundamentally good – as he had argued against the Manichaeans –, but now he stressed that it has been corrupted (*corrupta*) or damaged (*vitiata*) through sin. This was a significant shift in Augustine’s thought.

As the result of his renewed study of the writings of Paul, Augustine came to the conclusion that the original state of man had been lost through the sin of Adam and that this change affected both the stability of the soul and the clarity with which the law of nature could be perceived. In the original state, there was a harmony of body and soul because the rational soul was in control of the desires (*concupiscentiae*) of the body. In man’s present state, however, the desires of the body overwhelm the soul and impair its stability. This does not mean that the soul no longer possesses free will, but rather that the damaged will is very limited in its ability to perform good. In *On the Spirit and the Letter*, Augustine actually asserts that sin has deleted the natural law in the heart: “In consequence of this sinfulness, the law of God is erased out of their hearts” (Chapter 47), but then in the following section (Chapter 48), he modifies this statement by allowing a certain knowledge of the natural law even among the most ungodly: “Still, since God’s image has not been so completely erased in the soul of man by the stain of earthly affections, as to have left remaining there not even the merest lineaments of it whence it might be justly said that man, even in the ungodliness of his life, does, or appreciates, some things contained in the law.” Augustine seems to sense that human beings would no longer be truly human without some vague knowledge of natural law. In our terminology, a complete loss of natural law in the heart would indeed reduce human beings to brute animals. We would still be individuals with genes, and we would still have brains superior to those of other animals. But we would no longer have a *world*.

There would no longer be an event in which the written law resonated with the natural law of the heart, and the disclosing and concealing of nature as creation would disappear altogether. Language would cease to be creative in its disclosing and concealing of all things, and in eviscerated form, it would become a mere tool for communicating information.

> *Just as we saw in the previous section that the disclosing in the context of creation shows itself as "creating and sustaining" and the concealing as an "unfathomable mystery", we now see that this event of nature has a moral dimension that speaks directly to human beings.*

Having discussed the connection between nature and law, we turn again to the issue of the *oneness* of nature. In our treatment of Heraclitus, we saw the way in which the oneness of nature was expressed in the event of disclosing and concealing that occurs in the medium of language (*logos*). We also saw that the structuring character of language was associated with the divine law that lies at the heart of all civil and moral law. As Heraclitus stated in Fragment 114: "For all human laws are nourished by the law of God, for this rules as far as it wills, and suffices for all, and prevails over all." So the oneness of the event of disclosing and concealing is at the same time the oneness of the medium of the event, i.e. language, and due to its structuring character, the oneness of language implies the oneness of natural law. In Stoic philosophy, the thought of Heraclitus was adopted and modified so that the oneness of nature acquired a new dimension. By focusing on two constitutive elements in nature, Chrysippus introduced the notion of a dynamic continuum in the universe that involved tensile movement. This continuum was also known as the *pneuma* or spirit that permeates all things. As we have seen, Max Jammer considered this Stoic concept to be the predecessor of the modern field concept in physics. Just as the *pneuma* of the Stoics was thought to hold together the entire universe, the force fields of quantum physics are thought mutatis mutandis to perform the same function.

Physical evidence of the connectivity of all things was provided some years ago by an experiment performed by the physicist Alain Aspect. The phenomenon disclosed in this experiment has become known as quantum entanglement. The background of the actual experiment was Albert Einstein's attempt to disprove the basic concepts of quantum physics. To this end, he along with his colleagues Podolsky and Rosen devised a thought experiment in 1935 that in their opinion would demonstrate the absurdity of quantum physics. At that time, no one was able to construct an experiment to actually test Einstein's hypothesis, and so it remained simply a thought experiment for decades. However, when Alain Aspect actually constructed such an experiment in 1983, the results were astounding. Not only did this experiment confirm the basic concepts of quantum physics, but it also demonstrated a non-causal relationship between spatially separated quantum events. Aspect's experiment used photon pairs that were separated spatially far enough that the transmission of a signal from one to the other was not possible even at the velocity of light. Without any possibility of physical communication between the two photons, a change in the state of one resulted in a correlated change in the state of the other. This result gave rise to the term non-locality because the connectivity of the two events does not seem to lie within a time-space continuum.

Although the details of the Aspect experiment need not concern us here, an analogy will provide an intuitive understanding of the non-causal connections. Let us consider the situation of identical twins – we'll call them Jim and Bill – living in the eighteenth century before the dawn of modern communication. Consider further that Jim lives in Boston and that Bill lives in London. Now everyday each of them takes a 20-minute walk around the block in his respective neighborhood. Jim leaves his home daily at 10:00 a.m., whereas Bill leaves his at 3:00 p.m. Given the five hour time difference between Boston and London, this means that the two men are taking walks at the same time. For each of these men, there are two possibilities for circling the block; starting from their respective houses, they can circle it clockwise or counter clockwise. Now it turns out that Jim has no particular pattern to his choice of clockwise or counter clockwise; quite arbitrarily, he either goes one way or the other. So far there is nothing particularly unusual about this situation. What is unusual, however, is the inexplicable correlation between Jim's choice and Bill's choice. Then on examination, we discover that Bill always chooses counter clockwise when Jim chooses clockwise. Conversely, Bill chooses clockwise when Jim chooses counter clockwise. Since there is no possibility of communication between the two and since Jim's choice is always arbitrary, the correlation of their choices defies explanation within the space-time continuum that is usually assumed in establishing causal relationships.

The phenomenon of quantum entanglement has led to much speculation about the underlying character of reality, and as one might expect, there has been no shortage of attempts to combine this element of physics with mysticism. Setting aside such speculation, however, Hans Primas, who was Professor of Chemistry at the ETH in Zürich, Switzerland, wrote about the undeniable implications of quantum entanglement: "The system that from a classical point of view appears to consist of two particles is in fact and truth one undivided whole. The experiment of Aspect proves … that the material world cannot always be divided into spatially separable elements."[5] At the very least, the results of the Aspect experiment call into question the reductionism of Richard Dawkins and others who are convinced – in spite of such evidence to the contrary – that reality can be grasped most accurately through a reductionistic ap-

[5] HANS PRIMAS, "Umdenken in der Naturwissenschaft", *GAIA*, No. 1, 1992, p. 9 f. The quote in the text above is my translation. See also HARALD ATMANSPACHER, "Remembering Hans Primas (1928–2014)", *Mind & Matter,* Vol. 12(2), 2014, pp. 341–348 and BRUSH, *Naturwissenschaft als Herausforderung für die Theologie*, p. 312.

proach that divides the object of investigation into discrete parts, whether these parts be cells or atoms.

We are not suggesting that there is an identity between the Stoic notion of connectivity in the universe and the non-locality of quantum physics. The former is clearly a philosophical idea, whereas the latter is based on experimental data of the scientific community. Nevertheless, the similarity of the two concepts is striking and perhaps worth pursuing. Of course, non-locality in and of itself would not seem to be particularly relevant to the human situation, but as an analogy, it may aide us in understanding the oneness of the universe that is relevant for the constitution of human beings and their interpersonal relationships.

Given the preceding emphasis on oneness, it should not surprise the reader that we have ignored some well-known distinctions that are usually discussed in regard to nature. From the time of Aristotle, the distinctions between living and non-living, between organic and inorganic, between plants and animals have been considered fundamental. Admittedly, these distinctions have proven useful in the history of science, but for an understanding of nature as such, i.e. nature as disclosing and concealing, they are quite irrelevant. The disclosing and concealing of Mt. Rigi in Central Switzerland is not fundamentally different from the disclosing and concealing of Shibayama's flower or of Edward O. Wilson's ants. More pertinent than the organic/inorganic distinction would be the distinction commonly designated as the difference between "nature" and culture. Obviously, "nature" in this sense is quite different from the understanding of nature presented in the present work. Nevertheless, the distinction is worth discussing. When we speak of the distinction between "nature" and culture, we have in mind a difference produced by the intervention of human activity into the realm of things in their pristine state. Specifically, the intervention is understood as a *cultivation* of nature for the benefit of the individual and society. Note that the words "culture" and "cultivation" are derived from the Latin root *colo*, meaning to "cultivate" or to "till" (the land). Consider, for instance, the difference between an oak tree standing in a pristine forest and an oak tree nicely trimmed and planted in the lawn of a homeowner. The difference becomes even more apparent with increased cultivation as in the case of a Bonsai. So "nature" in the nature/culture distinction means "untouched by human hands", "not cultivated by humans". Clearly, both *uncultivated* and *cultivated* things fall under our definition of nature as the event of disclosing and concealing. Therefore, it behooves us to replace the everyday distinction between nature and culture with the more accurate distinction between cultivated things and uncultivated things.

This distinction gains in significance when culture is dominated by technology. One might not recognize a great difference between a wild rose and a cultivated rose, but the artificial rose reveals something quite different. Whereas the wild rose discloses the gift character of nature, the artificial rose discloses the human expertise in designing an object. On the one hand, we see the event as pure gift; on the other hand, we observe the technological control of the event. In the artificial rose, it is primarily the genius of the human being that is revealed, while the source of all creativity withdraws and hides itself.

> *We are now able to add a further element to our understanding of nature. Nature as the event of creating and sustaining with the character of an unfathomable mystery not only exhibits a moral dimension, but also a fundamental distinction between cultivated and uncultivated within the connectivity of all things. The oneness of nature does not allow for a separation of the cultivated and uncultivated, but rather only for a distinction – a distinction that can assume many different forms depending on the character of the cultivation.*

Finally, we come to inquire explicitly about *human* nature. Of course, this topic has already been addressed in connection with natural law when we discussed the inscription of the natural law in the hearts of men, but now we must broaden our understanding of human nature because it is precisely in *human* nature that we recognize clearly the *deficit inherent in nature itself.* The Apostle Paul comments on this aspect of nature in his Letter to the Romans: "for the creation was subjected to futility (ματαιότης), not of its own will but by the will of him who subjected it in hope" (8: 20). The actual word order in the Greek text places "futility" (ματαιότης) at the beginning of the sentence, thus emphasizing the emptiness, the vanity, and the purposelessness of the creation. Obviously, this text stands in contrast to Romans 1:18 ff. where Paul maintains that the power and divinity of God are revealed in the creation. In view of this, we are definitely faced with a problem of interpretation, and as we soon discover, any possible interpretation is rendered difficult due to the scarcity of available evidence.

Aside from the dictionary meaning of the word ματαιότης, Paul's reference in verse 21 to the "bondage to decay" provides our only clue to his understanding of the "futility of creation". What we can assert with some confidence is this: Paul's "futility of creation" points to a deficit in the created order just as Augustine's concept of sin limited the ability of human beings to perceive the natural law of the heart. In both cases, there is a lack of goodness, but in neither case does the deficiency have the last word. Even in the condition of sin, the natural law remains in the heart so that the conscience cannot be totally abolished. And in spite of the futility of creation, the creating and sustaining power of God is still manifested in the appearing and concealing of all things. Beyond these general statements about the deficit in nature, we can only proceed by a closer examination of *human* nature, and in the following, we will see how the deficit in nature becomes apparent in the experience of loneliness and in the lack of balance in human beings.

Although depth psychology does not enjoy in the twenty-first century the status that it once had, it can still provide a fruitful starting point for our discussion. Accordingly, we begin with the psychological distinction between conscious and unconscious experience. The concept of the unconscious is often associated with the work of Sigmund Freud. In the early years of the twentieth century, the Austrian physician published his groundbreaking book entitled *The Interpretation of Dreams* (*Die Traumdeutung,* 1900), followed by two articles "The Unconscious" (*Das Unbewußte*, 1915) and "Repression" (*Verdrängung*, 1915) in which he laid the foundation for the psychoanalytic understanding of the human mind. Of course, Freud was not the first person to treat the concept of the unconscious, but he was the first to develop the idea that consciousness and the unconscious are two separate systems of the mind that operate on distinctly different principles. Since Descartes, the concept of consciousness had dominated Western philosophical thought, although it was recognized that the concept was extremely problematic. In particular, the relationship between consciousness and the body proved difficult to explain. However, in his article "The Unconscious", Freud addressed a different problem and argued that it was impossible to explain the phenomenon of consciousness without postulating an unconscious system that interacted with it. The so-called Freudian slip, e.g. those instances in which a person says something unintended, indicates that the conscious process is being influenced by another unconscious system. In subsequent years, Freud modified his understanding of the unconscious and published in 1923 "The Ego and the Id" (*Das Ich und das Es*). The genesis of Freud's thought on the unconscious is very interesting, but not really relevant for our topic. Thus, an explanation of a simple example of the relationship between consciousness and the unconscious should be adequate.

Consider the case of a female patient who suffers severe anxiety because of an animal phobia. As a child, the patient experienced something so traumatic that she could not bear to think about it consciously, and so she repressed the thought into the unconscious. Yet, in the unconscious system, the anxiety associated with this thought did not simply dissipate, but rather it attached itself to another thought that was less painful to the conscious mind. The result of this change was that the original anxiety associated with the traumatic event became associated with a harmless animal such a dog. So when the female patient as an adult encountered a dog, she was overwhelmed with anxiety. Therapeutically, Freud saw the solution to this problem in the psychoanalytic techniques through which it was possible to integrate the memory of the traumatic event into the present consciousness of the patient. He was convinced that the animal phobia would be overcome as soon as the patient realized the actual source of the anxiety. The crucial point of such examples is the possibility of integrating unconscious content into consciousness. In our terminology, this would amount to disclosing something that was hidden. But there are both psychological and philosophical reasons for thinking that the region of the unconscious reaches far beyond the limits of integration. Freud himself sensed this fact when he postulated the notion of primal repression (*Urverdrängung*), but this state of affairs became even clearer in the work of his colleague C. G. Jung. When Jung introduced the concept of the collective unconscious in contradistinction to the individual unconscious, he posited in effect a realm of unconscious content that extends far beyond the capacity of the individual to integrate the unconscious into consciousness. Significantly, such unconscious content, although it remains hidden from consciousness, is fundamentally different from the mystery of nature that we have discussed. The mystery of nature is not some *content* that might or might not be assimilable into consciousness. Instead, the mystery of nature is a constitutive element in the *event* of disclosing and concealing. This is the oneness of nature that cannot be captured in the psychological distinction between consciousness and the unconscious, whether the latter be understood in the Freudian or the Jungian sense. To be sure, the conscious/unconscious distinction may be helpful in some situations, but it proves to be inadequate as a defining trait of human nature.

Meanwhile, it should not have escaped our notice that the concept of the unconscious was developed as a correlate to the concept of consciousness, which became a central philosophical concept in the writings of Descartes and in the philosophical tradition that followed him. Just as the concept of the unconscious has proven to be problematic, reflection upon the primacy of the Cartesian consciousness reveals that Descartes' *cogito* is equally as problematic as Freud's unconscious. In his attempt to secure a region of human freedom alongside the materialistic, deterministic world of science, Descartes drew a fundamental distinction between two types of substance: the thinking substance (*res cogitans*) and the extended, dimensional substance (*res extensa*). Whereas the extended substance (*res extensa*) was considered to be the world of physics where all interactions are determined by strict laws, the thinking substance (*res cogitans*) was identified with human consciousness and was thought to be free from the deterministic laws of physics.

Unfortunately, this distinction of substances had the unintended result of isolating human consciousness from the outside world, and Descartes himself was not able to offer a plausible explanation for the interaction between the two substances. For example, the *thought* of raising my hand to vote in an assembly and the actual *movement* of my hand were in the philosophy of Descartes two separate occurrences that took place in two separate substances. Furthermore, Descartes' distinction raised serious questions about the reality of the world outside of consciousness as well as about the reality of other minds. Although we have, according to Descartes, immediate experience of our own consciousness, we must simply infer that other human beings have consciousness. Without doubt, Descartes' philosophy has contributed to the extreme individualistic character of modern consciousness and has led indirectly to the problem of isolation and loneliness in contemporary societies.

One might have expected the isolation of individuals in modern society to be overcome by the development of various modes of communication. However, it has become abundantly evident that communication technology has not been able to alleviate the burden of isolation. Although technology has produced the means to stay "connected" with other people over the entire world, the experienced loneliness has at the same time become more intense. According to a study of the global insurer and health services company Cigna, loneliness has become an alarming problem for many Americans today. Particularly disturbing is the fact that young Americans between the ages of 18 and 22 seem to be the loneliest. That's a sobering thought. Precisely those Americans who grew up with computers and iPhones, i.e. those who are most connected in the electronic world, are the loneliest individuals in our society. It is an unsustainable situation that can easily lead to substance addiction, and it certainly increases the danger of today's youth falling prey to the lure of fanatical religious groups.

In his three volume work entitled *The Information Age*, Manuel Castells has analyzed in detail the problems that have arisen out of the technological focus on electronic communication. The interconnections between globalization and communication led Castells to distinguish between two types of space: the "physical space" as we know it and what he terms "the space of flows". The "space of flows" is an electronically created space in which capital, information, technology, organizational interactions, and images flow.[6] When Castells first published volume one of his work in 1996, he maintained that the space of flows had become the dominant experience of space for the managerial elites in society, whereas the majority of people in society conduct their lives in physical space with its interpersonal relationships. He wrote: "In short: elites are cosmopolitan, people are local. The space of power and wealth is projected throughout the world, while people's life and experience is rooted in places, in their culture, in their history."[7] Unfortunately, the last two decades have altered this situation dramatically so that it is no longer clear that "people's life and experience is rooted in places, in their culture, in their history". The development of the iPhone and the almost universal practice of using the device on a daily, if not hourly, basis have

---

[6] CASTELLS, *The Information Age,* Vol. 1: *The Rise of the Network Society*, Ch. 6, "The Space of Flows".

[7] CASTELLS, *The Information Age,* Vol. 1, p. 446.

lessened the distance between Castells' elites and ordinary citizens. That notwithstanding, Castells' distinction between local space and electronic space remains valid, and many of the negative consequences that he predicted as a result of the dominance of electronic space have become a reality in our society. Above all, Castells' thesis that the space of flows is characterized by *power*, whereas local space is the realm of *meaning* has found confirmation in contemporary society. If a person living in the twenty-first century does not have a personal website, a Facebook account, and a Twitter account as well as an iPhone, that person is virtually unable to impact an audience. The power of disseminating ideas and of influencing others is inextricably tied to the space of flows. Meaning, on the other hand, can only be discovered and cultivated locally, i.e. in interpersonal relationships. This split between *power* and *meaning* in modern societies is a problem that we have not even begun to address.

If the electronic "social" media is not capable of overcoming the problem of loneliness, but on the contrary has exacerbated the problem, the next solution offering itself to us would be the establishment of more personal contact. Instead of communicating via satellite with each other, we should focus on forming clubs and discussion groups in which we come into immediate contact with others. Certainly this would be preferable to electronic communication, but it still does not address the root problem of modern societies. It is our understanding of human nature that has separated us from each other and that has produced an unprecedented sense of isolation and loneliness. Even when we meet in groups, we still think of ourselves as individuals, each with his or her own separate consciousness. For this reason, human beings can also feel incredibly lonely in a group; that is, the mere presence of others does not guarantee a sense of belongingness and community.

New insight into the phenomenon of loneliness and community was provided by the Swiss psychiatrist Medard Boss, who was one of the co-founders of the Daseinsanalysis approach to psychotherapy. In an article entitled "Loneliness and Community" (*Einsamkeit und Gemeinschaft*)[8], Boss discussed the inseparable relationship between loneliness and community and thereby demonstrated that it is only possible to be lonely, if community is an essential aspect of human nature. The experience of the absence of the other person is not simply an experience of nothing, but rather it is the experience of the other person *as* absent. That is, loneliness is always a particular mode of community; it is the experience of the lack of something that belongs to us. The Greeks expressed the difference between absolute nothingness and relative nothingness through the phrases: τὸ οὐ όν and τὸ μὴ όν, both of which are usually translated as "non-being". But non-being in the first sense is absolute, whereas non-being in the second sense is relative. The relative non-being is not totally separated from being, and therefore it still bears the impression of being in some way. So it is with loneliness. It is not simply the experience of being alone absolutely, but rather the experience of missing the community to which one essentially belongs. Being alone is a fundamental denial of human nature because belongingness is essential to human existence. Both the Greek and the Latin roots of the English word "existence" point to this openness for other human beings. Literally, the word means "to stand out", and in "standing out", humans are in contact with other human beings. In view of this, the modern image of the independent, self-sufficient individual is an illusion. Belongingness and interdependence are the fundamental reality of human existence.

Given the understanding of nature presented earlier in this chapter, it should be apparent that we are in agreement with Boss concerning the necessity of describing human nature in less individualistic terms. The oneness and connectivity of nature discussed in the last section find their confirmation in Boss' conviction that belongingness and interdependence are fundamental to human existence. Nevertheless, the sources that we have investigated in previous chapters lead us to conclusions

[8] MEDARD BOSS, "Einsamkeit und Gemeinschaft", *Daseinsanalyse*, Vol. 1, No. 1, 1984, pp. 6–22.

that extend beyond the realm of psychology. The moral dimension of the event of nature that speaks to human beings presupposes an *openness* of human nature for that which nature proclaims, and it is precisely this openness that makes the belongingness and interdependence possible. The unique disclosing event of human nature can be characterized as an *openness for the appearing of nature as a gift, an openness for the creative, sustaining power manifested in nature, an openness for the world as a matrix of interpersonal relationships and an openness for the belongingness and interdependence of all human beings*. On the other hand, the concealing event of human nature can be described as the *unfathomable mystery, the nothingness, the abyss and the consuming fire of God's presence* that form the boundaries of human existence. These are, of course, not really two events, but one. The disclosing of the sustaining power of God in nature is at the same time the concealing of the consuming fire of God's presence. The word "concealing" should not be interpreted as though it meant "to make totally absent". The concealing of the consuming fire is a withdrawing that is experienced at times quite vividly.

If the elements of belongingness and interdependence in human nature hold the prospect of overcoming the loneliness in modern societies, we might well consider authentic *community-building* to be a *moral imperative* inherent in human nature itself.[9] For, immanent moral laws in human beings not only guide their conduct (both permissively and restrictively), but more fundamentally such laws enhance human nature. Let us return for a moment to the ancient Stoics. As we have seen, the Stoics interpreted Heraclitus' harmony of opposites as a dynamic tension between opposites. In the *pneuma* or breath that permeates the universe, there is, according to Chrysippus, a blending of the two constitutive elements hot and cold, and this blending forms the dynamic continuum of the universe that expands and contracts. Since the movement is a simultaneous activity in opposition directions, a dynamic tension between

[9] See BRUSH, *In Search of the Common Good*, 2016, Ch. 7.

the opposites occurs. We maintain that an analogous phenomenon is at work in human nature. It is no longer a dynamic tension of opposites, but rather a *balancing of polarities* that enhances human nature. In this context, it would be possible to demonstrate that the moral imperative of community-building grows out of the necessity of balancing the polarity of life and the spirit. For the present, however, we will concentrate on the polarity between power and force.

We begin by distinguishing between power, force, and violence and note that *power* is quite distinct from *force* in the political, societal, and personal realms.[10] Whereas force compels and coerces, power persuades and convinces. Whereas the physical world is the medium of force, language is the medium of power. We speak of moving heavy objects by sheer force regardless of whether the force is produced directly by the exertion of human muscles or by machines designed by humans. In either case, the force is applied according to the laws of physics, and the objects are moved from one place to another. If similar forces are applied to human "objects", then they too can be compelled to move in this or that direction. In general, we can coerce other human beings to obey our will either by the threat or by the actual exercise of force. The intensity of the force can range from a slap in the face to the use of abusive physical restraint, but the principle remains the same. We coerce others to obey our will by the use of force. When such force becomes destructive of life and property, as in the case of warfare, then the boundary has been crossed from force to *violence*. Through violence, we not only coerce others, we destroy them.

In contrast to both force and violence, *power* has the uncanny quality of changing people's hearts and minds without the use of coercion. A dramatic speech, for instance, can have tremendous power. Properly conducted diplomacy can have a powerful impact. The mere presence of persons whom we respect can convey considerable power. As we said, *lan-*

[10] In this section, I am indebted to HANNAH ARENDT for her analysis in *On Violence* (1970).

guage is the medium of power, but the language that conveys power need not always be *verbally* expressed. According to Heraclitus, the Word (*logos*) is the gathering of what is needful into an ordered pattern, and the message of nature, according to Psalm 19, is communicated in language without any audible expression. As we know, the silence expression of love can be extremely powerful in forming interpersonal relationships.

Power, understood in its relationship to language, has become very difficult for us to grasp because of the shift in thinking that has resulted from the development of modern science and the incorporation of the term "power" into physics. As I demonstrated in my book on faith in the age of science, the new scientific concept of power that developed in the seventeenth and eighteenth centuries eclipsed the older and more fundamental concept by merging it with the concept of force.[11] In elementary physics books, we learn about the mathematical connections between force and power. Work in terms of physics is defined as the product of the displacement of an object and the force acting on the object. In turn, power is defined as the time rate at which work is done. The common units of power are either kilowatt or horsepower. In any case, the physicist's concept of power is directly related to force, and as a result the experiential contrast between the two has been obscured.

We can already observe the emergence of a new concept of force in the writings of Johannes Kepler, but it was in the work of Sir Isaac Newton that the notion of force/power really began to replace power. In what became known as the "Newtonian World Machine", the entire universe was thought to be moved by physical forces. Since everything that took place in this mechanical world was caused by some physical force, even God's interaction with the world was conceived in this manner. Whereas the theological tradition had always spoken of God's omnipotence, meaning God's attribute of being all-powerful, the mechanical world of physical forces led to the notion of God's attribute of being all-forceful. With this shift in meaning, the power of God in the medium of language was

[11] BRUSH, *Glauben als Ereignis: Selbst, Kraft, Zeit, Leben,* 2011, pp. 159–182.

concealed, and this eclipse of divine power eventually extended into all areas of society where force became the only means of dealing with relationships, whether these relationships were to nature or to other human beings. So today, the hallmark of our relationship to nature is force. Likewise, the standard of our relationship to other persons has become force, spilling over quite often into raw violence. In this context, power has totally lost its meaning. In its prescientific meaning, power had much more in common with love and respect than it did with force and violence. Power draws people into agreement; force coerces them into obedience. In classical Greek, the difference between power and force was expressed in the words βία (force) and δύναμις (power), and it is significant that the Lord's Prayer attributes power to God. We do not pray: "For thine is the kingdom and the *force* and the glory forever", but rather "thine is the *power*".

Of course, we are not suggesting that force is never necessary. We are simply saying that it is crucial to recognize the fundamental difference between force and power and to strive for a balance between the two. The importance of balancing force and power in the actualization of human nature can be seen clearly in the case of interpersonal relationships, particularly in extreme cases of imbalance. At one end of the spectrum, we find the extreme case of imbalance, whereby the individual exerts excessive force in almost every situation to the detriment of others. At the other end is the extreme case, whereby the individual relies almost completely on the power of language, even when force appears to be necessary for the restoration of order. Finding the proper balance is never easy, and it must be discovered anew in every critical situation.

Furthermore, the process of establishing this balance is complicated by the fact that the two elements, force and power, are not equally at our disposal. As we saw above, the disclosing event of human nature is an *openness for the world as world*, and the concealing event of human nature is the *presence of the nothingness* that continually threatens human existence. Since these two are really one event, the openness of human nature not only makes possible belongingness and interdependence, but it also exposes us to the threat of extinction. This threat is real and cannot be ignored, and we must exert force in order to deal with it successfully. Such was the insight expressed in the so-called "domination command" of Genesis 1:28: "God said to them, 'Be fruitful and multiply, and fill the earth and subdue it; and have *dominion* over [it]'." This passage was never intended as license to abuse the environment, but rather as a recognition that nature itself requires from us a modicum of force. On the other hand, the disclosing event of nature also brings to light God's creative power; it allows us to perceive the world as God's gift to us; and it grants us participation in the divine creative power.

Because of these two elements – the necessity of exercising force and the gift of creative power –, the balancing of force and power in human nature can also be observed within the phenomenon of language. Inasmuch as we participate in the power of God, our utilitarian language based on grammar and semantics acquires a creative dimension that transcends the technological structure of means/ends. The balance between communicating information in language and manifesting the creative power of God in language is an essential part of human nature. The attempt to manufacture a computer program that can successfully simulate a human conversation is interesting from the standpoint of technology, but its success would be tantamount to a demise of human nature. Perhaps, the communication of information would be facilitated, but the element of transcending creativity would be lost.

The relationship between power and force is not the only polarity in human nature; there are also the polarities of time and eternity and of life and the spirit. The natural law (*lex naturalis*) in humans demands the balancing of these polarities. In the next chapter, we will have occasion to consider the polarity of time and eternity, and at the same time, we will gain some insight into the way in which it intersects with the polarity of life and the spirit.

Chapter 7

"Nature and Life"

As we approach the end of our discussion on nature, it seems appropriate to return to the arguments of Richard Dawkins and to address the concept of life explicitly. The astute reader will have noticed that Dawkins as a biologist was primarily concerned about *life*, whereas we have been concentrating on an understanding of *nature*. The reason for this apparent difference in emphasis lies to some extent in Dawkins' treatment of his subject matter. Simply stated, Dawkins commits the logical fallacy of drawing a general conclusion from a particular proposition. His particular proposition is that life was not created by God, but rather that it originated spontaneously on earth. His general conclusion is that there is no Watchmaker who created the universe. Dawkins is so convinced of his atheistic views that it never occurs to him that God could have created the universe, even if life itself originated spontaneously. To the extent that his arguments about life are valid, they do not in any way support his atheistic position.

In Dawkins' defense, however, it seems likely that he was misled somewhat on this point by William Paley's emphasis on the organic world as it appears in Chapter III of his *Natural Theology* as well as in subsequent chapters. Still, Paley's book as a whole does not simply deal with the organic world, but rather more generally with nature including the inorganic as well as the organic realms. The full title of Paley's work was: *Natural Theology or Evidence of the Existence and Attributes of the Deity, collected from the appearances of nature*, published 1802.

The phrase "*appearances of nature*" is important because it signals the breadth of Paley's interest, and as a matter of fact, the Watchmaker argument does not mention the organic world at all. Paley's classic argument in Chapter I reads as follows:

> In crossing a heath, suppose I pitched my foot against a *stone*, and were asked how the stone came to be there; I might possibly answer, that, for any thing I knew to the contrary, it had lain there forever: nor would it perhaps be very easy to show the absurdity of this answer. But suppose I had found a *watch* upon the ground, and it should be inquired how the watch happened to be in that place; I should hardly think of the answer which I had before given, that for any thing I knew, the watch might have always been there. Yet why should not this answer serve for the watch as well as for the stone? why is it not as admissible in the second case, as in the first? For this reason, and for no other, viz. that, when we come to inspect the watch, we perceive (what we could not discover in the stone) that its several parts are framed and put together for a purpose, *e.g.* that they are so formed and adjusted as to produce motion, and that motion so regulated as to point out the hour of the day; that, if the different parts had been differently shaped from what they are, of a different size from what they are, or placed after any other manner, or in any other order, than that in which they are placed, either no motion at all would have been carried on in the machine, or none which would have answered the use that is now served by it. To reckon up a few of the plainest of these parts, and of their offices, all tending to one result: – We see a cylindrical box containing a coiled elastic spring, which, by its endeavour to relax itself, turns round the box. We next observe a flexible chain (ar-

> tificially wrought for the sake of flexure), communicating the action of the spring from the box to the fusee. We then find a series of wheels, the teeth of which catch in, and apply to, each other, conducting the motion from the fusee to the balance, and from the balance to the pointer; and at the same time, by the size and shape of those wheels, so regulating that motion, as to terminate in causing an index, by an equable and measured progression, to pass over a given space in a given time. We take notice that the wheels are made of brass in order to keep them from rust; the springs of steel, no other metal being so elastic; that over the face of the watch there is placed a glass, a material employed in no other part of the work, but in the room of which, if their [sic] had been any other than a transparent substance, the hour could not be seen without opening the case. This mechanism being observed (it requires indeed an examination of the instrument, and perhaps some previous knowledge of the subject, to perceive and understand it; but being once, as we have said, observed and understood), the inference, we think, is inevitable, that the watch must have had a maker: that there must have existed, at some time, and at some place or other, an artificer or artificers, who formed it for the purpose which we find it actually to answer; who comprehended its construction, and designed its use.[1]

Unlike Dawkins, I have quoted Paley's entire Watchmaker argument. Since this argument has been the subject of so much criticism, it seems only fair that we have the argument in its entirety before us. When Dawkins quoted his abridged version of Paley's argument, he appended

---

[1] William Paley, *Natural Theology or Evidences of the Existence and Attributes of the Deity – Collected from the Appearances of Nature,* (1802), 1818, pp. 9–11. It is interesting to note that Charles Darwin completed his theological exams in Cambridge in 1831. So he may well have been familiar with the 1818 edition.

to the Watchmaker argument of Chapter I the first sentence of Chapter III where Paley refers to nature in general before beginning his discussion of the human eye.[2] This chapter is entitled "Application of the Argument" and begins as follows: "for every indication of contrivance, every manifestation of design, which existed in the watch, exists in the works of *nature*; with the difference, on the side of nature, of being greater and more, and that in a degree which exceeds all computation."[3] It is surprising that Dawkins quotes this passage without realizing that it implicitly expands the applicability of the Watchmaker argument beyond the phenomenon of life. To be sure, Paley presents in Chapter III an application of the Watchmaker argument to the organic world, focusing on the human eye, but examples from the organic world are not the only application of his argument. Moreover, it is significant that the Watchmaker argument goes into great detail about the *mechanical parts* of the watch and does not even mention the phenomenon of *life*. Paley's argument in Chapter I is based strictly on design in the *universe*, and if Dawkins had not omitted the portion of the argument concerning the motion of the watch's parts, he might have realized how the argument prepares the reader for Chapter XXII entitled "Astronomy".

In a section of Chapter XXII in which Paley discusses centripetal forces and gravitational force, he writes: "Our second proposition is, that whilst the possible laws of variation were infinite, the *admissible* laws, or the laws compatible with the preservation of the system, lie within narrow limits. If the attracting force had varied according to any *direct* law of the distance, let it have been what it would, great destruction and confusion would have taken place."[4] By "possible laws of variation", Paley means that the strength of the force of gravity could have been based on different proportions of distance and mass. That is, there is no strictly logical reason why the force must vary inversely with the square of the

---

[2] DAWKINS, *The Blind Watchmaker*, p. 9.

[3] PALEY, *Natural Theology*, p. 22 (italics added).

[4] PALEY, p. 326.

distance between the objects involved. Had the force *increased* with the distance between the objects, the results would have been catastrophic. Thus, some choice of the mathematical relationships must have been made, and in Paley's mind, this choice indicates once again a designer. The correctness of Paley's physics need not concern us here. The point is that his arguments for the existence of God are not limited, as Dawkins would have us believe, to the question of life.

It is interesting to note that several modern physicists and cosmologists have puzzled over the mathematical coincidences that enabled the formation of our universe. If one assumes a static universe as Paley did, the modern problem never emerges, but as soon as one assumes that the universe exploded out of a singularity some 13.7 billion years ago, the expansion rate becomes a crucial factor in the formation of matter. For example, if the rate of expansion one second after the Big-Bang had been a hundred thousand million millionth smaller, then the universe would have collapsed until the gravitational pull before it reaches its present state. On the other hand, if the expansion rate had been a millionth greater, then the stars and planets would not have formed. The theoretical physicist and mathematician Freeman Dyson commented on the mathematical coincidences in the universe in this way: "Being a scientist, trained in the habits of thought and language of the twentieth century rather than the eighteenth, I do not claim that the architecture of the universe proves the existence of God. I claim only that the architecture of the universe is consistent with the hypothesis that mind plays an essential role in its functioning."[5] Dyson does not speculate about the character of mind, but parallels with the Stoic idea of *logos* in the universe suggest themselves immediately. The Stoics were convinced that the universe is deeply rational, and they explained the rational character of the universe, which included for them moral law, as the result of the *pneuma* that permeates everything.

[5] FREEMAN DYSON, *Disturbing the Universe*, 1979, p. 251.

The comments of Paley and Dyson are not cited here in order to prove the reality of God. They are simply intended to broaden our perspective and allow us to see the limitations of Dawkins' argument. The atheistic thesis that he maintains cannot be proven from his arguments constructed solely on the basis of evolutionary biology. Still, the question remains about his understanding of life. As we have seen, he never offers any explanation of his understanding of *nature*, but one might overlook this deficiency seeing that his professional expertise is limited to biology. On the other hand, we have every right to expect him to provide a clear definition of *life*, since this concept is crucial for his entire presentation.

As I understand Dawkins, he takes a two-pronged approach to the question of life. In Chapter 5, he attempts to define life or at least to explain what life is, and then in Chapter 6, he addresses the problem of the origin of life. From the outset of Chapter 5, the polemical tone of his argument is apparent, and one gets the distinct impression that his primary aim is to discredit his opponents' views rather than to present a clear concept of his own. In particular, Dawkins finds the idea of a "life force" repugnant, whether it be in the form of the *élan vital* of Henri Bergson or in the form of the Stoic *pneuma*. He writes: "What lies at the heart of every living thing is not a fire, not warm breath, not a 'spark of life'. It is information, words, instructions. … If you want to understand life … think about information technology."[6] So far Dawkins' position, even if untenable, seems clear enough. Life is information, and there is nothing mysterious about information. If one does not find information technology mysterious, then one should also acknowledge that there is nothing mysterious about life. Just like non-living things in the world, living things are composed of molecules. "What is special is that these molecules are put together in much more complicated patterns than the molecules of nonliving things, and this putting together is done by following programs, sets of instructions for how to develop. …"[7]

[6] DAWKINS, *The Blind Watchmaker*, p. 159.
[7] DAWKINS, p. 158.

So again, life is defined as information, i.e. as a set of instructions, but this definition of life, even if clear, is woefully inadequate. Not even Dawkins finds this definition adequate because living things reproduce themselves in a way that is hardly predicable of information. The conclusion is inevitable: Something else must be added in order to distinguish *living* information from *computer* information. In attempting to describe this “something else”, Dawkins resorts to terms such as “ingredients” and “properties”, and this is the point at which the discussion becomes very murky. Given the context of his comments, the more appropriate designation seems to be “property”, and the most important of the three properties that he mentions is the property of self-replication. Thus, the distinguishing factor between computer information and DNA information is the *property* of self-replicating. Then, Dawkins shifts his terminology and refers to self-copying *entities* or replicators and explains that these self-replicating entities are the driving force of the evolutionary process. Since self-replication is a *property* of DNA information, a self-replicating *entity* or replicator must be self-replicating information. Still, it seems odd to call information of any sort an entity; at the very least, it violates our usual understanding of the word “entity”, which derives from the Latin *ens* meaning “being”. Going a step further, Dawkins assumes a causal chain of events in evolution so that the replicators become the causal factor in the process. But in the absence of a life force, these replicators must be the cause of themselves. So in order to eliminate any trace of mystery in the phenomenon of life, Dawkins arrives at an understanding of life as self-replicating information that is its own cause. That is to say, if one were to ask the question about the cause of the replicator, the only possible answer is that the replicator causes itself, i.e. it is *causa sui*. The appeal to self-causation is, however, very problematic for Dawkins since the notion of self-causation is clearly a prescientific concept, as we shall see below. So at this point, Dawkins finds himself in a dilemma. In order to reject the prescientific concept of a life force, he must either appeal to equally prescientific concept of self-causation or completely abandon the category of causation at the very fountainhead of life, which would seem to contradict the scientific framework of his analysis.

Apparently, Dawkins opts for the concept of self-causation, and as a result, the biological definition of life becomes hopelessly entangled in philosophical-theological ideas that date back to the time of Plotinus. In its Greek form (αἴτιον ἑαυτοῦ meaning "cause of itself"), Plotinus was the first thinker to develop the notion of self-causation[8], and it was later adopted into the Latin tradition by Marius Victorinus and Augustine. In general, the idea of aseity was applied to God, but Augustine also considered the human soul to be self-moving. In view of the history of the concept, the idea of self-causation is very ill-suited as a means of eliminating the mystery of life. The whole notion of something causing itself seems uniquely odd, if not downright mysterious. Of course, the process of replication can be analyzed and described, but there always remains the mystery of *why* it happens. Why does a replicator replicate? For the working scientist, this is probably not a central question, but for the philosopher or theologian, it is just as central as Heidegger's question in the opening sentence of his work on metaphysics: *Warum ist überhaupt Seiendes und nicht vielmehr Nichts?* (Why is there anything at all instead of Nothing?).[9] In summary, Dawkins does not and cannot answer the question of "why" with regard to life, and in the end, the only way to escape the mystery of life is to disallow the question.

In Chapter 6, Dawkins deals with the origin of replicators, which would be, of course, a primary concern to the creationists. Whereas he explained in Chapter 5 that replicators "must somehow, as a consequence of the ordinary laws of physics, come into being", he proposes now to explain how this happened and why it is unnecessary to assume a Creator. But the task that Dawkins sets before himself exceeds the present

---

[8] Plotinus, *Enneads*, VI. 8, Ch. 14.

[9] Martin Heidegger, *Einführung in die Metaphysik* (Introduction to Metaphysics), (1953), 1987, p. 1.

explanatory capacity of science. So after presenting several theories on the origin of life, he honestly admits that the problem remains unsolved. In spite of this, he rejects the suggestion that there is anything mysterious about the origin of life and assures us that any scientific explanation, even if grossly inadequate, is preferrable to a theological solution – "preferrable" presumably because a theological solution does not fit into the framework of his scientific views. For the scientist, however, the difficulty in explaining the origin of life goes beyond the current gaps in our knowledge. In the entire discussion of possible solutions to the question of the origin of life, there is the underlying assumption that one could explain an event that occurred some 3.7 billion years ago based on the results of a laboratory experiment performed in the present. The validity of this assumption is far from obvious. Even if biologists could demonstrate experimentally in a laboratory how life *might* have originated, the experiment would demonstrate nothing more than the *possibility* that it actually happened that way. The *beginning* of biological life as such is not a repeatable event, and therefore it will always remain somewhat shrouded in mystery.

In the end, Dawkins offers no clear definition of life. He attains clarity only in asserting what he rejects, and he clearly rejects the idea that life is in any way mysterious. Apparently, the word "mysterious" means for him that "something" transcends in principle the explanatory capacity of science. At this point, the metaphysical thrust of Dawkins' thought becomes quite apparent. He cannot conceive of anything in the universe that does not fit into the framework of science; science itself is for him the ultimate philosophy. That is, science or scientific thinking has the capacity to explain everything in the universe. Yet within the framework of science, specifically evolutionary biology, he is unable to give an adequate account of nature or life. So his entire enterprise fails because he claims more than he can deliver. Of course, this diminishes in no way his expertise in biology nor does it reduce the importance of his contributions to the scientific community. His failure lies in going beyond the undeniable limitations of scientific thinking.

If we approach the question of life from the standpoint of *natural thinking* as we have described it in Chapter 5, we must first turn to the historical sources that we have investigated. Consider, for instance, Heraclitus' statement in Fragment 30: "This world, the same for all, neither any of the gods nor any man has made, but it always was, and is, and will be, an *ever-living* fire, kindled in due measure, and in due measure extinguished." Leaving aside Heraclitus' conviction that the world is everlasting, that it always was and always will be, let us focus our attention on his description of the world as "an ever-living fire, kindled in due measure, and in due measure extinguished". The process of kindling and extinguishing is familiar to us now from our previous investigation of Heraclitus' fragments. It expresses the continual appearing and concealing of nature, and inasmuch as the appearing and concealing is described as "an ever-living fire", it is identified with Zeus who with his thunderbolt steers all things (Fragment 64). Still, Fragment 30 does not speak explicitly of *nature* (φύσις), but rather of an *ever-living* fire (πῦρ ἀείζωον), which raises the question concerning the connection between *nature* and *life*.

In everyday parlance, we think of life as a more restricted concept than nature; "nature" encompasses living things, but also non-living things. As Dawkins tells us, there are living molecules and non-living molecules. In this sense, "living" is contrasted with that which does not live and has never lived. A stone, for instance, is a collection of non-living molecules. But living is also contrasted with dying, and accordingly life is contrasted with death. A stone lying on a pathway is non-living, but nobody would describe it as dead. Likewise, nobody would describe the deceased at a funeral as non-living. The experience of accompanying an individual in his last living moments can hardly be described as a transition from living molecules to non-living molecules.

Something else is happening here, and this "something else" presses us to inquire further into the phenomenon of life.

First of all, it is important to note that Heraclitus employs a verb form in Fragment 30 in order to build the compound "ever-living" (ἀείζωον): ζῶον is the participle of the verb ζῆν, which means "to live". From this, it is clear that Heraclitus is thinking of an *event*, not an abstract concept. The verb's dictionary form (first person, singular, present tense) is ζάω, and according to classical philologists[10], the verb ζάω was formed from the well-known prefix ζα that occurs in other Greek words and has the effect of *intensifying* or *strengthening* the meaning of the word to which it is prefixed.[11] Take, for example, the Greek word for "strong" μένος. By prefixing ζα, the adjective ζαμενής is formed which means "very strong". Of course, ζα does not appear in the verb ζάω as a prefix, but rather as the verb stem. Nevertheless, if we interpret the verb in the context of Fragment 30, we arrive at an understanding of the verb that is very similar to the meaning of the prefix; thus, Fragment 30 tells us that *life is an intensifying of the appearing and concealing of nature*. So life for Heraclitus was not a subcategory of nature; life is the appearing and concealing of nature in its purest form. Clearly, Heraclitus' understanding of life has nothing to do with life in the modern biological sense. On the other hand, we do find in Stoic thought some of the ideas that approach a biological understanding and that have evoked the disdain of biologists such as Dawkins.

As we have seen, the Stoics took over many ideas from Heraclitus and modified them in ways that would have been quite foreign to the Ephesian. In his *On the Nature of the Gods*, Cicero reports the Stoic view of life and its connection to fire, and in his description, the difference between Heraclitus and the Stoics becomes very apparent. Cicero writes: "It is a fact that all things which undergo nurture and growth

---

[10] See, for example, HERBERT WEIR SMYTH, *Greek Grammar,* (1920), 1984, p. 250.

[11] See HEIDEGGER's discussion in: *Der Anfang des abendländischen Denkens: Heraklit*, Gesamtausgabe, II. Abteilung, Vorlesungen, 1923–1944, Bd. 55, 1979, S. 93–96.

contain within themselves a power of heat without which they could not be nurtured and grow. For everything which is hot and fiery is roused and activated by its own movement; but a thing which is nourished and grows has a definite and regular movement; as long as this remains in us, so long sensation and life remain, but when the heat has been chilled and extinguished, we ourselves die and are extinguished. ... Therefore every living thing, whether animal or vegetable, is alive on account of the heat enclosed within it. From this it must be understood that the element heat has within itself a vital force which pervades the whole world. We shall recognize this more readily from a more detailed account of this all-penetrating fieriness in its entirety."[12] The influence of Aristotle on Stoic thought is evident in the fact that life is now restricted in some way to plants and animals, which brings the concept closer to the modern view of biology.[13] Nevertheless, the vital force (*vis vitalis*) of life is described as an "all-penetrating fieriness" that permeates the entire universe. So from the standpoint of the vital force, nature itself is living, and therefore life cannot really be considered a subcategory of nature.

If we turn from our Greek and Roman sources to the Ancient Near East, we find that there are similarities, but also significant differences between the understandings of life in the two regions. In both cases, life was generally understood as a vitality or force, but in the Hebrew literature, an important distinction was introduced into the idea of vitality because of the transcendence of God over nature. Parallel to the fundamental difference between God and human beings, a distinction between "being" and "having" became central to the idea of life. Whereas God *is* life, human beings *have* life as a gift from God. For this reason, we find a more intentional emphasis on human beings as opposed either to plants and other animals, or to the universe as a whole.

Broadly speaking, the idea of life referred to the vitality that an individual enjoyed throughout a certain span of time. The Hebrew word for

---

[12] CICERO, *On the Nature of the Gods* (De natura deorum), Bk. II, Ch. 9–11.

[13] See, for example, ARISTOTLE, *On the Soul* (De anima), Bk. B, 413a f.

"life" (חַיִּים) could also mean "years of life" in reference to the whole of that which the individual has experienced. Perhaps we come closer to the Hebrew thought on life in thinking about the biography of an individual. In any case, one of the characteristics of Hebrew thought was its emphatic *value judgment of life*. Life is not only good, it is seen as the ultimate good. So we read in Job 2:4: "All that a man has he will give for his life." And again in Proverbs 3:16, where Wisdom is described: "Long life is in her right hand; in her left hand are riches and honor." Even in times of distress when life seemed hardly worth living, the value of life was not forgotten as the writer of Ecclesiastes reminds us in verse 9:4: "But he who is joined with all the living has hope, for a living dog is better than a dead lion." This quotation from Ecclesiastes is particularly interesting because it associates life with hope. Life in the thinking of the author was not simply physical life. Life involved an openness for possibilities that engender hope for the future. From these brief comments, the difference between the Hebrew and the Stoic view of life becomes very clear. Unlike the Stoics, the ancient Israelites could never have considered the voluntary termination of life as good. For they viewed life as a gift from God; that is, they thought that life arises out of the creative activity of the deity. If God is the source of life, then God can be named "the living God" (אֱלֹהִים חַיִּים), as we read in Deuteronomy 5:26.

As we can see, the description of life in the Hebrew Bible also has very little to do with the modern concept of biological life. To be sure, the Hebrew concept involved the physical presence of the individual, the necessity of nourishment, the recognition of the progression from birth to death, but all of this was viewed in the *context of relationships*. The individual had a relationship to the produce of the land, to the immediate and extended family, to the community, and finally to God, the source of all vitality and creative power. These relationships constituted life. In contrast to the Stoic view, life was no longer conceived as a cosmic principle, but rather it was viewed in the relationship between God and man. Nothing could set this understanding more sharply apart from the modern biological understanding than the phrase "the living God". If life is essentially divine, it is wholly non-materialistic.

When we turn from the Hebrew Bible to the explicitly Christian writings of the New Testament, we find that further distinctions have been introduced into the idea of life as vitality. First and foremost, there is a *new temporal distinction between present life and future life*. Both of these are associated with vitality, but in different ways, and this is apparent in the distinction between corruptible life and incorruptible life. Life in its truest form is thought to be incorruptible, whereas the present life of the individual is corruptible and thus characterized by reduced vitality. Because of the vitality of the future life, it is also called "eternal life" (ζωὴ αἰώνιος). So we read, for instance, in the Gospel of Matthew that a young rich man came to Jesus inquiring about eternal life: "Teacher, what good deed must I do, to have eternal life?" As the text explains, his present life was abounding with material possessions, but the vitality or power of real life was missing. So the young man approaches Jesus with the question about eternal life.

In the writings of Paul, we find another variation: The present life can be described as "life in the flesh" in contrast to future life, which is "life in the spirit". In Galatians 6:8, Paul writes: "For he who sows to his own flesh will from the flesh reap corruption; but he who sows to the Spirit will from the Spirit reap eternal life." The anthropological terms "flesh" and "spirit" should not be interpreted materialistically, but rather relationally. That is, both present life and future life are constituted through a pattern of relationships. Likewise, the terms "flesh" and "spirit" designate different modes of life that are constituted in different relationships. Living in relationship to the material world is the essence of the present life, but living in relationship to God constitutes the future life.[14]

---

[14] The primacy of relationships is expressed by the Apostle Paul through the use of the Greek dative. See GERHARD EBELING's discussion of Galatians 2:19 in: *Die Wahrheit des Evangeliums*, 1981, p. 191 f.

If the future life is constituted by living in relationship to God, the question arises as to how this is to be understood. In today's world, the discussion between Christians and atheists often revolves around the question of God's existence, but in the thought of the New Testament writers, the future eternal life is not dependent upon believing that God exists since the reality of God was generally assumed by everyone. Rather, eternal life was thought to be granted through faith in Jesus: "every one who sees the Son and believes in him should have eternal life" (John 6:40). Since faith in Jesus means simply trusting his word, language comes into view again, this time in connection with life. Just as language was central to the appearing and concealing of nature, trusting the language of Jesus becomes central to the intensifying of the appearing and concealing of nature, i.e. to life. Faith, then, as a response to language is the path through which future life is attained. This correlation between word and faith is fundamental for understanding the Christian view of life.

In our discussion to this point, present life and future life have already appeared as somehow interrelated. For it is in our present life that we hear the word to which we respond with faith and enter into future life. If we understand this statement purely in the context of technological time, i.e. time as a series of points, the future life would seem to lie on a timeline somewhere beyond the present. However, this is not the concept of time predominant in the New Testament. Instead, we must think again about integrated time in which past, present, and future are interrelated since both Paul and John maintained that *eternal life* is to some extent *already present*. In the Gospel of John, this is even more evident than in the letters of Paul. According to John, eternal life, i.e. the future life of incorruptibility, is already present in the experience of the believer, and therefore, death has already been overcome by the fullness of life. With these brief remarks, we must conclude our theological exposition of life in the New Testament since a more thorough treatment of the topic would exceed the bounds of our investigation. For our purposes, we can draw from the preceding discussion several important conclusions. *First of all, life as understood in the New Testament is fundamentally relational and involves integrated time, i.e. the interrelatedness of past, present, and future. Secondly, life exhibits a polarity between time and eternity. Thirdly, life always occurs as a linguistic event.*

Now these three conclusions from the textual analysis require a more systematic exposition in order to incorporate them into our understanding of nature in general. Although these characteristics of life are not really separable, we will discuss them separately for the sake of clarity. We begin with the *relationality of life* and delve deeper into this aspect by reflecting on life in connection with death. Such reflection demands that we step back from our everyday manner of thinking because we usually think about life and death as quite unrelated. We normally talk about life without any thought of death, and when death does come into view, it appears as a boundary situation in our lives. Dominated as we are by the technological experience of time, we think of our lives as a series of points on a line or as a one-way street that leads from birth into the dead-end of death. As long as we are living, we travel along the road relatively unconcerned about the dead-end that awaits us. This understanding of life and death corresponds to the biological scheme of modern science. Just as life is defined biologically, so also death is understood from the standpoint of biology.

Although there may be an element of truth in this scheme, it cannot account for our actual experiences with life and death. Consider, for example, what happens when a cherished member of our family dies. We are overcome with grief in a double sense; we mourn for the person who died, but we also mourn for ourselves. We mourn the loss of life in the deceased, and we mourn the loss of a relationship in our own lives – a relationship that was literally a part of us. That is, a part of us dies with the deceased. So death cannot simply be explained in biological terms because it inevitably involves the existential loss of vitality in the midst of life. It is the severing of a relationship that was constitutive for our lives. Life is fundamentally a matrix of relationships, and it is the harmonious exchange in these relationships that grants vitality to us. Since death is the loss of vitality, it is not simply an occurrence at the temporal end of physical life. Death is a constant threat to life; it is the root source of human anxiety; and it can actually occur *in* life (understood as a biological system). This means that a person can fall victim to the threat of death to such an extent that he dies while still physically present. When a person experiences the loss of all meaningful relationships, he can actually commit physical suicide in order to escape the death that he experiences in the midst of life. In this context, life and death become a contrast between *community* and *isolation*, a contrast between harmonious relationships and severed relationships.

In dealing with the relationality of life, we have already touched upon the problem of integrated time, but we must now consider explicitly the way in which past, present, and future constitute the relationality of life. In Chapter 5, we discussed integrated time in connection with the contrast between the scientific mode of thinking and the natural mode of thinking. It may be helpful at this point to review our previous discussion before we demonstrate the relevance of integrated time for an understanding of life.

The scientific mode of thinking operates on the assumption that time is a series of points. Calculations can be made at t_1, t_2, t_3 and so forth in order to arrive at certain scientific conclusions. For example, the momentum of an object at point d_3 moving along a plane can be calculated from Newton's law if we know the mass and velocity of the object at d_3. The velocity, in turn, is dependent on the distance traversed between two points in time. In this context, there is no apparent need to consider the way in which past, present, and future tenses are interrelated. Nevertheless, this interrelatedness is the more fundamental concept of time from which the technological clock-time is derived.

Whereas technological clock-time can be measured, the interrelatedness of tensed time defies such segmentation. Consider again the tenses of the English language. Events that have already occurred belong to the past; events that are taking place now belong to the present; and events that have not yet occurred belong to the future. As we have noted, it is possible to discuss the tenses of time without any reference to numbers. Nevertheless, it may seem at first glance that the three tenses represent a series like our clock-time, albeit a series that begins with past and ends with future. But this similarity with clock-time is only apparent, and as soon as other tenses such as the progressive and the present perfect are considered, it becomes clear that the tenses describe *events* and their relevance, not *points in a series*. Furthermore, the description of the events occurs in language. These reflections lead us to the following conclusion: *Time as a series of points has an essential connection with numbers, whereas time as a description of events is inherently related to language.* Just as the words in a sentence hang together and convey a meaning, the tenses of time are interrelated and enable unified experiences. The interrelatedness of past, present, and future is evidence in the experience of promise and fulfillment; what was promised in the past and anticipated in the future is fulfilled in the present. Past, present, and future are not three *points* in a series; they are interwoven with each other to create a *unified experience*. If we look for similes to describe this difference, we could say that clock-time is like a *string of beads*, whereas tensed time is like a *woven cloth*.

The interrelatedness of tensed time together with the relationality of life brings us to our second conclusion mentioned above: Life exhibits a *polarity between time and eternity*. In discussing this polarity, it is important to remember that time in this context is to be understood fundamentally as integrated time; time is the interrelatedness of past, present, and future. That is, we must not fall into the trap of assuming a technological concept of time as a series of points. Likewise, we must guard against the assumption that eternity can be grasped in the context of our technological clock-time. If we assume that time is a series of points and that the life of an individual can be represented as a series of points from birth to death, then eternal life would seem to be the state of the individual *after* death, and for this reason, it is common to speak about the eternal life as *afterlife*. This usage of the word "eternal" is, however, unsatisfactory because it indicates a further point in the series. It is as if the life of the person took place in time from point A to point B, and then afterlife began at point C and continued forever in an endless series. But afterlife in this sense is really *everlasting*, not *eternal*. The word "eternity" has in the philosophical as well as in the theological tradition a different meaning, and this meaning can only be grasped if we move beyond the clock-time that is so predominant in our society.

In his *Timaios*, Plato described time as the "moving image of eternity", whereby he meant first of all that time and eternity are not to be separated as though eternity were timeless.[15] Time and eternity belong together fundamentally, and in some way, time reflects eternity. As Plato says: It is the moving image of eternity. It is not necessary in the context of our investigation to pursue a detailed interpretation of Plato's phrase. For our purposes, it suffices to say that *eternity is the perfection or completion of time*. That is, *when time occurs in its purity as a flawless integration of past, present, and future, it is the image of eternity*. In the experience of eternity *in* time, everything has its proper place, nothing is lost. In order to understand this experience, we must call to mind those elevated moments of life, moments of intense joy, when we experienced a *completion* of time in which past and future seemed to coalesce in the present. This experience of the perfection of time without a hint of loss, untainted by melancholy, and free from anxiety is the experience of *eternity* in time. However, these glimpses of eternity are not yet "eternal life" in the New Testament sense because they are ephemeral experiences emerging out of fortuitous situations.

[15] PLATO, *Timaios*, 37d5: εἰκὼ δ' ἐπενόει κινητόν τινα αἰῶνος ποιῆσαι. See the study by GERNOT BÖHME, *Idee und Kosmos: Platons Zeitlehre – Eine Einführung in seine theoretische Philosophie*, Philosophische Abhandlungen, Bd. 66, 1996.

Eternal life in the New Testament sense is not ephemeral. To be sure, the experience of eternal life may not always be as intense as the individual wishes, but eternal life brings about a fundamental change in the polarity between time and eternity so that a completion of time is experienced not only in joy, but also in grief. The Apostle Paul calls this completion of time "life in the Spirit". Thus, the inseparable connection between the polarity of time and eternity and relationality of life begins to emerge. Life as a matrix of relationships is constituted in the polarity between time and eternity, but the possible variations of balancing this polarity can be characterized as "life in the flesh" or "life in the Spirit". That is, "life in the flesh" and "life in the spirit" are designations for the dominating power extending over the entire polarity of time and eternity. When the polarity of time and eternity is actualized in such a way that the harmonious interrelatedness of past, present, and future is dominant in forming the relationality of life, we speak of "life in the Spirit" or simply "eternal life".

On the other hand, when the polarity of time and eternity is actualized in such a way that the interrelatedness of part, present, and future is distorted, we designate it as "life in the flesh". In this case, the interrelatedness of past, present, and future is so skewed that the individual suffers under the burden of a crass materialism. Such an individual may experience the past affectively as tainted by guilt and the future as a source of anxiety. Between guilt and anxiety, the present may be disturbed by a bitterness toward others and an insatiable desire for possessions. As the interrelatedness of past, present, and future becomes more and more fragmented, time emerges as a series of points, and "life in the flesh" becomes "life in a materialistic world" dominated by the technological experience of time. This does not mean that technological clock-time cannot be experienced in life when life unfolds as the harmonious interrelatedness of past, present, and future. If this were the case, the development of clocks would never have taken place, and the scientific mode of thinking would not have been possible. It is simply a question of *pre-*

dominance in the intensified appearing and concealing that we call “life”. In “life in the Spirit”, the technological concept of time is never dominant. Dominant is this: *the harmonious interweaving of past, present, and future that issues forth in the relationality of life known as “eternal life”.*

Finally, life always emerges as a *linguistic event*, be it “life in the flesh” or “life in the spirit” (eternal life). As we have seen, the terms “flesh” and “spirit” designate different ways in which the polarity of time and eternity is balanced, that is, different ways in which life is constituted through relationships. In both cases, the relationships are established through language. Language in this context does not mean simply a particular spoken language such as German or English, although a particular language may be involved. As we learned from Heraclitus, language (*logos*) has a much broader meaning than the usual semantical understanding of the modern era. More essentially, language is the process of gathering and structuring that is manifested in particular languages. In the interest of clarity, however, we will consider language for the moment as a system of thought embodied in a particular language. Both the language of the biologist and that of the historian may be English, but the fundamental thoughts embodied in their experience of the English language are different. For this reason, the language of the biologist and the language of the historian bring different things to light; they allow different things to appear, thus necessarily concealing other things. In short, the linguistic events of appearing and concealing are different, and therefore, different relationships are established from which different modes of life emerge.

In considering the New Testament understanding of life, we observed a correlation between language and faith, whereby faith in Jesus meant simply trusting his word. If the word “faith” seems too narrowly religious, we could easily translate the New Testament word for “faith” (πίστις) as “trust” or perhaps even as “confidence”. *So trust as a response to language is the path through which life is constituted, and this holds true whether we are speaking about life in the flesh or life in the spirit.* The present life in the flesh is contingent upon our confidence in a matrix of ideas and concepts embedded in our everyday and professional language. Scientists pride themselves on being open for new ideas, but in truth, their openness is very limited. In order to pursue a scientific endeavor, it is necessary to embrace an underlying system of thought, which cannot be called into question. To be sure, details can be questioned, and new avenues of thought can be pursued. But the very foundation of the scientific endeavor – what counts as truth, what qualifies as evidence, how to validate an assertion, the correlation between "nature" and mathematics – all of these elements must be embraced on "faith". There is no Cartesian certainty; first principles can never be proven. The only possible validation of the underlying principles of science would be utilitarian. If it works, it is correct – which, of course, begs the question as to what it means for something "to work". In my opinion, it reflects more intellectual integrity to simply admit that first principles are unprovable. To my knowledge, Euclid never tried to prove his axioms, and as it turned out, his fifth postulate was wrong. In short, faith or trust is not only a religious concept. Trust is a necessary condition of life in general, and it is inseparably oriented toward language. This correlation between word and faith is fundamental for understanding the Christian view of life, but it is also indispensable for the scientist and for life in a secular society.

In light of our discussion, the conclusion seems inevitable that Dawkins' attempt to discredit the religious views that do not fit into his framework of thought is contingent upon the acceptance on faith of *his* framework of thought. If he really intends to *prove* his point, the argument is hopelessly circular. On the other hand, even if one does accept his basic premises, the whole argument loses its force because true conclusions do not follow from false premises, and many of his philosophical and theological premises are patently false. Furthermore, *certain* conclusions do not follow from *hypothetical* premises. Just as I am committed to the tradition of Western philosophy and Christian theology, Dawkins is committed to a scientific framework that utilizes a particular set of concepts and an accepted method of investigation. Neither commitment is provable in the sense of logical argumentation or empirical evidence. The empirical evidence claimed by Dawkins is always filtered through the concepts that he holds to be valid. That is, the very selection of empirical data and the weighting of its importance cannot be separated from the existing theories and the hypotheses being tested. The final commitment to a context of thought embedded in a language is a matter of faith or trust. Nobody devotes his life to pursuing an investigation in a particular direction without being convinced that the chosen direction holds the promise of bearing fruit. We can trust that we are right, but Cartesian certainty is not possible. The role played by peer groups in the scientific community can imbue at times the researcher with a false sense of confidence and certainty. But positive peer reviewing of one's work does not in any way eliminate the possibility that the entire group could be wrong. This line of argumentation is not intended to convert the atheistic scientist into a believer in the Christian sense. It is simply intended to clarify the role of trust in the life of the atheist as well as in the life of the Christian. The correlation between language and trust cannot be removed from the life of the atheistic scientist because it is constitutive for his life.

As we near the end of this chapter, we need to set in relief once again the distinctions between *nature*, *human nature*, and *life*. As we understand *nature*, it is not a thing or a collection of things, but rather an event. Nature happens and when it happens, it has the character of disclosing and concealing. The disclosing can best be described as a creating and sustaining, whereas the concealing occurs as an unfathomable mystery. The event of nature also has a moral dimension that addresses human beings and guides their conduct. The unique disclosing event of *human nature* can be characterized as an *openness* for the creative, sustaining power as a gift, an openness for the world as a matrix of interpersonal relationships and an openness for the belongingness and interdependence of all human beings. On the other hand, the concealing event of human nature can be described as the unfathomable mystery, the nothingness, the abyss and the consuming fire of God's presence that form the boundaries of human existence. Inasmuch as *life* is the intensification of nature, it is simply the appearing and concealing of nature in its purest form. Still, the intensification itself sets life somewhat apart from nature in general, and this dimension has often been expressed in the notion of vitality. Moreover, life acquires new dimensions at the level of human beings because of the interrelatedness of past, present, and future and because of the polarities of force and power, of time and eternity, and of life and the spirit. The fact that these polarities are, for the most part, out of balance points to a deficit in nature that seems to be just as fundamental as the essential goodness of nature. Finally, the distinction between "life in the flesh" (materialistic life) and "life in the spirit" (eternal life), which was recognized within the Christian tradition, emphasizes the way in which language and faith are determinative for the quality of life.

Human *nature* has been defined in relationship to nature in general, but human *life* has been defined ultimately in relationship to God. The natural mode of thinking that we have employed demanded such an approach and led to the following insight: God is the giver of life, while human beings are the recipients of the gift. So ultimately, life is a relational concept. We live or we die in particular relationships – first and foremost, in relationship to God, but then also, in relationship to our world. That these two relationships are intertwined and therefore not really separable should be clear from our previous treatment of the topic. This philosophical, theological understanding of life does not negate the biologist's concepts of living forms, but rather it provides a context in which to understand the latter. The biologist's concepts arise out of the materialistic framework of modern science; they are not necessarily wrong within their proper framework, but they are severely limited as general principles. Our understanding of life does not seek to refute the scientific work of scientists such as Richard Dawkins. It is not his science that I am challenging, it is his broad philosophical and theological claim that I find untenable. In developing an understanding of “life” within the narrow framework of contemporary science, he believes that he has provided a more or less complete account of the whole. But in truth, he has only demonstrated the blindness that is so characteristic of many contemporary scientists. His claim that he can verify his atheistic views on the basis of evolutionary biology is more reminiscent of the hybris of Oedipus Rex than of the serious, reflective thought of Johannes Kepler. Unfortunately, the “blind watch” has become blind for its own blindness. Contrary to what Dawkins seems to think, he has not discovered the Archimedes’ point to move the world.

Conclusion

The Problem of Definitions and the Admissibility of Evidence

As we have seen in our analysis of the arguments of Richard Dawkins and William Paley, both writers focused on the argument for the existence of God from design, and both utilized empirical evidence to support their respectful claims – Paley being for the argument, Dawkins being against it. The argument from design in the universe and in living beings in particular originated among the Stoics and was reported in some detail in the writings of Cicero. For historical reasons, William Paley chose this argument form in his classic work *Natural Theology*, and Dawkins followed him inasmuch as he concentrated on refuting the design argument in *The Blind Watchmaker*. Interestingly enough, neither of these writers proves anything conclusively. Paley himself was aware that his argument was based on analogy and that a rigorous proof of the existence of God was impossible. Whether Dawkins was really clear on the logical status of his arguments remains somewhat unclear. In essence, Paley simply tried to demonstrate that there is design in the universe and that such design indicates beyond any reasonable doubt the existence of a Designer or Creator. Dawkins, on the other hand, presented voluminous empirical data showing that there is every reason to doubt the existence of such a Creator because the apparent design can be explained in terms of evolutionary biology.

In my opinion, the arguments on both sides suffer from several difficulties. To begin, both writers are very careless in defining terms. As we have seen, the word "existence" is ill-suited when used in reference to the reality of God if we understand the word in its root meaning as "standing out". Existence as "standing out" characterizes human beings, but not God. For this reason, the systematic theologian Paul Tillich insisted repeatedly in his writings that the whole concept of existence implied a time-space continuum that contradicts the meaning of the word "God". Tillich was often criticized by conservatives for his insistence that God does not *exist*, but simply *is*. When Thomas Aquinas set out to demonstrate the reality of God, he did not write about *existence*, but rather about the *reality* or the *actuality* of God, i.e. the sheer "to be" (*esse*) of God. The question for Thomas was: *Utrum Deus sit* ("Whether God would *be*" or better "Whether there is God"). This issue may seem at first glance to be a mere matter of semantics, but it really is crucial for any understanding of God to recognize that God is not a superman or super-being among other beings and thus subject to the conditions of existence. Tillich himself often substituted the phrase "the *ground* of being" for the word "God" in order to emphasize that God is not a being among other beings. Such philosophical language may be helpful in some circles, but it is not a phrase that is completely at home in the theological tradition. In any case, it should be apparent that God as the ground of being is a non-theistic (not atheistic) understanding of God.

A second problem with the arguments of Paley and Dawkins lies in the concept of evidence. In both cases, the evidence under consideration seems to be "empirical" in some sense, although they present different types of evidence and at times offer radically different interpretations of the same evidence. It is worth remembering that the full title of Paley's work is: *Natural Theology or Evidence of the Existence and Attributes of the Deity, collected from the appearances of nature.* Paley is not presenting a logical demonstration of the existence of God – his method is rhetorical, analogical, and probabilistic –, but rather he is pointing to the "appearances of nature" that he judges to be evidence of God's existence. On the other hand, Dawkins presents "scientific" evidence that in his mind irrefutably confirms the evolutionary theory of Charles Darwin (with the necessary corrections and additions based on modern genetics). Regardless of how one judges the arguments of Paley and Dawkins, it seems to me undeniable that Dawkins' evidence is much more theoretically laden from the outset than that of Paley. Consider the human eye, for instance. When Paley talks about the human eye, his evidence is very direct. That is, he is considering the human eye as it immediately appears. In contrast, Dawkins is forced in his refutation of design to introduce very indirect evidence of the human eye – evidence that from the beginning is overladen with theoretical concepts. That is to say, he cannot simply take the human eye as it appears today as his sole or even primary evidence. This does not mean that Dawkins' entire argument is wrong; it simply means that his evidence is not as weighty as he would like to think.

Whereas Paley considered the evidence from *appearances* as empirical, Dawkins in concert with modern science relies on *empirical* evidence in the scientific sense. The phrase "empirical evidence" is such a common element in technological thinking that we rarely consider carefully its meaning. The word "evidence" is, of course, a Latin derivative from the word *videre* meaning "to see", and as soon as we add the prefix *e* (i.e. *ex*), it assumes the meaning "manifest", "clear" or "evident". The other part of the phrase, namely "empirical", adds the notion of experience, and in the early days of science, such experience was almost always based on the five senses. In this case, the word "empirical" functioned restrictively to limit the kind of evidence admissible. So not everything that was evident and manifest was necessarily accepted as relevant to the scientific enterprise, but only that evidence based on information from the five senses. At this point, one wonders how it would be possible to distinguish between evidence that is manifested *in some way* and evidence that is manifested *through the five senses*. Either we must accept that all valid evidence is not necessarily empirical, or the phrase "empirical evidence" becomes redundant. Of course, the scientists of the seventeenth century never really held themselves consistently to these distinctions, but it was clearly built into the phrase "empirical evidence".

In today's science, however, the phrase "empirical evidence" has lost its meaning to a great extent for two reasons. Firstly, some of the major advances in modern science have been made with little or no *empirical* evidence. Albert Einstein's development of the General Theory of Relativity is a classic example. To be sure, there has been subsequent confirmation of the theory based on *empirical* data, but originally the actual *evidence* for the theory was purely mathematical. Secondly, the instrumentation and methods of measurement utilized in modern science often produce a long path from the event under investigation to the sense experience of the investigator. As a result, the accepted evidence is only indirectly empirical in the usual sense. What the investigator calls "empirical" may be no more than the image on a computer screen that has been processed through various complicated programs. In the area of evolutionary biology, the problem of empirical evidence is exacerbated by the fact that events of the past are no longer available for examination. The origin of life on earth is a past event that cannot be duplicated in the present as the *origin of life on earth.* Whatever may be accomplished in a laboratory is a present event whose relevance to the actual origin can only be inferred. The point of these reflections is this: If we intend to talk about the actuality of God from the standpoint of evidence, we must be clear on the kind of evidence that we consider admissible.

A third problem with the arguments of Paley and Dawkins is the understanding of God assumed in their respective arguments. Paley's understanding of God is clearly theistic in the sense of eighteenth century theism, whereas Dawkins seems to have only a vague idea of "something" irrational that does not fit into the framework of scientific thinking. Again, this is a crucial matter because any conversation about the reality or non-reality of God becomes hopelessly confused if the discussion participants do not share to some extent a common understanding of the word "God". Put simply, what could it possibly mean to say "God does not exist", if we do not know the meaning of the word "God"? If the atheist seriously considers the question concerning God's existence or the reality of God, he must have some idea of what the word "God" means. If the word "God" has absolutely no meaning for the atheist, then the question itself and consequently the answer to the question are meaningless.

Suppose that I ask the atheist this question: "Does the centrifugal bumble-puppy exist?" He may not feel comfortable answering with a simple "yes" or "no". He may well respond: "I don't know what 'centrifugal bumble-puppy' means, and therefore I can't say whether or not such a thing exists." But let's suppose that he has read Aldous Huxley's *Brave New World* and knows that a centrifugal bumble-puppy is not a thing, but rather a children's game. Then, the atheist might well respond: "The question makes no sense. How can you say that a game exists?" Let's go a step further and suppose that six children are playing this game. Now, if I ask the atheist his opinion about the existence of the six children, he will not hesitate to say that the children do, in fact, exist. But what if I ask him about the existence of the number six? Then he may not find an answer so easily. Our entire world functions apparently on the basis of numbers. It is difficult to imagine what would happen to our economy if all the numbers in the world suddenly disappeared? And yet, as important as numbers are, it is not clear that it makes any sense to say that they exist. Still, the atheist might cut off this line of reasoning and object that everyone knows what the word "God" means. "It refers to a being, and beings unlike numbers either exist or they don't exist." He may even go further and say: "The word refers to an all-powerful being, a being with personal traits, that created the world, that interacts causally with the world, but is separate from the world. And either this being exists or it doesn't exist." This is basically the theistic concept of God held by William Paley, and if all of us were to accept this definition, the debate could be conducted in a meaningful manner. However, this understanding of the word "God" is not accepted today by all Christians nor, for that matter, by all adherents of other religions. For this reason alone, further discussion on the matter is necessary.

Trapped in the Dialectic between Technology and Religion

The theory of evolution that was originally proposed by Charles Darwin and that was developed further by biologists such as Julian Huxley has shed much light on the biological-chemical constitution of human beings. It has answered many questions about structures of the human body and the relationship between humans and animals. But it has done all of this from a very limited perspective. Evolutionary biology employs, as we have seen, a particular set of concepts that correspond to a particular vocabulary. Regrettably, many of its proponents have failed to recognize the limited perspective from which they view the organic world, and accordingly they have attempted to draw universal conclusions from particular results. The consequences of this attempt have been very detrimental to Western societies. In the hands of the Darwinists, Darwin's work on the *descent of man* – interesting as it is as a scientific endeavour – has contributed to the *descent of human nature*. As a result of Darwin's theory of evolution, the understanding of human nature in the Western world has literally descended to the point that there is very little perceptible difference between human beings and animals. I am not suggesting that the theory of evolution is the only historical cause of this development. On the contrary, the creationists themselves have contributed unwittingly to the problem by abandoning serious theological thinking and adopting a technological mode of thought in their debate with the evolutionists.

The creation/evolution debate that has raged almost uninterruptedly since the publication of Darwin's *The Descent of Man* has focused, for the most part, on the question whether human beings were created in their present form by a divine being or they evolved over billions of years from very primitive life forms. Although Christian conservatives may perceive this debate as crucial, it has in my opinion much less theological relevance than they suppose. Much more important than the question of *origin* is our present understanding of *human nature*. It is *this* problem and not the question of origin that has led to the ethical crisis of the present. We talk about "human rights", but we really do not know what the phrase means because we do not know what it means to be *human*. The entire debate about the origin of human beings distracts from more fundamental problems and contributes little to an understanding of human rights since the argumentation takes place within the realm of technology.

The irony of the present debate between the atheistic evolutionists and the Christian creationists is that both groups fall into the category of believers in the broadest sense. As the ideological bent of the departments of humanities at our major universities spread into the science departments, Darwinism morphed into an ideology that can no longer be questioned. Like the Marxist ideology of East Germany (the old DDR) before the fall of the Berlin Wall, Darwinism has taken on the characteristics of a religious creed to which "respectable" scientists are expected to adhere. Any scientist who questions the Darwinian dogma will be promptly reprimanded by his peers and discredited in the mainstream media. There was a time when one could consider Darwinism simply to be the dominant paradigm of biology in much the same sense that Newtonian physics was the dominant paradigm of physics before the work of Albert Einstein. But today, Darwinism is not simply a paradigm in the sense of Thomas Kuhn's *The Structure of Scientific Revolutions*. It is a creed that is defended by its adherents with religious fervor.

The broader context of this development is the politicization of science as a whole. Step by step the scientific community has abandoned its original objectivity by adopting a political-societal ideology that prejudices the direction of its research as well as the presentation of its results to the general public. This ideology, which emanated from the humanities, has roots in both the Frankfurt School of Marxism (Critical Theory) and in the postmodern nihilism of the French deconstructionists. It exhibits many characteristics of a religion including the rigid adherence to certain dogmas, even in the face of contrary evidence. Currently, the scientific community seems to be trapped in the dialectic between technology and "religion", and there is no indication that it is capable of moving beyond this point.

On the other hand, the creationists are no less trapped in the dialectic between technology and religion than the atheistic evolutionists. The attempts of the creationists to argue against Darwinism operate fundamentally on the level of biology and arrive at theological ideas only as a conclusion to a chain of scientific data. Additionally, the claim that intelligent design implies an intelligent designer is faulty. There is no logical reason to assume that *intelligible* design implies anything other than a certain orderliness in nature. In the end, the creationist simply believes the creed of God's creation, just as the atheist believes the creed of Darwinism. On both sides, the main arguments take place on the level of technology in the broadest sense, but the conclusions make an unsupported leap into metaphysics. In spite of the often hostile tension between the evolutionists and the creationists, the proponents of both groups remain trapped in the *same* dialectic between technology and religion. The difference is this: The creationists move from religion to technology, whereas the evolutionists move from technology to religion. The dialectical movement in both directions has contributed to the politicization of science and to the radicalization of religion. This situation poses questions that cannot be answered in the present work. For instance: Does the technological mode of thinking contain an element that tends toward religion fervor and dogmatic belief? And further: Does the contemporary form of conservative Christianity contain an element that leads its adherents into the realm of technology? Answers to such questions might well benefit both the creationist and the evolutionist.

The Self-Inflicted Blindness

One of the salient features of modern natural science is that it lacks an understanding of nature. The biologist, for instance, understands cells, DNA, replicators etc., but he has no clear understanding of nature as a whole. The reductionism of modern science has led to a proliferation of specialties dealing with this or that abstracted segment of nature, but nature itself always withdraws from view before the scrutinizing, analytical eyes of the scientist. In the previous chapters, we have tried to bring nature more clearly into view through a consideration of noted philosophers and theologians.

In moving beyond the narrow vision of science, it was necessary to contrast the dominant technological mode of thinking with the natural mode of thinking as we have described it. The reductionistic, analytical thinking of science is incapable of grasping nature as a whole, i.e. nature *as* nature, and inevitably it considers a dissected portion of nature to be in some sense representative of the whole. The assumption that we can understand the whole of nature by analyzing and dissecting portions of it is nothing short of a bias that cannot be supported either logically or empirically. As we have seen, the natural mode of thinking involves an integrated experience of time and is deeply linguistic; both of these traits combine to render it historical in a twofold sense. Firstly, natural thinking necessitates the investigation of historical documents, and for this reason we have focused on the thought of two philosophers and two theologians. Secondly, natural mode of thinking is historical in the sense that the investigator himself must recognize his own thinking as a part of the movement of history. This means that natural thinking can claim neither certainty nor finality for its results.

Our previous discussion of the technological and the natural mode of thinking may have given rise to the impression that the two are completely separate. This is certainly not the case. On the contrary, the technological mode emerges out of the natural mode and bears the marks of its heritage. Consider the phenomenon of time. The natural mode of thinking proceeds from an integrated experience of time in which the past, the present, and the future are interwoven. As we have pointed out previously, the interwoven character of time is very apparent in the correlation of promise and fulfillment. The promise that was made in the past and the fulfillment that is anticipated in the future intersect in the present and form a unified experience of time. Without this fundamental human experience, the clock-time of the scientist could never have developed. What the scientist designates as t_1, t_2, t_3 etc. in his laboratory experiment is simply a dissection of the unified experience of time manifested in promise and fulfillment. One should not conclude from this that the understanding of the physicist or the biologist is wrong, but rather that it is very limited. Inasmuch as the time designations of the experiment are grounded in the natural experience of time, they bear the marks of their heritage and can lead to significant advances in thought. But when the investigator absolutizes this mode of thought, he falls prey to the prejudices of an assumed metaphysics and becomes the victim of a self-inflicted blindness – a situation that is all the more tragic because the scientist, unlike Oedipus, does not recognize his own blindness.

Epilogue

As we have demonstrated in our discussion, Dawkins does not seem to have any clear concept of God in *The Blind Watchmaker*, and so it was to be hoped that some of the obscurities of this early work would be clarified in his 2006 publication of *The God Delusion*. Unfortunately, this hope was not fulfilled. Of the two works, the former is by far superior to the latter. *The Blind Watchmaker* may have suffered from definitional problems and from a misunderstanding of philosophical and theological concepts, but the *The God Delusion* is a New York Times Bestseller intended to amuse and entertain. Some readers may indeed be amused by it, but I suspect that most religious fundamentalists will be offended by Dawkins' trivial handling of serious material. Unlike the earlier work of Dawkins, this one contains an endless series of stories and antidotes, but very little substantive material. It would be a daunting task to critique this work from the standpoint of history, philosophy, or theology. Let it suffice for me to point out at random some of the glaring mistakes and misunderstandings.

Early in the book Dawkins attempts to discredit Christianity by claiming that it has been a major source of violence in the world. On page 58, for instance, after he has criticized Islamic violence, he writes: "Christianity, too, was spread by the sword, wielded first by Roman hands after the Emperor Constantine raised it from eccentric cult to official religion, then by the Crusaders. ..." This is one of Dawkins' many attempts to discredit Christianity as well as all other religions by claiming that they are the primary source of violence in the world. As a matter of historical accuracy, it was not Constantine, but rather Theodosius who in A.D. 380

elevated Christianity to the status of official religion of the Roman Empire. That notwithstanding, it is certainly true that the Edict of Constantine in A.D. 346 led to a period of Christian intolerance and persecution toward those of other persuasions. On the other hand, it is also true – which Dawkins neglects to mention – that the Christians themselves had been subjected to brutal violence until the time of Constantine. Sad as it is, violence has been a constant factor in human history. One need only consider the invasion of Europe by Atilla the Hun in the fifth century or the dictatorship of Joseph Stalin in the twentieth century to verify the fact that violence has plagued the world quite apart from the influence of any religion. There is absolutely no historical evidence that the Huns were religiously motivated, and yet their savagery is legendary. As for Stalin and later for Chairman Mao, the reports speak for themselves: unprecedented violence without religious motivation. In fact, the atheistic communistic platform is based on revolution – not the bloodless type of revolution that occurred in England in 1688, but the violent type exemplified by the uprising of the proletariat in Europe culminating in the Bolshevik Revolution. In various Prefaces to the *Manifest der Kommunistischen Partei* (1848), Engels praised the use of violence in order to spread the communist doctrine.[16] In more recent times, the world has witnessed the Tiananmen Square Massacre of 1989. And currently, we are observing under the leadership of Xi Jinping the brutality of the Chinese Communist Party in Hong Kong as well as in Mulan where millions of Uyghur Muslims are being persecuted and held in concentration camps. Of course, one could argue – depending on one's political views – that the communist inspired revolutions in Europe yielded positive results, but the religious leaders of the seventeenth century could make the same claim about the outcome of the Forty Years War in the German-speaking world. To approve the

[16] In a newspaper article in 1848, KARL MARX wrote: "there is only one way in which the murderous death agonies of the old society and the bloody birth throes of the new society can be shortened, simplified and concentrated, and that way is revolutionary terror" (*Neue Rheinische Zeitung*, No. 136, transl. by Marx-Engels Institute).

one and condemn the other involves a value judgment. Indisputable is this: Violence was manifest in both cases. My point in relating these historical events is simply to demonstrate the obvious prejudice of Dawkins in discussing the role of Christianity in the history of violence. Human history is fraught with violence, and it is absurd to single out religion as its source. One must remember, however, that Dawkins' work is a New York Times Bestseller, not a serious treatment of historical data.

Dawkins' contribution to an understanding of the word "God" is presented near the beginning of *The God Delusion.* He does not refer to it as a definition, but rather as a hypothesis that he intends to refute, namely the hypothesis that there exists "a superhuman, supernatural intelligence who deliberately designed and created the universe and everything in it, including us".[17] It should be noted that Dawkins is fixated on the idea of creation in his entire refutation of Christianity. One would be hard pressed to find an instance of such a narrow understanding of the word "God" in the entire theological tradition, but I suppose that Dawkins is entitled to formulate his own "definition". The problem is that his "definition" restricts any possible dialogue to a narrow group of fundamentalists who, in his mind, represent the entire breadth of Christian thought. In addition, Dawkins' hypothesis is problematic from the standpoint of the biblical text. Apparently, he is unaware that the belief in the creation of the world was a rather late development in Israelite thought. The first glimpses of this belief can be found in some of the psalms where the sustaining power of God (*creatio continua*) in the world is described, but not until postexilic times do we find a creation narrative about the beginning of the world. Of course, Dawkins is not really seeking respectful dialogue with informed Christians and trained theologians because he is convinced that science holds the answers to all possible questions relevant to humans beings and the universe. As he asserts later in the book, "I am arguing that … the God question is not in principle and forever

[17] Dawkins, *The God Delusion,* 2006, p. 52.

outside the remit of science."[18] So for Dawkins, science is the ultimate metaphysics or religion, if you like. Whether he realizes it or not, this attitude renders him as dogmatic and inflexible as the fundamentalists whom he opposes.

Before leaving Dawkins' *The God Delusion*, I feel obligated to mention his attempted refutation of classical arguments for the "existence" of God. Although he focused in his earlier work almost exclusively on the design argument of William Paley, he extends the scope of his criticism in this work to include the famous ontological argument of Anselm of Canterbury as well as the five arguments of Thomas Aquinas. Just as Dawkins demonstrates a lack of historical consciousness in dealing with biblical literature, he shows in his discussion of Anselm and Thomas Aquinas a complete lack of understanding of the basic philosophical concepts involved.

Anselm was born in 1033 near Aosta in what was then Burgundy. In 1093, he became the Archbishop of Canterbury, and before his death in 1109, he penned several theological treatises that have left a lasting mark on the theological and philosophical traditions of Western societies. Of these writings, the *Proslogion* is undoubtedly the best known because it contains the so-called ontological or a priori proof for the reality of God. Actually, the designation "ontological argument" does not stem from Anselm himself. It is first attested in the eighteenth century and was possibly coined by Kant who rejected Anselm's argument. In any case, Anselm tells us in Section Two of Chapter Two that he intends to demonstrate *Quod vere sit Deus* ("that God really is" or more loosely "that God is a reality"). In order to do this, he formulates the phrase: *aliquid quo maius nihil cogitari potest* ("something in comparison with which nothing greater can be conceived"), and then he asserts that this is exactly what we mean when we refer to God. Finally, he claims that one becomes involved in a logical contradiction if one says that "something in comparison with which nothing greater can be conceived" is

[18] DAWKINS, p. 96.

present only in *thought* and not in *reality*. The validity of the argument in this form depends on the assumption that "greatness" means "perfection" and that "being in reality" is a perfection. That is, Anselm holds that the *thought* of God cannot be separated from the *reality* of God. He who forms the correct concept of God already affirms the reality of God.

Anselm's argument is difficult to follow because it presupposes a connection between "being in thought" and "being in reality" that is very foreign to the modern mind. Thomas Aquinas rejected the ontological argument; Descartes developed the argument in his *Meditations*; Leibniz defended it; and Kant attacked it. In the twentieth century, Charles Hartshorne, probably the most famous student of Alfred North Whitehead, formulated a version of it in terms of modal logic and Kurt Gödel did the same. Given the history of the ontological argument, it is nothing less than breathtaking when Dawkins dismisses it as "infantile".[19] The argument may not be valid, and as a matter of fact, the Vatican Council of the Roman Catholic Church has officially deemed it as invalid, but to dismiss it as "infantile" is really beneath the dignity of a scholar. In his defense, Dawkins does admit that as a scientist he has difficulty accepting any conclusion that is not substantiated by "data from the real world". Apparently, "data from the real world" means for Dawkins empirical evidence, which is itself problematic as we have seen previously. In any case, Dawkins' assertion leaves the mathematician wondering about the status of a perfect right triangle since there seems to be no empirical evidence for it. Be that as it may, Dawkins' rejection of purely logical arguments would eliminate the entire field of formal logic and render Kurt Gödel's incompleteness theorems "infantile". It would also entail the impossibility of applying any formal system of logic to a semantic system.

In his *Summa Theologiae*, Thomas Aquinas presents five arguments for the reality of God that proceed from observations of the physical world, but that depend ultimately on philosophical concepts. They are

---

[19] DAWKINS, p. 104.

in order: 1) the argument from motion, 2) the argument from efficient cause, 3) the argument from contingency, 4) the argument from degrees of perfection and 5) the teleological argument. It would exceed the bounds of an epilogue to interpret the five arguments of Thomas. It is also unnecessary since the literature on the subject is voluminous. Nevertheless, I do regard it as important to point out the obvious errors in Dawkins' interpretation.

In his usual demeaning style, Dawkins assures us first of all that the five arguments of Thomas Aquinas can easily be "exposed as vacuous".[20] Presumably, he is so confident of his interpretation that he does not bother to analyze the arguments carefully, nor does he investigate the philosophical background of the terms involved. The first three arguments Dawkins lumps together because all three are based on the impossibility of an infinite regress, and, in Dawkins' mind, this means that all three say basically the same thing. Unfortunately, Dawkins does not recognize that it is crucial to define "infinite regress". I suspect that he is thinking of an infinite regress in a mathematical sense, although it is impossible to be sure based on his vague comments. Had he bothered to investigate the background of these arguments, he would have discovered that the argument from motion, for instance, was taken from Aristotle (*Metaphysics*, XII, 8) and that "motion" must be understood in the broad sense of the transition from potency to act. Apparently, Dawkins thinks that Thomas was referring to *local* motion in the sense of Newtonian physics; this would explain his confusion about motion and efficient cause. Such a confusion is quite surprising given that Thomas is very explicit about the meaning of the term "motion". In Question 2, Article 3, Thomas writes: "For motion is nothing else than the reduction of something from potentiality to actuality" (*Movere enim nihil aliud est quam educere aliquid de potentia in actum*). From this, it should be clear that the infinite regress of the first argument is neither mathematical nor temporal, but rather ontological. It is the modal sequence from potential-

---

[20] DAWKINS, p. 100.

ity to actuality that Thomas deems impossible, not a temporal sequence leading back to the beginning of time. In fact, Thomas Aquinas did not think that it was possible philosophically to prove that the world had a beginning, and as we know, Aristotle himself thought that the world extended backward in time indefinitely. So an infinite regress in time could not play a role in the five philosophical arguments of the *Summa Theologiae*. The argument of Thomas from motion simply claims that the reality of the world, its sheer being there, requires an explanation.

After Dawkins has criticized the notion of infinite regress, he writes: "there is absolutely no reason to endow that terminator [i.e. the terminator of the infinite regress] with any of the properties normally ascribed to God: omnipotence, omniscience, goodness, creativity of design. …"[21] From this comment, it is not clear whether Dawkins recognizes that the five arguments of Thomas are not intended to establish the attributes of God. On the contrary, Thomas simply states that the conclusion of each argument is that which everyone understands to be God. In the case of motion, an ultimate ground for the reality of motion in the world must be something unmoved, and this is what everyone understands to be God (*et hoc omnes intelligunt Deum*). Now that may not be, in fact, what everyone understands to be God, but that is what Thomas says. And if we set out to discuss his arguments, we should at least try to understand what he intended. In these five classical arguments, Thomas intends to establish the fundamental distinction between reason and faith, between that which is by nature is knowable about God and that which must be believed. The background of this distinction can be traced back to the Apostle Paul and found expression in the writings of Augustine, as we have seen. In considering the arguments of Thomas, it is this *distinction*, not the applicability of certain *attributes* that is decisive.

In my critique of Dawkins' *The Blind Watchmaker*, I charged that he was very restricted within a narrow Anglocentric perspective when he discusses religion. This judgment seems to be confirmed by his erro-

[21] Dawkins, p. 101.

neous assumption that a *teleological* argument and an argument from *design* are identical. In reading Dawkins' comments on Thomas' teleological argument, it is apparent that he is thinking about the theology of William Paley, not the argument of Thomas Aquinas. The teleological argument of Thomas is based on the concept of final cause as found in the philosophy of Aristotle (*Physics*, 194b16 and *Metaphysics* 1013a24 f.), and it has little resemblance to Paley's concept of design created by a Creator. As we have noted, Thomas does not assume the Christian doctrine of creation in his five arguments for the reality of God. The design argument claims that the world was so designed by an intelligent Creator that everything fits together. For instance, the fruit tree produces fruit so that man and other animals can be nourished. This is Stoic thought, not Thomistic. The internal finality argument of Thomas is concerned with the fruit itself reaching its perfection. When the fruit becomes mature, it has reached its goal or telos. This is the concept of the final cause as understood by Aristotle and Thomas, and plainly it would not have sufficed for Paley's purposes. Dawkins' claim that the fifth argument of Thomas Aquinas is an argument from design is patently false. Even in a book intended to entertain the reader, such confusion of philosophical concepts could and should have been avoided. In my opinion, the only lesson to be drawn from Dawkins' attempted refutation of classical theological arguments is this: He is hopelessly fixated on the notion of design. Intelligent Design is his declared opponent, and he sees it everywhere. Nota bene: I am not suggesting that either the argument from final cause or the argument from design is valid. I am simply pointing out that Dawkins' treatment of the topic is fraught with so many errors that it is useless as a basis for drawing any reasonable conclusions.

Quite apart from Dawkins, the ontological argument of Anselm and the five arguments of Thomas Aquinas are historically interesting and may be of some value in clarifying the question of God even in a modern society. Of the two types of argument, the *a priori* or ontological argument of Anselm certainly holds the greatest potential for actually proving anything. Anyone interested in logic can hardly ignore the modal argument of Kurt Gödel. Nevertheless, I am not convinced that Christianity really accomplishes very much in trying to *prove* God's reality. Even in the most sophisticated proof, a definition of God is necessary, and this is always the weakest point of the argument. The truth is that we really do not know what God is. This does not mean that we have no knowledge of God whatsoever, but it does mean that our knowledge is too limited to form anything approaching the necessary premises for a logical proof. Few Christian theologians perceived this situation as clearly as the German Reformer Martin Luther, who often drew the distinction between the hidden God (*Deus absconditus*) and the revealed God (*Deus revelatus*). What we know about God is simply that which has been manifested to us; the depth of the reality of God remains a mystery of which we only on rare occasions gain a glimpse. These reflections are totally in line with the thoughts of the Apostle Paul when he writes in Romans 1:19 f.: "For what can be known about God is plain to them, because God has shown it to them. Ever since the creation of the world his invisible nature, namely, his eternal power and deity, has been clearly perceived in the things that have been made." Lest we forget, Paul is not talking here about faith or belief in God. He is talking about something that is manifest to everyone because the most basic evidence for the reality of God is always immediate.

Bibliography

PL = Patrologia Latina
LCL = Loeb Classical Library

Aquinas, Thomas. *On Truth* (De veritate), Question 1.

_____. *Summa Theologiae*, Prima Secundae, Questions 90–97.

Arendt, Hannah. *On Violence*,1970.

Aristotle. *Metaphysica*, Oxford Classical Texts, ed. W. Jaeger, 1957.

_____. *Metaphysics*, transl. by Hippocrates Apostle. (1966). 1975.

_____. *On the Heavens*, in: LCL, Vol. 338, ed. W.K.C. Gutherie, (1939), 1986.

_____. *On the Soul* (De anima), in: LCL, Vol. 288.

_____. *Parts of Animals* (De partibus animalium), in: LCL, Vol. 332.

_____. *Physics* (Physica), Oxford Classical Texts, ed. W. D. Ross, 1951.

Arnim, Ioannes. *Stoicorum Veterum Fragmenta,* Vol. II, (1903), 1964.

Atmanspacher, Harald. "Remembering Hans Primas (1928–2014)", *Mind & Matter*, Vol. 12(2), 2014, pp. 341–348.

Augustine. *Against Faustus the Manichean* (Contra Faustum Manicheum), in: Migne, PL, Vol. 42.

_____. *Confessions* (Confessionum libri tredecim), in: Migne, PL, Vol. 32.

_____. *Diverse Questions* (De diversis questionibus liber unus), in: Migne, PL, Vol. 40.

_____. *Expositions on the Psalms* (Enarrationes in Psalmos,), in: Migne, PL, Vol. 37.

_____. *On Christian Doctrine* (De doctrina christiana), in: Migne, PL, Vol. 34, and in: Corpus christianorum Latinorum, Vol. 32.

_____. *On Free Will* (De libero arbitrio), in: Migne, PL, Vol. 32.
_____. *On Genesis against the Manicheans* (De Genesi contra Manichaeos), in: Migne, PL, Vol. 34.
_____. *On the Nature of the Good* (De natura boni), in: Migne, PL, Vol. 42.
_____. *On the Sermon on the Mount* (De Sermone Domini in Monte) in: Migne, PL, Vol. 34.
_____. *On the Spirit and the Letter* (De spiritu et littera), in: Migne, PL, Vol. 44.
_____. *On the Trinity* (De trinitate) in: Migne, PL, Vol. 42.
_____. *On true religion* (De vera religione), in: Migne, PL, Vol. 34.
_____. *Sermons, No. 126* (Sermones, 126), ed. by A. Mai in: Migne, Patrologia Latina Supplementa.
_____. *The City of God* (De civitate dei), in: Migne, PL, Vol. 41.
_____. *The literal Commentary on Genesis* (De Genesi ad litteram), in: Migne, PL, Vol. 34, and in: Corpus Scriptorum Ecclesiasticorum Latinorum, Vol. 28.
_____. *Treatise on the Gospel of John* (In Joannis Evangelium tractatus, CXXIV), in: Migne, PL, Vol. 35.
_____. *Unfinished literal Commentary on Genesis* (De Genesi ad litteram inperfectus), in: Migne, PL, Vol. 34.
Böhme, Gernot. *Idee und Kosmos: Platons Zeitlehre – Eine Einführung in seine theoretische Philosophie*, Philosophische Abhandlungen, Bd. 66, 1996.
Boss, Medard. "Einsamkeit und Gemeinschaft", *Daseinsanalyse*, Vol. 1, No. 1, 1984, pp. 6–22.
Brush, Jack E. *Glauben als Ereignis: Selbst, Kraft, Zeit, Leben*, 2011.
_____. *Naturwissenschaft als Herausforderung für die Theologie: Eine historisch-systematische Darstellung*, 2008.
_____. *In Search of the Common Good: Guideposts for concerned Citizens*, 2016.

Castells, Manuel. *The Information Age*, Vol. 1: *The Rise of the Network Society*, (1996), 2010.
Chomsky, Noam. “Language and Cognition”, *The Future of the Cognitive Revolution*, ed. David Johnson and Christina Erneling, 1997, pp. 1–31.
Cicero. *Academics* (Academica), Bk. I, in: LCL, Vol. 268.
_____. *First Philippic* (Oratio Philippica prima), in: LCL, Vol. 189.
_____. *Letters to Atticus,* in: LCL, Vol. 7.
_____. *Letters to Quintus*, in: LCL, Vol. 462.
_____. *Oration for Milo* (Oratio pro Milone), in: LCL, Vol. 252.
_____. *On Duties* (De officiis), in: LCL, Vol. 30.
_____. *On the Commonwealth* (De re publica), in LCL, Vol. 213.
_____. *On the Ends of Good and Evil* (De finibus bonorum et malorum), in: LCL, Vol. 40.
_____. *On the Laws* (De legibus), in: LCL, Vol. 213.
_____. *On the Nature of the Gods* (De natura deorum), in: LCL, Vol. 268.
_____. *Oration for Cluentius* (Oratio pro Cluentio), in: LCL, Vol. 198.
_____. *Tusculan Disputations* (Disputationes Tusculanae), in: LCL, Vol. 141.
[Cicero]. *Rhetorica ad Herennium*, in: LCL, Vol. 403.
Dalferth, Ingolf U. “Theismus”, *Theologische Realenzyklopädie*, Studienausgabe, Vol. 33, 2006, pp. 196–205.
Darwin, Charles. *The Descent of Man*, Vol. 1, 1871.
Dawkins, Richard. *The Blind Watchmaker*, (1987), 1996.
_____. *The God Delusion,* 2006.
Diels, Hermann. *Die Fragmente der Vorsokratiker*, Vol. 1, 1903.
Dyck, Andrew. *Commentary on Cicero's De Legibus*, 2004.
Dyson, Freeman. *Disturbing the Universe*, 1979.
Ebeling, Gerhard. *Die Wahrheit des Evangeliums*, 1981.
Einstein, Albert. “Religion and Science”, *Ideas and Opinions*, 1954.

Evers, Dirk. "Nature als Schöpfung", *Naturphilosophie: Ein Lehr-u. Studienbuch*, ed. Thomas Kirchhof, Nicole C. Karafyllis, et al, (2017), 2020. pp. 23–31.

Flusser, David. "Noachitische Gebote", *Theologische Realenzyklopädie*, Studienausgabe, Part II, pp. 582–585.

Fortin, Ernest L. "Augustine, Thomas Aquinas, and the Problem of Natural Law", *Classical Christianity and the Political Order, Collected Essays of Ernest Fortin*, Vol. 2, ed. J. Brian Benestad, 1996.

Freud, Sigmund. *Die Traumdeutung*, 1900.

Heidegger, Martin. *Der Anfang des abendländischen Denkens: Heraklit,* Gesamtausgabe, II. Abteilung, Vorlesungen, 1923–1944, Vol. 55, 1979.

_____. *Einführung in die Metaphysik* (Introduction to Metaphysics), (1953), 1987.

Homer, *Odyssey*, Bk. IX.

Horsley, Richard. "The Law of Nature in Philo and Cicero", *Harvard Theological Review*, Vol. 71, issue 1–2, 1978, pp. 35–59.

Hübner, Jürgen. *Die neue Verantwortung für das Leben*, 1986.

_____. *Die Theologie Johannes Keplers zwischen Orthodoxie und Naturwissenschaft,* 1975.

_____. *Die Welt als Gottes Schöpfung: Zum Verhältnis von Theologie und Naturwissenschaft heute*, 1982.

Jammer, Max. "Feld, Feldtheorie", *Historisches Wörterbuch der Philosophie*, Vol. 2, 1972, pp. 923–926.

Kafatos, Menas and Nadeau, Robert. *The Conscious Universe*, 1990.

Kepler, Johannes. *Briefe 1590–1599*, Gesammelte Werke, Vol. XIII, Number 91.

_____. *Mysterium Cosmographicum*, Gesammelte Werke, Vol. I, (1987), 2013.

Köster, Helmut. "φύσις", *The Theological Dictionary of the New Testament*, Vol. 9, ed. Gerhard Friedrich pp. 251–277.

Laertius, Diogenes. *Lives of Eminent Philosophers*, Bks. 6 –10, in: LCL, Vol. 185.
Long, A. A. and Sedley, D. N. *The Hellenistic Philosophers*, Vol. 1, (1987), 2013.
Luther. "Enarratio Psalmi 51", *Weimarer Ausgabe*, Vol. 40, Part 2.
Mayr, Ernst. "What Evolution is", *Edge* (www.edge.org), ed. John Brockman. 12. 31. 1999.
Meyer, Stephen C. *Darwin's Doubt: The Explosive Origin of Animal Life and the Case for Intelligent Design*, revised ed. 2014.
Michelson, Abraham Albert. *Light Waves and their Uses*, (1903), 1907.
Nietzsche. *Die Philosophie im tragischen Zeitalter der Griechen*, Späteres Vorwort, Abschnitt 8, [1873].
Orenstein, David I. and Blaikie, Linda Ford. *Godless Grace*, 2015.
Paley, William. *Natural Theology or Evidences of the Existence and Attributes of the Deity – Collected from the Appearances of Nature*, (1802), 1818.
_____. *Evidences of Christianity*, 1794.
Patrick, G. T. W. *The Fragments of Heraclitus*, 2013.
Philo. *On Abraham*, in: LCL, Vol. 289.
_____. On *Providence, Fragment* I, in: LCL, Vol. 363.
Plato. *Symposium*, 191e–192a.
_____. *Timaios*, 37d5.
Plotinus. *Enneads*, in: LCL, Vol. 446.
Primas, Hans. "Umdenken in der Naturwissenschaft", *GAIA*, No. 1, 1992.
Rose, Steven. *Lifelines: Biology Beyond Determinism*, 1998.
Sandbach, F. H. *The Stoics*, (1975), 1994.
Ruden, Sarah. *Paul among the People: The Apostle Reinterpreted and Reimagined in his own Time*, 2010.
Schadewaldt, Wolfgang. *Hellas und Herperien*, Vol. I, (1960), 1970.
Schleiermacher, Friedrich. *Herakleitos, der dunkle, von Ephesos,* 1808, Kritische Gesamtausgabe, 1. Abteilung, Vol. 6, pp. 101–241.

Seneca. *The Moral Letters to Lucilium* (Ad Lucilium epistulae morales), Letter 9, in: LCL, Vol. 5.

Shaftesbury, Anthony Cooper. *An Inquiry Concerning Virtue or Merit*, (1699), 1904.

Shibayama, Zenkei. *A Flower Does Not Talk*, (1970), 1988.

Sophocles. *The Oedipus Cycle*, transl. by Dudley Fitts and Robert Fitzgerald, (1939), 1977.

Whitehead, Alfred North. *Process and Reality,* (1929), Corrected Edition, ed. by David Ray Griffin and Donald W. Sherburne, 1978.

Wilson, R. McL. “Mani and Manichaeism“, *The Encyclopedia of Philosophy*, (1967), 1972, Vol. 5, pp. 149f.

Philosophy in Dialogue / Philosophie im Dialog
edited by Prof. Dr. Janez Juhant (University of Ljubljana) and
Ass. Prof. Dr. Vojko Strahovnik (University of Ljubljana)

 Bojan Žalec

Essays on Franz Weber
Slovenian philosopher Franz Weber (or France Veber) (1890 – 1975) was the most important philosopher in Slovenia in the last two decades before the Second World War. He was the first professor of philosophy at the Faculty of Arts, University of Ljubljana (founded 1919). He emerged from the Graz school of Alexius Meinong, founder of the object theory. He brought the object theory to Slovenia and complemented it with his original theory of direct experience of reality. The book is a concise comprehensive presentation of Weber's philosophy and its development, with an emphasis on his theory of knowledge, social philosophy, and philosophy of culture that were all grounded in his philosophical psychology. He advocated (Slavic) agrarianism and cooperativism.
vol. 6, 2021, ca. 144 pp., ca. 29,90 €, br., ISBN-CH 978-3-643-91125-4

Vojko Strahovnik
Global Ethics
Perspectives on Global Justice
The book discusses selected issues related to global ethics and global justice. Among its central topics are: defining the notions of global ethics and global justice, dimensions of justice and the questions of universal standards of justice, moral disagreement and moral dialogue, agents of global justice, status justice and membership, restitutive and restorative justice in historical context and context of communities, the role of reactive moral attitudes (shame, guilt) in reconciliation, intercultural and interreligious dialogue, the role of intellectual humility and epistemic justice, and culture of fear and religious (in)tolerance. The core unifying theme of the entire book is the focus on justice (in its various forms) as one of the most significant ethical challenges of the contemporary world.
Bd. 5, 2019, 128 S., 29,90 €, br., ISBN 978-3-643-91124-7

Nadja Furlan Stante; Anja Zalta; Maja Lamberger Khatib (Eds.)
Women against war system
Bd. 4, 2018, 176 S., 29,90 €, br., ISBN 978-3-643-90918-3

Vojko Strahovnik; Bojan Žalec (Eds.)
Religion, Violence, and Ideology
Reflections on the Challenges of Postmodern World
Bd. 3, 2016, 108 S., 29,90 €, br., ISBN 978-3-643-90774-5

Bojan Žalec
Genocide, Totalitarianism and Multiculturalism
Perspectives in the Light of Solidary Personalism
Bd. 2, 2015, 112 S., 29,90 €, br., ISBN 978-3-643-90617-5

Janez Juhant; Vojko Strahovnik (Eds.)
Dialogue in the Global World
From Ideologies to Persons
Bd. 1, 2014, 144 S., 29,90 €, br., ISBN 978-3-643-90497-3

LIT Verlag Berlin – Münster – Wien – Zürich – London
Auslieferung Deutschland / Österreich / Schweiz: siehe Impressumsseite

Forum Religionskritik

Lutz Pohle
Etikettenschwindel als System
Warum der „Heiligen Kirche“ Volk und Priester abhanden kommen
Bd. 19, 2021, ca. 160 S., ca. 24,90 €, br., ISBN 978-3-643-14983-1

Werner A. Müller
Gottesvorstellungen und Leben nach dem Tod
Märchenhaftes und Mythen des christlichen und islamischen Glaubens im Lichte historischer und naturwissenschaftlicher Forschung
Das Buch fasst zusammen, wie der Glaube an einen persönlichen Gott und an ein Leben nach dem Tode entstanden ist. Die Aussagen von Religionen werden durchleuchtet, Ungereimtheiten, Widersprüchliches und Märchenhaftes aufgezeigt und mit Ergebnissen der historischen und heutigen naturwissenschaftlichen und neurologischen Forschung konfrontiert
Bd. 18, 2021, ca. 104 S., ca. 19,90 €, br., ISBN 978-3-643-14887-2

Udo Kern
Karl Marx und der Neue Atheismus
Toleranz – mit Verstand, Herz, Gemüt und Hoffnung gestaltet – wird von Religion und Atheismus begreiflich, einleuchtend, evident erwartet und verlangt. Das gilt sowohl für Karl Marx als auch für den Neuen Atheismus und die Religion. Der russische Literaturkritiker Michail Michailovitsch Bachtin hat Recht: „Der Glaube lebt dicht an der Grenze zum Atheismus, schaut ihn an und versteht ihn; der Atheismus lebt dicht an der Grenze des Glaubens und versteht den Glauben.“
Bd. 17, 2020, 152 S., 29,90 €, br., ISBN 978-3-643-14801-8

Edda Lechner
Von der Kirche zum Kommunismus
Einblicke und Folgerungen nach lehrreichen Auseinandersetzungen. Mit Anhang „Religionsfreiheit und linke Politik“
Welche bedeutende Rolle die Achtundsechziger-Bewegung auch in der Kirche spielte, zeigt sich in dem hier geschilderten Fall der Pastorin Edda Groth/Lechner. Von den „revolutionären“ Ideen beeinflusst, erklärte sie in ihrer Konfirmations-Predigt 1974, „dass Mao Gott näher stehe als alle Päpste und Bischöfe der letzten 1000 Jahre“. Es gehe darum, dass auch Christen sich gegen den Kapitalismus und für den Sozialismus einsetzten. Das führte zu einem heftigen hier ausführlich geschilderten Konflikt innerhalb der Gemeinde und mit der Kirchenleitung in Schleswig-Holstein, zu ihrem Kirchenaustritt und der atheistischen Erkenntnis, „dass uns kein höh’res Wesen rettet“.
Bd. 16, 2020, 420 S., 34,90 €, br., ISBN 978-3-643-14197-2

Michael Francisci de Insulis OP
Determinatio De Antichristo. Traktat über den Antichrist
Editionem curavit Walter Simon. Herausgegeben und eingeleitet von Walter Simon
Der Dominikaner Michael Francisci de Insulis, Rektor der Ordensschule in Köln, nahm am 19. Oktober 1478 im Rahmen einer akademischen Veranstaltung Stellung zu Gerüchten, im Orient sei der seit langem geweissagte Antichrist zur Welt gekommen. Ein Schreiben, das diese Behauptung verbreitete, musste auf seine Glaubwürdigkeit hin geprüft werden. Zur Identifizierung des erwarteten Widersachers, der die Endzeit ankündigt, greift Michael Francisci altbekannte Stellen der Heiligen Schrift auf und beruft sich auf die Autoritäten der Kirchenlehre, vor allem auf Thomas von Aquin und Vinzenz Ferrer.
Bd. 15, 2021, ca. 120 S., ca. 39,90 €, br., ISBN 978-3-643-13842-2

Karl Richard Ziegert
Die Verkäufer des „perfect life“
Über die Amerikanisierung der Religion und den Untergang der EKD-Kirchenwelt in Deutschland
Bd. 14, 2015, 468 S., 39,90 €, br., ISBN 978-3-643-13013-6

Forum Religionsphilosophie

Udo Kern
Karl Marx und das Judentum
Bd. 43, 2021, ca. 152 S., ca. 29,90 €, br., ISBN 978-3-643-14979-4

Adolf Hochmuth
Evolutives Christentum
Versuch einer Kritik der christlichen Vernunft
Die religiöse, die christliche und kirchliche Großwetterlage erscheint am Beginn des 3. Jahrtausends unübersehbar eingetrübt. Als die größte Konfession tritt der Agnostizismus zumindest in der westlichen Welt auf. Christliche Vernunft muss sich als mit den Natur- und den Humanwissenschaften vereinbar erweisen und muss eine immer schon in ihr angelegte evolutive DNA zu Wort kommen lassen. Die aufklärerischen Impulse des Christentums dürfen in großem Selbstbewusstsein allen anderen Religionen und einer billigen Wellness-Esoterik gegenüber intellektuell offen bekannt werden.
Bd. 41, 2021, ca. 296 S., ca. 39,90 €, br., ISBN 978-3-643-14915-2

Matthias Vonarburg
Der Mensch und seine Vollendung
Die Frage nach der Himmelsehe im Kontext christlicher Eschatologie
Das hier vorliegende Werk ist ein Beitrag zur christlichen Eschatologie und geht der Frage nach, ob es bei den Beziehungen unter den Heiligen von Gott intendierte Unterschiede qualitativer Art gibt. Über das Vorstellungsmodell der Himmelsehe wird dabei eine mögliche Beantwortung hergeleitet und der spekulativ gewonnene Topos von der praegerichtlichen Offenlegung als Novum in die Diskussion eingeführt.
Bd. 40, 2021, 152 S., 24,90 €, br., ISBN 978-3-643-80319-1

Udo Kern
Das Leben, das Sein und das Nichts
Ein philosophisch-theologischer Diskurs
Philosophisch-theologisch relevante Themen bestimmen dieses Buch. Udo Kerns Partner des überzeitlichen 'Gesprächs' sind Hans-Walter Wolff, Karl Marx, Ludwig Wittgenstein, Max Picard, Gerhard Ebeling, Martin Heidegger, Hans Jonas, Albert Schweitzer, Gerd Theißen, Dietrich Bonhoeffer, Karl Jaspers und Meister Eckhart.
Die Realität der Sprache *spricht* unsere Wirklichkeit. Dabei erkennen wir die Grenzen unserer Welt. Hierbei ist auch die Urzeithaftigkeit des Schweigens geltend. Das Sprachlichsein bestimmt unser Sein. Das Leben erweist sich individual und gesellschaftlich als Unterwegssein. Dieses selbst wird nur durch das Leben erkannt. Barmherzigkeit erbaut hier. Das bewahrt nicht vor dem Nichts. Fundamental zu beachten ist *Proverbia* 4,23: „Behüte dein Herz mit allem Fleiß; denn daraus quillt das Leben."
Bd. 39, 2020, 336 S., 39,90 €, br., ISBN 978-3-643-14618-2

Robert Ernst
Theologische Fragen im Lichte mystischer Offenbarungen
Herausgegeben von Matthias Bücker-de Silva
Der Band des geistlichen Grenzgängers und profunden Kenners christlicher Mystik, Robert Ernst, behandelt das sehr weite Spektrum des Offenbarungs-Glaubens: Werke der Adrienne von Speyr und des Jakob Lorber – Das Problem der Reinkarnation – Die Erscheinungen Gottes im Alten Testament und die Menschwerdung Gottes im Neuen Testament – Die Eucharistierede im Johannesevangelium – Das Problem des Wunders – Die Stufen der Vollkommenheit – Die Astralsphäre.
Der Autor untersucht charismatische Kundgaben und Erfahrungen auf ihren Wert als Hilfe für die Theologie.
Robert Ernst (1909 – 1997) war Seelsorger und katholischer Priester und der wohl produktivste Autor im deutschsprachigen Grenzraum Ostbelgiens.
Bd. 38, 2020, 186 S., 24,90 €, br., ISBN 978-3-643-14366-2

LIT Verlag Berlin – Münster – Wien – Zürich – London
Auslieferung Deutschland / Österreich / Schweiz: siehe Impressumsseite